OPERA ANECDOTES

OPERA
ANECDOTES

ETHAN MORDDEN

OXFORD UNIVERSITY PRESS
New York   Oxford

Oxford University Press

Oxford   New York   Toronto
Delhi   Bombay   Calcutta   Madras   Karachi
Petaling Jaya   Singapore   Hong Kong   Tokyo
Nairobi   Dar es Salaam   Cape Town
Melbourne   Auckland

and associated companies in
Berlin   Ibadan

Copyright © 1985 by Ethan Mordden

First published in 1985 by Oxford University Press, Inc.,
198 Madison Avenue, New York, New York 10016-4314

First issued as an Oxford University Press paperback, 1988

Oxford is a registered trademark of Oxford University Press

Library of Congress Cataloging in Publication Data
Mordden, Ethan
Opera anecdotes.
Includes index.
1. Opera—Anecdotes, facetiae, satire, etc.
I. Title. ML1700.M72   1985   782.1   85-4818
ISBN 0-19-503600-X
ISBN 0-19-505661-2 (PBK)

8   10   9   7

Printed in the United States of America

To Robert Jacobson

PREFACE

These are my retellings of opera's tales, classic and arcane, derived from lore and literature. I have sifted the libraries for authentic versions, but a sense of what is theatrical and humanistically insightful has impelled me more than literal reconstruction—especially as most anecdotes are fictions in the first place, products of town gossip, imaginative journalists, *pensées de l'escalier,* uninhibited translators, or even opera people themselves, embellishing the legends as they pass them on. Like the elements of a mythology, anecdotes help us to understand a subject, but generally they are not to be taken reportorially.

I have not imposed a quota of fame upon the whole; the collection represents the best stories, not necessarily the "best" people. Yet there is history here; for if many of the tales are silly, many others are telling. They bring us close to a moment in which art is invented, revised, elaborated. The chararacters of opera's adventures are so vital and stimulating that almost anything they do enlightens us.

The author wishes to acknowledge his editor Sheldon Meyer, who continues to observe ideals of gentility and culture in a profession that is beginning to lose them. Leona Capeless put a keen eye on the manuscript—another vanishing amenity, knowledgeable editing. The vivacious Joellyn Ausanka runs a trim office, and designers Frederick Schneider and Leslie Phillips must be congratulated for their grace in making a busy text both handsome and readable. And, as ever, my agent Dorothy Pittman functions as a combination of lawyer, first critic, and best friend.

New York   E.C.M.
May 1985

CONTENTS

Overture

Because so many of opera's most typical stories evoke the capers of divas and divos, let's launch our tour with a sampling of the stars in glory or disaster, waxing witty or dull, playing magnanimous or self-intent.

Identity Crisis

A soprano, on tour in Mexico, was captured by bandits who turned out to be music lovers unwilling to molest a daughter of art. They agreed to let her go—*if* she proved that she was indeed a prima donna of the opera.

"How can I do that?" she asked.

"Sing!"

"What? Sing in a cavern? Sing before rabble? Without footlights, makeup, costumes? No lords in the boxes? No critics in the pit? No bouquets hurled at the curtain? *No money in the box office?*"

"Let her go," sighed the bandit chief. "She's a prima donna, all right."

Next, to Bayreuth, for an encounter of two great Wagnerians:

Gracious Diva

During one of the early Wagner festivals, young Lillian Nordica, a star on the rise, crossed paths with veteran Lilli Lehmann, who had helped open Bayreuth in 1876 and was now the Brünnhilde of the day. Nordica has hopes of singing Lehmann's roles, and wishes to pay her respects, colleague to colleague.

"May I call on you, Madam Lehmann?"

Lehmann eyes Nordica as Brünnhilde might an overzealous Schwertleite. "I am not taking any pupils this season!" she snaps.

We'll be seeing a lot more of this professional courtesy, but now, for a change of register, to Victorian England and its favorite tenor, Sims Reeves:

In Which We Learn Why Opera Is a Noble Art

A railway porter, recognizing Reeves while he was waiting to make a connection, put to him an interesting question. The singer reputedly earned a great deal of money, yet could not be said to work very hard for it—hardly at all, as far as the porter saw it. Yet the porter worked very hard indeed and earned very little, perhaps as little as a tenth of what Reeves earned. Wasn't that so?

Reeves smiled. "How much do you earn?"

"Eighteen shillings a week, all the year 'round."

"Right," said Reeves, and burst into the singer's traditional major-key octave scale: "Do, mi, sol, do!" With a flourish, he concluded, "There, my man—there's a year of your salary made in four notes!"

Reeves stood out in his day for his refusal to italianize his name, as many Britons and Americans did. But when it comes to certain antics, one cannot beat tenors of the authentic native flavor:

An Inscription in a Guest Book

Giuseppe Fancelli, who was perhaps less intelligent than tenors generally hope to be, was writing his name in the autograph book of the Liverpool Philharmonic Society. He did well enough, though he had to omit his first name (utterly beyond his powers) and inadvertently dropped a bit of the last (the c and one of the ls). Alas, he decided to append to his name his own rave review, to wit: *Primo tenore assoluto*. The first two words he got down, but "assoluto" gave him trouble. The inkwell spilled, his fingers smudged and blotched, and he never was sure how to get through the last three syllables of "assoluto."

What he left on the page of the Society's album was

FANELI PRIMO TENORE ASS

Fancelli was not much of a musician, either; and could scarcely act. He did have a notable high C, and for that much may be forgiven. But second-raters beware the public:

Pagliacci with Interpolations

Two traditional tales of audience participation in a regrettable performance have best been rendered by raconteur Walter Slezak, who places both in a *Pagliacci* in Naples. The first episode finds the baritone delivering a questionable Prologue; anyway, this audience questions it, with jeers and yells.

"Perchè fischiate a me?" the singer responds. "Aspettate il tenore!": Why whistle at me? Wait till you hear the tenor!

Then comes the poor soprano, who makes a rough job of the Balla-tella, after which, astonishingly, come cries of *bis!*—the demand for an encore. She grants the repeat, no less unevenly than the first time, and still the gallery screams for an encore while those downstairs protest in horror. *"Bis!"* screams the gallery. *"Basta!"* cries the orchestra: *Enough!* At last a lone voice calls out from upstairs, "Deve cantarla fina che non lo conosce!": She'll sing it till she gets it right!

Even less appreciated are the dilettantes who decide that opera is easy:

Hold, Enough!

In Victorian England, a doting father arranged for his daughter, an amateur singer, to perform at a concert. Came the day, the man was gout-ridden and could not attend, but he anxiously awaited his wife's report.

"She could *not* have been better received!" crowed Mama when they returned.

"There were some Italians in the house, Papa!" said the budding prima donna. "And *they* took me for Madame Pasta herself!"

"What? My word!"

"Yes, Papa. For I had scarcely sung a dozen notes when the Italians began to cry, "Basta! Basta!"

Even the great names can suffer indignities:

A Cutting Remark

The late-nineteenth-century tenor Joseph Capoul was so popular that he set a fashion in men's hairstyles, the "coiffure à la Capoul." In the barbershop once, Capoul was asked how he wanted his hair cut, and, somewhat meekly, for his fame embarrassed him, he requested it à la Capoul.

"I am sorry, Monsieur," replied the barber, turning Capoul's head this way and that. "You don't have the head to carry off that style. Perhaps à la de Reszke?"

Thus we learn the hazards of being humble in a profession that can prize only resolute self-belief. Here's a classic lesson in the art of asserting oneself:

How To Get Your Way at La Scala

You scream, you threaten, you rave, and you stomp out.

Or you do what Beverly Sills did—finally, after wasting her time not screaming and not raving—when preparing for her Scala debut in Rossini's *L'Assedio di Corinto*. Originally, Renata Scotto was to have sung Sills's role of Pamira, but cancelled when she became pregnant. Unfortunately, Sills not only got Scotto's role but Scotto's costume, a gown in gold that favored the Italian's coloring, not Sills's. The designer, Nicola Benois, agreed with Sills that the costume should be remade in silver, and the wardrobe mistress agreed to make the switch. *Sì, sì; everything will be fine.*

At the dress parade, when the clothes are held up under the lights, there was Sills's gown—in gold. Sills spoke up. *Silver*, not gold, right? Sì, sì; everything will be fine.

Sills began to wonder about that but held her temper till the day of the first piano dress rehearsal, when she found her costume hanging in her dressing room in, yes: gold.

Epiphany. Sills took the dress, walked onstage, had the wardrobe mistress summoned, and got more or less the third assurance that everything would be fine.

So Sills took the costume, folded it, borrowed the wardrobe mistress's shears, and cut the costume into halves. Then, smiling, Sills told her to go back to her workroom and *make the costume in silver.*

One soprano who could have given Sills lessons in prima donna strategy is Maria Jeritza. Here she is in her famous Metropolitan Opera bout with Beniamino Gigli:

The Gigli-Jeritza War

No way around it: those two just did not get along. Met manager Giulio Gatti-Casazza thought their chemistry as a duo comparable to that of Caruso and Farrar and liked to cast them together, but it sabotaged the love plots somewhat when she would wriggle in his embrace till he lost his footing, or when she would throw herself at him with such force that he went crashing into the scenery. The worst of it was the performance of Giordano's *Fedora* in which, following the text, he rejected her—but so violently that she staggered across the stage and just saved herself from falling into the orchestra pit. She had wrenched something, but furiously refused his help, and sang the rest of the scene prone on the floor.*

Backstage, he said it was an accident.

She said he had tried to kill her.

"Defend my honor!" she cried to her husband, Baron von Popper, who habitually spent her performances backstage. "Challenge that man to a duel!"

The Baron did no such thing, but still the tenor was troubled, for the press celebrated the event as the nasty outcome of an ego feud, proposing the analysis that he had at length tired of her shenanigans and purposely Given Her a Push.

Then she told Gatti she would never sing with That Man again.

"Rubbish," says Gatti. "You're singing *Tosca* together in two weeks."

Tosca went well till the bows, when she refused to share the calls with him. Shrugging it off, he bowed alone and went home. So did most of the audience. But her claque stayed on, calling for their idol. At last she appeared, sobbing in the arms of conductor Giuseppe Bamboschek, to deliver the classic line, "Gigli not nice to me!"

Backstage, Jeritza became hysterical, and Gatti had to be called out of bed to come to the opera house and soothe her. This took most of the night, of course; Jeritza was running on Viennese time, which clocks one's legend in feudhours. "Rubbish," Gatti kept muttering to himself, for some reason. "Rubbish."

Let us continue more or less on this note in a medley of Fun with Sopranos Through the Ages.

The Diva Edits the Score

Francesca Cuzzoni, they say, was sometimes difficult for the sport of it; but Handel was tougher. One day, Cuzzoni announced that she didn't like a certain piece Handel had just played for her.

"I would like a fresh air to sing," she haughtily told him. "That one doesn't suit me, if you please!"

Handel flew at her in a rage, shouting, "I alvays knew you vere a fery tevil. But I shall now let you know zat I am Beelzebup, ze prince of de tevils! You vant fresh air! I giff you some fresh air!"

---

* Of course Jeritza was famous for singing Tosca's "Vissi d'arte" prone on the floor, so the *Fedora* mishap is something less than *azione drastica*. Still, singing opera horizontally is more comfortable when one does it by romantic invention rather than by brute force.

He then dragged Cuzzoni to an open window and was about to heave her into the street when she suddenly decided that she'd be thrilled to sing that delightful little aria after all.

The Show Must Go On

Mary Ann Paton, heroine of Weber's *Oberon* in its world premiere, was invited to a party by a parvenu couple who so insisted when she declined that she decided to put in an appearance for form's sake. As usual in those days, the ladies spelled each other at the piano, with "Cease Your Funning" and "Di tanti palpiti," and no doubt they were quite fine. But it was Paton whom the hosts had in mind from the start, and came the moment when they asked her to second the amateurs with her professional expertise.

Paton politely begged the company's indulgence.

"What, not sing, Miss Paton?" cried her hostess. "But I announced you to my guests! It is the very reason for the party, indeed it is!"

"That alters the matter," said Paton. "When a singer is announced, a singer must perform."

"I should say."

And Paton gave concert, full repertory plus encores. The next morning, to the hostess's shock, she sent around her bill for £50.

When a singer is announced, an impresaria must pay.

Did This Really Happen?

The great contralto Ernestine Schumann-Heink was Czech by birth and German by musical training but American by cultural adoption; she must have been one of the few public figures to have sons fighting on both sides in World War I. Schumann-Heink was hefty, lovable, and a superb artist—but in this vignette, passed from buff to buff over the years, she is simply a woman with a German accent in that Great American Invention, the drugstore.

"I'd like some powder, please," she tells the clerk.

"Mennen's?"

"No. Vimmen's."

"And would you like it scented?"

"No, I'll take it vit me."

A First in Greats

Theatre critic James Agate asked music critic Neville Cardus who were the three finest actresses he had seen.

Cardus considered. "Peggy Ashcroft and Edith Evans would certainly be near the top of my list. But my all-time favorite is Lotte Lehmann."

"I'm not talking about opera singers," said Agate, annoyed. "I'm talking about actresses."

"So am I!"

The Flip Side

All her life, Joan Hammond's most successful recording was "O my beloved father" ("O mio babbino caro," Lauretta's aria from Puccini's *Gianni Schicchi*), which bore a similarly quaint translation of "Vissi d'arte" on the verso of the disc. When Hammond sang Tosca at Covent Garden, a neophyte in the gallery, while applauding "Vissi d'arte," turned to a friend and enthused, "I hope she'll sing the other side of the record next!"

Enter Arroyo

Under Rudolf Bing the Met pursued a course of racial integration, bringing black artists in for roles large and small. Janet Collins, a dancer, was the first. Marian Anderson was the notable veteran. Leontyne Price was the outstanding debutante. Not long after Price's debut, in *Il Trovatore*, Martina Arroyo joined the firm, quite appropriately, as the Heavenly Voice in *Don Carlos*. Heading into the Met one day, Arroyo was welcomed by a doorman as "Miss Price."

Says Arroyo, "I'm the other one, honey."

Madame Dorothy Parker Addresses Her Fans

Parker couldn't sing opera, but she could play the diva when the mood was upon her. One day, around the time that Maria Jeritza made her spectacular Met debut and Geraldine Farrar her spectacular Met farewell—in short, when the Manhattan air was full of sopranos—Parker and Alexander Woollcott took a ride in an open carriage. Stalled in traffic, they watched crowds of pedestrians hustling past them, crowds that might well have served Jeritza on her cheerful debut or Farrar on her brave farewell. And Parker is thinking of the opera, and the opera people, and the opera buffs, and that . . . *peculiar* music . . . and she suddenly rises, blowing kisses in all directions.

"I promise to come back one day and sing Carmen for you!" she cries.

Let us now pull back for the longer view and take in a few adventures in the management of great opera companies. First, off to La Scala around the turn of the present century, in the great days of Gatti-Casazza:

An Elephant at the Opera

Gatti's Milan seasons featured Donizetti's *Linda di Chamounix* with Rosina Storchio. Because the opera was modest in scope and was being given with cuts, it was thought advisable to bill it with a spectacular ballet, *Amor*—based, roughly, on the history of Italy from the Creation to the Battle of Legnano, when a league of Italian city-states defeated Barbarossa. One scene of *Amor,* set in ancient Rome, called for horses, an ox, and an elephant.

The elephant engaged for *Amor,* one Papus, attracted some attention when his trainer led him from the railroad station to the theatre. They traveled at evening, and by back streets; but the lights of a streetcar unnerved the beast, and he ran slightly wild, arousing the interest of the police.

"He's under arrest!" cried a constable.

"Never!" said Papus' trainer. "This is an artist of the Scala opera house!"

The police drew back respectfully, and order was restored. However, once ensconced at the opera house, Papus grew doleful. The world of velvet and jewels was not for him, it seems; perhaps he didn't like the music to *Amor,* for few if any did. To cheer him up, a monkey was brought in, one Pirri, and the two made a delightful and delighted pair. His morale restored, Papus made a great success in *Amor.* Some critics thought him quite the best thing on stage (after Storchio, of course; but it was a close consideration), and the public was entranced. Papus became the rage of Milan.

Then, one evening, just before the doors were to open, Papus's companion Pirri broke off his chain and bounded about the auditorium, eluding all attempts at capture. Outside, the public banged on the doors, demanding to know what the delay was about; inside, Scala officials chased Pirri through the galleries and boxes.

At length Gatti called for a gun, having decided to shoot Pirri regardless of the effect this might have on Papus's performance. Luckily, Pirri's trainer turned up just then and gave a whistle: the monkey immediately jumped down and ran to him as if he, Pirri, had pulled off a turn to equal that of the celebrated Papus.

The doors now opened and the Scala audience, as understanding as ever, filed into the theatre chanting, "Down with the management!"

A touch of history now, as we view, in three stories, the rise, feud, and fall of several opera companies that happened to be in the same place at the same time:

The Opera House War

A great city with one smallish opera house and a burgeoning aristocracy learned, by scientific method, that four hundred into eighteen won't go. Eighteen was the number of boxes in the opera house; but four hundred was the count of the people of fashion. Moreover, the city's most antique families held those eighteen boxes by seniority, shutting out and thereby infuriating the newer and financially better endowed names. This was before the era of the café and the theatre party; however free the tycoon in his business dealings, his social life was severely circumscribed. Where could his handsome wife display her *ton* but at the opera? How else accustom his sons and daughters to society but by receiving in their box at intermissions?

Legend tells that the wife of the most powerful man in the city, snubbed by the eighteen, asked her husband for a new opera house with which to overwhelm her rivals. Indeed, when word got out of the move to build a new theatre, many of the box shareholders in the older house joined up with the parvenus, because they themselves had been irritated by the strait exclusions of the eighteen boxes, and because they knew that the new theatre, to be built by merchants and bankers, would be so splendid that the old theatre would die.

It did. When the two houses began their competition, in 1883, the manager of the old house expressed annoyance that, because he had guided the available stars so thoroughly in his own operation, the new company scarcely needed to rehearse at all. There was consternation, too, among the old nobility who had remained faithful to their undersized, undecorated, but authentic old house. They had, in fact, attempted to buy off the parvenus and preclude construction of a second theatre by promising to establish new boxes in the old one.

New ones? Where?

Above the old ones. Beside them. Around them. Near them.

This was trivia to the founders of the new house. So they had pressed on and built a palace with abundant boxes. True, their repertory and casts were comparable with those of the older house, if more lavishly presented. True, too, their building was nothing to admire from the street; the manager of the old house called it a "yellow brewery." The interior lacked the great strolling spaces of Paris, Vienna, Milan. But the auditorium was larger than any, and its stage a gaping wonder. The older house was cozy, the new one a showplace. The old house was old guard, too confident and self-preserving to last. The new house was a demonstration of power. "I can't fight Wall Street," said the manager of the old house, as operagoers deserted it. Vaudeville claimed it, then dingy novelties. In 1926 it was demolished.

Forty years later, the new house was too.

> The new house was, of course, the old Metropolitan Opera, on Broadway between Thirty-ninth and Fortieth streets. The old house was the Academy of Music, on the north side of Fourteenth Street east of Union Square (not the later building of the same name, still standing across Fourteenth Street to the southeast and now a rock palace, the Palladium). The "four hundred," as the number of society's entitled, was in fact coined by Ward McAllister five years after the Met opened. He based the figure on the capacity of Mrs. Astor's ballroom. As Mrs. Astor held the Met's most choice box, first tier center, and thus dominated the Met and therefore Knickerbocker New York, founding census upon her social grip made perfect sense at the time. The manager of the Academy of Music during the raising of the Metropolitan was Colonel Mapleson. Both houses featured red and gold interiors.

Not Wanted on Voyage

One of the casualties of New York's opera house war was Max Maratzek, a conductor and impresario of an earlier day who was passed over when the Met organized its company. Critic Henry Krehbiel, wandering outside at an intermission during the Met's first season, spotted Maratzek on the sidewalk and asked him if he was attending the performance. He was—but from standing room: all the seats had been sold.

Moved that so distinguished a musician was so reduced after all he had done for New York's opera scene, Krehbiel offered Maratzek his own ticket, adding that some of the former impresario's colleagues were seated nearby and would be glad to salute him. Maratzek declined.

Krehbiel expressed regret that Maratzek had not been given the chance to lead the new house; Maratzek, too, regretted it: "When I heard the house was to be built, I did think that some of the stockholders would remember what I had done for opera. Some of the old-timers, who used to go to the Academy of Music and Astor Place Opera House when I was manager there, I thought, would recollect what companies I gave them."

Maratzek then rattled off the names of the great singers he had presented, the names of a bygone—or, better, a downtown—age. Fashionable New York had departed Fourteenth Street. "I thought," Maratzek went on, "somebody might remember this and the old man, and come to me and say, 'Max, you did a good deal for us once—let us do something for you now.' I didn't expect them to come and offer me the house, but I thought they might say this and add, 'Come, we'll make you head usher,' or 'You may have the bar.' But nobody came, and I'm out of it completely."

And he went back inside, to standing room.

The Second Opera House War

The Met, as New York's new (and soon enough only working) opera house, depended more on the rhetoric of its decor than on any distinction of performance to impress. It was some time before the various Met managers developed an identifiable production style or intent of repertory. In the meantime, impresario Oscar Hammerstein built his own opera house four blocks away, with the express hope of driving the Met out of public interest, even out of business.

Hammerstein was the most colorful impresario of a day that admired eccentricity in its celebrities. In his Prince Albert coat and high hat and carrying his gold-topped cane, he was a resplendent museum piece, insistently fashionable yet two generations out of fashion. He was heedless of money. His sons had to stick a five-dollar bill into his pocket whenever he went out, to ensure that he wouldn't embarrass himself in a restaurant or on the streetcar. He made fortunes in cigar manufacturing, real estate, and vaudeville, and constantly lost them—on opera.

Certainly, opera production is one of the most dependable ways to go bankrupt. Colonel Mapleson couldn't fight Wall Street? Hammerstein couldn't wait for the chance. His Manhattan Opera House was not only better than the Met: it was more artistic. "The people who come here," he announced from the stage on the last night of his first season, "come for the opera. I want no others. I am not trying to establish a society clientele."

From his first night, December 3, 1906, Hammerstein set up his rivalry with the Met in exactly these terms. Theirs was a hall of snobs; his was a temple of music. And while the Met did have box-office draws in Enrico Caruso and Geraldine Farrar, Hammerstein had the stylish tenor Alessandro Bonci, the theatrical baritone Maurice Renaud, the supreme Nellie Melba, the impressive conductor Cleofonte Campanini, all but Melba new to New York. The Met might strike back in preparing the first New York *Salome* with Olive Fremstad, a certain sensation; but it was so sensational that the Met board, led by J. P. Morgan, cancelled it after a public dress rehearsal—scheduled, rather obtusely, for Sunday afternoon and thus catching everyone right after church and (in many cases) a pungent sermon on the decadence of Oscar Wilde and Richard Strauss. Hammerstein calmly unveiled a *Rigoletto* with Melba, Bonci, and Renaud under Campanini, and the town flocked to his temple.

Luck rode with Hammerstein, and the Met leaders fumed as their own boxholders joined the public at the Manhattan. Almost nothing Hammerstein tried failed to go over. He put on *La Bohème* (in the face of the Met's exclusive arrangement with Puccini's publisher) with Melba, Emma Trentini (later Victor Herbert's original heroine in *Naughty Marietta*), Bonci, and Mario Sammarco. When Melba returned to England, Hammerstein produced Emma Calvé, the notable Carmen of the day. In his second season, he had a smash with *Les Contes d'Hoffmann*, then a novelty in New York; a sell-out debutante in Luisa Tetrazzini, perhaps the most ingratiating coloratura personality of all time; and, most telling of all, Mary Garden in the Garden specialties, Charpentier's *Louise*, Debussy's *Pelléas et Mélisande*, and Massenet's *Thaïs*. It was typical of the Manhattan's run of good fortune that even *Pelléas*, an admired dud everywhere else, was a hit for Hammerstein. Moreover, the impetuous impresario had evolved a clear artistic format to complement his anti-Wall Street social one: contemporary repertory featuring personable singing stars new to New York.

Finally the great Met bestirred itself, and in 1908 regrouped its forces under a new manager, Giulio Gatti-Casazza, and music director, Arturo Toscanini, both fresh from a controversial and extraordinary regime at La Scala. The Met immediately firmed up and became wonderful; under Toscanini, one tended to. At the same time, Hammerstein began making mistakes.

His third season, featuring his own *Salome* (with no Board to sabotage it), yet more Strauss in the first New York *Elektra*, and the debut of John McCormack, held to his formula. But he foolishly expanded his operation to Philadelphia, building a new opera house in a city that had enough of the art in the regular Met visits. He erred in bringing back to New York the soprano Lina Cavalieri, often called "the most beautiful singer in the world." Cavalieri's return was a deliberate act of war against the Met nobles, for Cavalieri had fleeced one Knickerbocker grandee and was said to be accepting the attentions of another. Worst of all, Hammerstein went out of his way to alienate his most crucial supporter, the extremely influential Mrs. Clarence Mackay, who had led many a society matron into the Manhattan. To tie it all up, Hammerstein quarrelled with Campanini as well. This was the extravagance of Hammerstein, an impresario most keen when striving toward a goal and most wasteful when he had attained it.

The occasion for the Hammerstein-Mackay rupture was a soiree Mrs. Mackay gave for heiress Beatrice Mills upon her marriage to a British earl. Violinist Mischa Elman was to play—and could Mr. Hammerstein's orchestra sit in as well? Despite his distaste for plutocrats, Hammerstein agreed. After all, Mrs Mackay had swelled his subscription list singlehandedly. He even sent the players to her complete with Campanini for no fee; they played *La Mer*, like much of the rest of Hammerstein's offerings fresh and thrilling. What with the Cinderella marriage, young Elman, and the veritable orchestra of the Manhattan Opera House, Mrs. Mackay's party was a smashing success, and she gratefully sent presents to those responsible—Campanini, a particular favorite, got an emerald ring. One person, however, did not get acknowledged, not even by letter.

Hammerstein.

Perhaps Mrs. Mackay avoided personal dealings with him because of his erratic sense of diplomacy. But he was offended all the same. He wrote her a letter ordering her never to set foot in his opera house again, and gave it to his son Arthur to deliver. Some time before, he had told Arthur to tell the Mackays to "go to hell" and Arthur had not passed the message on. Similarly, now, he destroyed the letter. But Hammerstein found out, wrote another, delivered it himself . . . and lost Mrs. Mackay, her many society friends, and Campanini, loyal to the Mackays and increasingly disillusioned with affairs in the opera house.

Thus Hammerstein tossed away social and artistic prestige; and the Philadelphia sideline was telling badly on his finances. Suddenly the Met stepped in and offered to buy him out. Why it happened just then is a mystery, for the state of Hammerstein's exchequer cannot have been a secret from the banker board of the Metropolitan. It may be that the flourishing of Cavalieri inflamed Met eminences, for there was a Dangerous Woman. In any case, at the very depth of Hammerstein's troubles, the Met proposed to pay him $1,200,000 for his promise not to produce any opera for ten years in New York, Philadelphia, Boston, and Chicago.

Arthur was overjoyed: the old man was bailed out just when he should, by rights, have gone under. Opera was a respectable passion, but it had several times cost Hammerstein's family everything they owned, and the crime of it was that everything *else* that Oscar tried turned to gold. He could build a vaudeville theatre, outfit it with personnel, plan the first season, and the thing would run itself forever after—but then he would sell it to start an opera company, never (of course!) in any available house. It had to be Hammerstein's own theatre! And there he would sit, on a kitchen chair in the wings, the eternal cigar clamped between his teeth, watching his singers, his operas, his music. A great man; but an unwise one. When Arthur brought his father the legal papers and money of the Met deal, Oscar was radiant. He announced that he had just bought property in London, and was now going to build the London Opera House and start all over.

"I'll never talk to you again," cried Arthur, "as long as I live!"

Composers

CHRISTOPH WILLIBALD GLUCK

"It is all very fine," he said of the opera of his day, *"but it doesn't draw blood."* When Gluck began, in the middle of the eighteenth century, opera was stagnant and decadent, a hash of castratos and prima donnas, of conventional subjects and contrived situations, of da capo arias and embellishments. When Gluck finished with opera, as Mozart was just coming into his era, the castrato was on the way out, the subjects were taking vital cues from the spoken stage, the arias had become elastic in structure, and the composers' war on excessive vocal display had begun. Yet Gluck was no shattering realist. "I do not wish to contradict nature," he once said. "I wish to enhance it."

He did, at least, contradict other composers of opera, who had led it down a dead-end of song for song's sake; in Gluck, song served story. Handel might be thought of as the chief exponent of the kind of opera Gluck's music theatre replaced; and this puts The Famous Story of Handel's Cook (a few pages hence) in a certain context. However, Handel only knew Gluck in the latter's youth, when he came to London to compose for the Haymarket Theatre—and compose, be it said, innocuously, right from the mold. Gluck's genius was slow to bite. By the time he was revitalizing opera, beginning with the Vienna premiere of *Orfeo ed Euridice* in 1762, Handel was dead. Still, the two had become great friends, Handel giving Gluck the much-quoted advice to bang out everything on the bass drum to reach the dull British sensibility, and Gluck hanging Handel's picture in his bedroom so he could gaze reverently upon his favorite composer the first thing every morning.

How sad that Handel did not live to enjoy Gluck's reform operas, and to take part, no doubt, in the controversy they created, with pamphlets, strange inventions, sudden retirements, and the politicization of art. The place was Paris and the time the 1770s, so everything was royalist or democrat, nationalist or transmontane, conciliatory or separatist. A Viennese from Bavaria by way of Bohemia, Gluck had to come to Paris to pursue his reform because French opera had always been more theatre-oriented than Italian opera. The French had a stronger sense of narrative, a more fluid balance of declamation and lyricism, and a varied vocal texture, with as much ensemble as solo work. By comparison, Italian opera was mere jingles.

Oddly, Gluck had worked the Italian model for decades before beginning his reform—and when he did begin, it was in Italian, and with a castrato hero: *Orfeo ed Euridice.* Then, in Paris, after launching himself with *Iphigénie en Aulide,* he revised *Orfeo* into *Orphée,* with a tenor hero, as if taking one small step backward to leap ahead. Not suprisingly, then, the following stories will take us to Paris, and many of the most important tales out of the eras after Gluck sustain the emphasis on Paris as the place where reform is affirmed (as with Rossini's *Guillaume Tell*) or contested (as with Wagner's *Tannhäuser*). If Paris throughout the nineteenth century was the international opera center, its days of renown began with Gluck and his, shall we say,

Challenge: "I only determined to publish the score of *Alceste,*" he wrote, "in the hope of finding imitators."

This statement is essential Gluck, for he was a composer who could articulate his principles. Unlike Verdi, who wrote as he saw fit, without reference to music-theatre theory, Gluck, once he found himself, wrote by aesthetic program. In this, he was like Berlioz and Wagner, a reformer who aimed to impose new imperatives of composition and performance upon an artistically corrupt system. If the public rejected one of Verdi's operas, Verdi would shrug; the public is always right. But Gluck, like Berlioz and Wagner, meant to bend the public to his will.

In Paris, he bent roughly half the public; the other half sought a champion in Niccolò Piccinni, to oppose Gluck's heroistic integrity with merry fun. Gluck was so *earnest,* said his foes: but Piccinni was delightful. Even his *tragédies* sounded like comedies. Thus erupted the Gluck-Piccinni War, a continuation of the decades-old "guerre des bouffons" ("the war over comedy"), in which conventional French opera, the *tragédie lyrique* of Lully and Rameau, was pitted against Italian melody, Italian singing, and Italian *opera buffa* in particular. Everyone in Paris had to take one side or the other, or jeopardize his cultural standing. One night at the Opéra, a Gluckiste was holding forth on the marvels of the Gluckian theatre. Gluck, he said, was "the first for grand effects, powerful, passionate, as warm as energetic, who rends your soul with a shout of despair. He is elevated even in his orchestral accompaniments—and who else blew life into your automatic chorus? In a word, he is the man to create the revolution in music that all sane men have been hoping for. True, I must admit that every once in a while he is a bit thunderous instead of melodic, but all the same—"

"So!" cried a neighbor. "You are a Piccinniste, then?"

"Hardly. I don't know a note of his music."

"What of it? You found a fault in Gluck—that makes you a Piccinniste!"

Typically, Gluck's anecdotes emphasize the artistic revolutionary, waging his own war-within-the-war against incompetent singers, impedient ballet dancers, and even orchestra players, unused to the psychologically commentative scoring that Gluck introduced into opera. As we will learn in the, yes, Famous Story of Handel's Cook, Gluck was not a musician's musician. But what he didn't know, he didn't need. And he did, as he hoped, find imitators. For decades after his death, his successors mined his work for its narrative concentration, its blending of opera's distinct elements and clarifying of their purpose. Perhaps in the end Gluck was a musician's musician: as the founder of modern opera.

The Famous Story of Handel's Cook

How great a composer was Gluck? Some say very great—*The Concise Oxford Dictionary of Opera* calls him "opera's second founder." Handel said not so great: "He knows no more uff counterpoint zan mein cook!"

Coffee-House Critique

Launching his reform of opera in Vienna, Gluck had to fight the reactionary Viennese public, to whom the very notion of "reform" was the promise of tedium. When *Alceste* was premiered in Vienna in 1767, one wit complained, "For nine days the theatre is closed, and on the tenth they reopen with a De Profundis!"

Gluck's Bass

The timbre of French singing often has a nasal quality irritating to those who are not French, and the bass Henri Larrivée was said to be most offensive in this regard. Gluck wrote leads for him in the two *Iphigénie* operas, which at any rate secured Larrivée's prominence, but . . . well, as one wag put it, "That nose has a really magnificent voice."

Gluck's Bass Does His Best

It was not Larrivée's timbre that annoyed Gluck, but his temper—or, better, the lack thereof. As Agamemnon in *Iphigénie en Aulide,* Larrivée sang as if he were a shepherd in some pastoral. How can one reinvent music theatre if the singers cannot *portray?*

Gluck tried to muster Larrivée, inspire him. Agamemnon is the greatest king in Greece and the head of all the Greek army in its greatest campaign yet. Troy and glory beckon! But he must sacrifice his daughter or risk divine ire. "Do you see, Larrivée?" Gluck asked, coaching the sluggish spirit. "Do you comprehend the tragic grandeur of the man?"

"Don't worry," said Larrivée. "Wait till I get into my costume—you won't recognize me."

A few days later, Gluck directed a full-dress runthrough. Some things were fine—the incomparable Sophie Arnould, for instance, as Iphigénie. Some things were drawbacks—the corps de ballet, especially. And some things were dull—such as Larrivée's interpretation, as uninflected as it had been when rehearsals began.

"Oh, Larrivée," Gluck moaned, as his dim Agamemnon struck a stock pose. "I recognize you!"

Gluck and the Ballet Master

Preparing the premiere of the new Paris version of *Orfeo,* Gluck had
to suffer the outrageous vanity of Gaëtan Vestris, who styled himself
"the god of the dance."

"If you are a god," Gluck urged him, "dance in heaven, not in my
opera."

But opera without ballet was unthinkable in Paris. "Write me a chaconne," said Vestris, planning his arabesques and pliés, and especially
his curtain calls.

"We are trying to depict life among the ancient Greeks," Gluck objected. "Do you think they knew what a chaconne is?"

"Didn't they?" asked Vestris, utterly amazed. "Life without the chaconne! How I pity them!"

A Gluck Story That Has Nothing To Do with Opera

Sugar was mysteriously disappearing from the kitchen of Gluck's
household, and his housekeeper, a devout miser, devised a trick to ex-
plode the mystery. Deftly catching a fly on the wing, she placed it in
the sugar bowl and covered it up. Later, she would see if the fly was
still there: if he was not, it proved that someone was pilfering sugar.

Sure enough, later the fly was gone. The housekeeper accused a servant; the servant protested his innocence. Disturbed by the noise, Gluck
came in in a fury—who dares interrupt his work? When the matter was
explained to him, the housekeeper certain she had her culprit and the
servant insisting he was no such thing, Gluck really lost his temper.

"I have been taking the sugar!" he cried. *"I* am the criminal! Que
voulez-vous? Is it off to the Bastille? Or may I return to my labor in
peace?"

Now the servant took up where the housekeeper left off, grumbling
about false accusations with no proof.

"This is intolerable!" Gluck roared. "Are you mad, or am I?"

"Oh, your excellency," came the reply. "Surely you would not keep
a servant who is mad?"

The Abbé Consoles with a Pun

In one of those classic stories that unfortunately sound a little dotty
several epochs later, Gluck witnesses the half-hearted applause for the
premiere of the revised French *Alceste* and runs out of the theatre in

despair. In the street, he happens upon the Abbé Arnauld. *"Alceste,"* cries Gluck, "is fallen!"

"Fallen from heaven!" says the good father.

> Later, in reflective irony, Gluck proved more eloquent than Arnauld. "This failure," he noted bitterly, "will make history in the taste of the French people."

Conflicted Calm

Repartee amuses and a pregnant encounter is fascinating, but the best anecdotes are those that illustrate a point in history or aesthetics: that instruct our understanding of how opera works. Here is one of the most famous such, because it occurs at precisely the moment when the costumed concert of castratos and prima donnas enforced its transformation into a theatre wired to a musical psychology.

The opera is *Iphigénie en Tauride*. Rehearsing Orestes' scene, "Dieux protecteurs de ces affreux rivages" (Gods of these savage shores), the orchestra came to the line, "Le calme rentre dans mon coeur!" (My heart is calm again) just as the violas had begun playing an obsessive figure that was anything but calm. Assuming that there must be some error in the copying of the parts, the orchestra broke off, but Gluck urged them on. There had been no mistake.

"He's lying!" Gluck explained. "He killed his mother! Keep playing!"

What Gluck Said to Piccinni

Gluck's story so emphasizes heroic idealism that this next tale becomes, in context, refreshingly cynical. At the height of the Parisian rivalry between Gluck's dynamically theatrical operas and Niccolò Piccinni's more conventionally tuneful ones, the two met for dinner. They themselves were cordial colleagues; it was their respective partisans who had created their "war." In fact, Gluck became quite confidential that evening, at least partly on the encouragement of wine, and told Piccinni, "The French are worthy people, but they make me laugh: they want song, yet don't know how to sing. My friend, you are celebrated through all Europe, and you work to sustain your fame. Eccellente! You give them fine music and what good does it do you? Believe me, here you must think of making money: and of nothing else!"

Diplomacy

The Gluck-Piccinni War never officially ended, for neither side would concede defeat, but it is certain that Gluck was not seriously challenged. Typically, when both men set texts on *Iphigénie en Tauride,* Gluck's was instantly acclaimed a masterpiece and Piccinni's was a fiasco.

In a way, the two composers themselves ended the war, simply by leaving Paris. Gluck suffered a crushing failure in *Echo et Narcisse,* immediately departed Paris for Vienna, and went into retirement. Piccinni lingered on, but the Revolution swept away his property and prestige, and he returned to Naples—where he gives us a last story. Somehow or other, Piccinni fell on the wrong side of Queen Carolina, the sister of Marie-Antoinette and as unattractive as the French queen was beautiful.

"Do you not think I resemble my sister?" Carolina asked Piccinni.

"There may be a family likeness, Your Majesty," Piccinni replied. "But no resemblance."

WOLFGANG AMADEUS MOZART

Of opera's major composers, Mozart may be the most difficult to write about, partly because of the mysterious perfection of the music and partly because the man's personality is elusive (despite a huge bequest of personal correspondence). What was Mozart like? Opinions, even among his contemporaries, differ. What *is* he like? Everyone agrees: the essential creator, a composer of composers. In symphonic, chamber, and instrumental music, Mozart is the most sacred territory, beyond criticism, and opera's spokesmen in particular revere him as monks do a saint. Richard Strauss, to name but one instance, offered any of his operas in exchange for a certain two bars of *Don Giovanni* that most listeners simply take for granted.*

That in itself is the point: the rightness of Mozart is so awesome that much of it only registers as genius, as conceived art, after alert study. Mozart is, above all, natural; or so we are told. So natural, so right, so perfect, that those who write of him often succumb to a mild case of icon worship. Listen to Peter Shaffer, author of the play *Amadeus:*

> Mozart's incomparability lies in the absolute nature of his achievements: the best of them cannot be even slightly rewritten without diminishment. Of course, great art always attests to the existence of absolutes: that is why the greatest offers the largest comfort—even as, temporarily, it can also induce the largest despair.

---

* The passage is the transition into the Maskers' Trio, two contiguous four-tone phrases from F Major into B Flat.

Shaffer himself spread despair among some Mozarteans for his treatment of the composer as an uncouth moron. But the classic tales give us either the impetuous *Wunderkind* who composed concertos before his hands were big enough to play them or the experimental genius who furiously accepted his talent as tending to the elite rather than to the popular. It's odd to think of Mozart as the "difficult" master of his Vienna: what could be more melodic, more basic, than Mozart? Yet his largely forgotten contemporaries had a stronger grasp on popular taste. A publisher warned Mozart to incline toward a more accessible style—meaning less dramatic, less self-absorbed—or risk losing his market. "Then I will write nothing more and go hungry," Mozart told him, "or may the devil take me." Later, he proposed *Don Giovanni* as having been composed "for myself and a few friends."

Mozart's anecdotes offer a contrast to those of Gluck, giving us the context of the all-purpose court composer of the Austro-Hungarian emperor (Mozart) after that of the free-lance opera specialist in Paris (Gluck). We see Mozart as conductor and instrumentalist, backstage and in the house, taking a historic early step in the Germanization of "German" opera with his Singspiel *Die Entführung aus dem Serail* (The Abduction from the Seraglio). But we saw Gluck only as an author of opera, theorist and producer as well as well as composer—at that, an internationalized composer who could sustain a series of reform operas in Italian and French but not in his own language, German.

Most contrasted of all is the two men's very different ways of dealing with opera's inherent problems. Gluck's masterpiece, *Iphigénie en Tauride* (1779), and Mozart's, *Don Giovanni* (1787), came forth but eight years apart; could any two operas be more unlike in form, characters, action? Gluck and Mozart seem yet farther apart when their greatest operas are compared, oeuvre to oeuvre: Gluck's all pursue a sole ideal in format while Mozart's blend different forms. Perhaps this is why Gluck remains the Great Reformer but Mozart the Great Composer. Gluck has no *Così Fan Tutte*, no *Zauberflöte*, much less a *Don Giovanni*.

Yet Gluck claims enlightening stories, virtually documents of art history, while Mozart's anecdotes seem trivial, amusing but not telling. They have been told from book to book, and will live as long as Mozart is heard, true writ. Yet their reach is not broad. The absolute, then, we hear in the music: not in the man.

"Anything To Declare?" "Just My Talent!"

Those travelers who are particularly susceptible to victimization by fastidious customs inspectors should do what Mozart did on his first trip to Vienna. At the customs house, matters threatened to slow the Mozarts up, so six-year-old Wolfgang pulled out his violin and treated the inspector to a concert.

The party was passed through in record time.

Mozart Stands Up to the Emperor

The Emperor of Austria-Hungary, Joseph II, supported Mozart's belief that German lands needed German opera, but wondered if *Die Ent-führung aus dem Serail* was the breakthrough work the culture needed. Joseph found it a little too fancy, too highly developed. He told Mozart, "There are too many notes in it."

"Just as many, Your Majesty," Mozart replied, "as there should be."

Surprise Entrance

Arriving in Berlin, Mozart learned that *Die Entführung* was on that night, and he hurried to the theatre. Unseen at the back of the house, he listened with growing consternation to the changes the singers had made—especially the customary pointless embellishments—while unwittingly moving forward through the audience. Just when he had reached the very edge of the orchestra players, some improvisation on stage outraged him and he cried out, "No! No! That's not how it goes!"

A few people recognized the intruder, and the house began to buzz with the news. But the singers fled to the wings in embarrassment, and some refused to go back onstage before so authoritative a spectator. Given what liberties they were taking with his composition, this was astutely discreet of them.

> Actually, liberties were normal for the place and time; it may well be that the performance was simply abominable and the guilty parties feared the composer's reproaches. In any case, Mozart had to go backstage and rally the singers personally before the opera could continue. Not a vastly intriguing episode, perhaps, but a famous one, recalled in countless retellings and even a number of engravings. In one alternate version, it is the orchestra that draws Mozart's fire, in amusingly dated Anecdotal Antique: "Not D Flat," he shouts. "D natural! You ought to play D natural, you rogues!"

Royalty Comprehends Genius

As the musicians were turning up for a piano concerto, Joseph II noticed that Mozart had troubled to compose for every player but himself.

"Where's your part?" the emperor asked.

Mozart touched his forehead. "Here."

The Cast Enthuses

Thespian belief holds that a terrible dress rehearsal promises a great performance; but there sometimes comes a certain moment in a rehearsal, not a calamitous one, when composition and performance blend together in such stimulating charisma that everyone knows he is witnessing the birth of a sure hit.

Such a moment occurred in the last full dress rehearsal of *Le Nozze di Figaro*, when Benucci, the Figaro, reached the big martial coda to "Non più andrai" in his biggest, grandest voice. Suddenly everybody—singers, orchestra players, and guests—was crying "Bravo, il maestro!" and "Viva, grande Mozart!" All turned to look upon the composer. "I shall never forget his little countenance when lighted up with the glowing rays of genius," wrote Michael Kelly, the Basilio and Curzio of the premiere. "It is as impossible to describe it, as it would be to paint sunbeams."

How To Be Popular

Of the composers prominent in Vienna when Mozart lived there, Vincente Martín y Soler was perhaps the most popular. "Many of his things are really pretty," Mozart remarked, "but in ten years' time no one will take any more notice of him."

This is not entirely true, for one melody from Martín's opera *Una Cosa Rara* is one of the most frequently heard tunes in opera today.

Because Mozart quoted it in the banquet scene of *Don Giovanni*.

The Viennese Were Not Amused

Don Giovanni triumphed on its world premiere in Prague, but when Mozart and his librettist Lorenzo da Ponte presented it to their fellow Viennese, the work failed to please. As court poet to Joseph II, da Ponte of course heard the Royal Opinion, at times more progressive than those of his subjects. "That opera is divine," said the Emperor. "It may even be more beautiful than *Figaro*. But such music is not meat for the teeth of my Viennese!"

When da Ponte repeated the comment to Mozart, the composer said quietly, "Give them time to chew on it."

Rossini's Opinion

Someone asked Rossini who was the greatest musician.

"Beethoven," came the reply.

"What of Mozart, then?"

"Oh, Mozart is not the greatest musician," Rossini answered. "He is the *only*."

GIOACCHINO ROSSINI

Rossini is one of the most misunderstood of composers, widely perceived as a tunesmith, a caterer in art, a maestro of divas at a time when Italian opera was simplistic and episodic. Then, too, there was the legend of the lazy, facile, witty gourmand of Royalist politics and "German" volume—"Signor Crescendo"—who carelessly spun out some forty operas and then, finding himself rich and popular in Paris, retired to give and attend parties, writing almost nothing for his last thirty-nine years. In short, Rossini is supposed to be a popular but not essential composer, gifted yet never especially committed.

On the contrary, Rossini contributed importantly to the development of opera, and was so unwilling to cater to unworthy audiences that his crushed idealism was a major factor in his early retirement. Facile Rossini was, following Webster's meaning of "ready, fluent," rather than "specious, superficial." As for lazy, how can we say this of the composer of forty operas?

Opera seria and *buffa* ("serious" and "comic") were the forms Rossini inherited when he launched his career in the 1810s, *seria* too often pretentious and *buffa* too often shallow. Mozart, of course, was exceptional, his *seria* endowed with a poetic naturalism and his *buffa* ennobled. But Mozart was inimitable. Reform had to start after Mozart, and it did: with Rossini. He gave *buffa* a startling glitter, no more; though his comedies were the best of the day, they did not change the course of opera history. But Rossini's serious pieces did. *Seria* had begun to turn into what is called *melodramma*, the tense da capo aria structures opened up and varied, and duets, trios, and choral ensembles enhancing the vocal texture and expediting dramatic motion. Rossini led this development vitally, at first respecting the limits set by the Italian public and then, toward the end of his Italian period, challenging them, drawing their attention beyond what was amusing in opera to what was enlightening.

There is no precise point at which Rossini broke away from business as usual. Yet, when he arrived in Paris in 1824 to run the Théâtre-Italien, he was considering alternatives to the generic noble characters, generic showpiece solos, and generic tidy act durations he had been working in. Paris, the musical capital of the world, had the least provincial audience, and Rossini learned French in order to create something splendid for the Opéra, something to exploit his talent instead of merely dropping in on it. The facile Signor Crescendo spent six months on the piano score of this new piece, and from its first night it remained an inspiration to every Italian composer—and a reproach to any who failed to meet its ideals: *Guillaume Tell*.

Comparing *William Tell* with Rossini's early comedy *The Barber of Seville* is not unlike listening to very late Verdi after very early. Yes, the autograph is consistent: but how different it looks! *Guillaume Tell* seemed to use all that was admirable in the growing new form of grand opera and reject all that was fill; at the same time, it was so beautifully planned a piece that it set grand opera into the form that would see it through fifty years of life. Ironically, it was too good for grand opera's audience, and fell out of the very fashion it created.

At least Rossini had the pleasure of spanning eras; one might almost say that he started just after Handel's *Giulio Cesare* and left off just before Verdi's *Macbeth*. Or was it a pleasure? Perhaps Rossini gave opera up in disappointment at the way his achievement was received. For years, his retirement prompted speculation from analysts. It was said that he was too easygoing to construct the complex works he himself had inspired. It was said that his well of melody had at last run dry. It was said that he feared a new work as risking his entire reputation: a success could hardly flatter his fame, but a fiasco could hurt it. He himself supposedly resented the eminence of Halévy and Meyerbeer, both working in *Tell*'s wake, and said, "I will return when the Jews have finished their Sabbath."

However, *Tell*'s contract called for a second opera, and Rossini was planning to base this second piece on Goethe's *Faust*. As he told the musician and journalist Ferdinand Hiller, four considerations prompted him in abandoning the theatre: first, a *Faust* mania that swept Paris and rendered his project supererogatory; second, the July Revolution, which undermined the contract and Rossini's Royal patronage; third, the passing of the Opéra from state into private jurisdiction; and lastly, the advanced age of Rossini's father, who wanted to return to Italy without having to die alone. To leave the theatre for a little while is happenstance; to return after a great while is a dare. Once gone, Rossini decided to stay away, voicing disapproval of the new composers, the new singers, the new stagecraft. Opera was becoming debased, he felt—and this only affirmed his Royalist aura, that air of *ancien régime*. Yet Rossini was artistically revolutionary—no Wagner, certainly, but no Handel, either.

None of this was clearly perceived by his contemporaries. Perhaps Rossini made it look too easy with his fleet and deft way with a pen; no one respects anyone who makes art fun. Furthermore, *Guillaume Tell*, the outstanding masterpiece of the era, was underrated by many because its apparent outgrowth—grand opera—was in fact a debased form of *Guillaume Tell*, like it but not as admirable. Years after, *Tell* inspired Verdi—*Don Carlos* is grand opera, and the influence is unmistakeable in *Aida* and *Otello*. Historians routinely note Verdi's "French" effects—Rossini invented them. So he had a long reach, after all. He must have sensed that he would, for some of the tart replies in these stories suggest a man who holds a very different opinion of his talent, and of his colleagues' talent, than they do. "Give us more *Barbers*," Beethoven urged; but Rossini had more than *opera buffa* to endow. Was he being mordantly ironic when, asked which of his operas

would survive, he cited only *The Barber,* the last act of *Otello,* and
the second of *Tell?*

An Ear for Music

The classic illustration of Rossini's amazing memory finds him, at age
fifteen or so, promising to get a copy of an aria for an amateur soprano
he wants to impress. But the head of the company performing the opera that contains the needed aria, himself the company's lead tenor, refuses to assist Rossini. Similarly, the company librarian says no. So
Rossini attends this opera, writes down the entire piece in piano score
from memory, and presents his handiwork to the stunned tenor.

"Impossible!" he says. "The librarian must have betrayed me!"

"Give me two more nights in the theatre," Rossini offers, "and I'll
copy down the orchestra score as well."

The tenor immediately befriends the young man and gives him a
commission to write an opera: a talent this acute is better used for you
than against.

> Incidentally, the story also illustrates Rossini's reputation as a lady's
> cavalier, one he was to sustain right through middle age.

Write It Again

Now for the classic instance of Rossini's melodic fecundity—and lazi-
ness. We find him composing a number in his bed, to keep warm on a
winter morning. The paper slips onto the floor out of reach. Rather
than brave the cold air to fetch it, Rossini simply starts over with a new
piece of paper . . . and a totally different piece.

> One of Rossini's first biographers, H. Sutherland Edwards, gives a more
> detailed version.
> A friend visits, and Rossini tells him, "I have just dropped a duet.
> Would you get it for me? It's somewhere under the bed." This done,
> Rossini shows his friend two pieces of manuscript score and asks,
> "Which do you like best? I have written two."
> "Nothing easier, surely, than to have picked it up?"
> "Nothing easier," Rossini replies, "than to write a new one."

Rossini Sets a Record

Rossini wrote *Il Barbiere di Siviglia* in thirteen days, it's said; and spent
the whole time in his dressing gown, unshaven.

"How ironic," a friend remarked, "that you wrote *The Barber* without shaving."

"But if I had shaved, I should have gone out. And if I had gone out, I should not have come back in time to finish *The Barber* in thirteen days!"

Il Barbiere di Roma

One morning, while rehearsing his *Torvaldo e Dorliska* for the Carnival season at Rome's Teatro Valle, Rossini was surprised to hear his barber say, "Till this evening, Maestro."

Rossini, about to leave the barber's shop, paused. "This evening?"

"Why yes, Maestro. Tonight is *Torvaldo*'s first orchestra rehearsal, is it not?"

"And what has *Torvaldo* to do with the case?"

"I play first clarinet in the orchestra."

Sure enough, that evening, there was the barber at the first clarinet's desk. Everyone commented on how gently Rossini discussed his mistakes with him, while storming at everyone else.

But then it doesn't do to upset a man who holds a razor to your throat every morning, does it?

The Great Trio

Adolphe Nourrit, the tenor who was to create Arnold in *Guillaume Tell*, and Nicolas-Prosper Levasseur, the bass who was to create Walter Fürst, were at Rossini's house while he was completing the opera's orchestration. Rossini suggested that they read through the trio in Act Two in which Fürst and Tell inform Arnold that his father has been killed by the Austrians; Rossini would fill in Tell's line.

As they sang, the two visitors were overwhelmed by the profound, sad beauty of the music, and when they finished, they could only throw themselves into Rossini's arms, too moved to speak. Levasseur wanted to sing the trio again, but Nourrit could not bear it. He was so taken with what he had sung that he had to cancel a concert for that evening.

"Poor Nourrit," said Rossini. "He's much too sensitive. This temperament of his will do him in one of these days."

Nourrit died a suicide.

M. l'Opéra Is Too Kind

Though *Guillaume Tell* became known among musicians and progressive cognoscenti as an extraordinary piece, the general public tired of it quickly. In its original run of fifty-six performances at the Opéra—a good but not spectacular stay—it lost the first scene of the third act and most of the fourth. Inferior casts further marred it. Finally, the Opéra dropped *Tell* from the repertory, retaining only Act Two (which has most of the plums: the soprano's "Sombre forêt," the big soprano-tenor love duet, the trio that so moved Nourrit, and the spectacular Massing of the Cantons) as a vocal diversion to texture mixed-grill evenings of ballet.

One day, Rossini met the director of the Opéra on the street. "Well, Maestro," says the impresario, anxious to show the composer that the Opéra is still looking after his treasure, "You are on the bills again tonight—we play the second act of *Guillaume Tell*."

"What," Rossini dryly replies, "the whole thing?"

Thoughtful Maestro

Strolling Paris with a friend, Rossini ran into Meyerbeer, who asked after his health. Rossini cited a string of calamities. Meyerbeer expressed all due dolor, and moved on; Rossini's friend then urged him to speed homeward to bed.

"My dear fellow, I feel perfectly fine," Rossini said. "But it so cheers our friend Meyerbeer to think that I'm at death's door that I hadn't the heart to disappoint him."

Another Meyerbeer Story

Meyerbeer died before Rossini, and the former's nephew, no great musician, composed a funeral march for his illustrious relation and showed it to Rossini.

"It's perfectly competent," said Rossini. "But I wonder if it wouldn't have been more delightful if you had died and your uncle had written the march."

Beware the Ut de Poitrine

One development that Rossini could never accustom himself to was tenors' tendency to sing high notes in chest voice, neglecting the sweet head voice of Rossini's youth. The chest voice was more thrilling; but what a din! When Enrico Tamberlik, the first to employ trumpeting chest tones on high C, paid a call, Rossini told his servant, "I shall be glad to see him—on the condition that he deposits his C outside with the coats. He can take it away with him the moment he leaves."

All'Autore dell'Bacio

The conductor Luigi Arditi, famous for the coloratura's showpiece waltz, "Il Bacio," appealed to Rossini to settle a confusion about the English Horn solo in *Guillaume Tell*'s overture. Arditi recalled it running a certain way, but his players kept insisting that they "had always played it *this* way." Which way was correct?

Taking up his visiting card, Rossini wrote out the correct figure on a little music staff, inscribed it "To the author of 'Il Bacio,' " and signed it.

The next time an English Horn presumed to know *Guillaume Tell* better than Arditi, the maestro whipped out his autographed treasure and settled the matter authoritatively. "Need I say," Arditi wrote in his memoirs, "that it was not without considerable satisfaction?"

Rossini on Wagner

Rossini was a celebrated purveyor of *table d'hôte*, so all Paris took note when he served a Wagnerian devoté a puddle of sauce without fish or meat—this, Rossini claimed, was the appropriate dish for someone who liked harmony without melody.

This and other tales denoting Rossini's dislike of Wagner swept Paris after the fiasco of *Tannhäuser*. But Rossini wrote a letter to a newspaper disclaiming them. He had no opinion of Wagner's music, he said, because he had not heard Wagner's music, except for the famous March from *Tannhäuser,* which he liked.

Wagner was so grateful that he paid a visit, and the two proceeded to discuss the state of the art, Wagner pointing out that in "Sois immobile" (Tell's address to his son before he shoots at the apple) Rossini had achieved a perfect wedding of music and drama—the very thing Wagner had been striving for all his life. Rossini wondered facetiously if he had been writing Wagner's Music of the Future without knowing it. Wagner answered that this was music for all time.

An impressive meeting of minds. But, as Rossini later remarked, "This is the man for whom the German people forgot Mozart."

The Strakosch Edition

Maurice Strakosch, impresario and musician, often devised his singers' embellishments, and became notorious for the amount of coloratura he could cram into an aria.

Once, in Paris, Strakosch took a singer to treat Rossini to their version of "Una voce poco fa."

"Very nice," says Rossini. "Who wrote it?"

Uh-oh. "Why . . . you did, Maestro."

"I? Never! *C'est une Strakoschonnerie!*"

A New Opera by Rossini!

For years, there were rumors: this company promises . . . That impresario is sure . . . A certain soprano has heard . . . And we are told that a wealthy aficionado at last determined to settle the matter and wrote to Rossini, by then removed to Italy. This Rossinian offered the composer a blank check for a new opera—and, lo, in the short term typical of Rossini's youth, a package was dispatched to the sponsor. A successor to *Tell!* How the man must have trembled as he cut the fastenings and pulled back the papers to reveal . . . a mortadella and a garlic sausage.

Catchy Tunes

Daniel-François-Esprit Auber was one of those composers who outraged Rossini by rising to fame in post-*Tell* Paris on a wave of twice-told tunes and situations. Still, Rossini retained his sense of humor. Attending Auber's latest *opéra comique,* Rossini kept saluting every time a major tune was heard, and at last a companion asked him what he was up to.

"Oh," said Rossini. "It's nothing, really. I'm just greeting old friends."

Rossini Dares the Pigeons

It was high time that Rossini take his place in stone among the immortals, and his friends collected a fortune to erect a monument to his art.

When the amount involved was quoted him, Rossini feigned amazement. "Give me the money," he said, "and I'll stand on the pedestal myself!"

GIACOMO MEYERBEER

Meyerbeer's fame was so fully invested that he tended to think of himself in the third person. "Hush!" he told a barking dog. "Meyerbeer's working!" Yet he is reviled by almost every commentator today, at least condescended to. His operas were flagrant rubbish well sung, we are told; or artful nonsense; or a triumph of stagecraft over art. It is one of opera's clichés that the fourth act of *Les Huguenots* is the exception to all this, especially the closing love duet, so intensely characterized that the opera's entire fifth act was often cut as anti-climactic. Even Wagner had to admire the duet's power to move and thrill—better yet, seemed to admit that there had been nothing like it before.

There was a great deal like it after, and this was Meyerbeer's problem. He was an original musician, but not a great one, so Meyerbeerean novelties that made no important effect on the average ear turned up, retuned and perfected, in other men's scores. No one, not even Wagner, failed to profit from Meyerbeer. They looted him for decades. By 1900, what had been good in Meyerbeer was better in everyone else, best in, say, *Aida, La Gioconda, Le Cid,* or *Die Königin von Saba*. Moreover, these later operas were easier to stage and sing. So Meyerbeer faded away.

There is no parallel in opera for such total eclipse after such prominence. Franz Schreker, wildly popular in German-speaking theatres in the 1910s and 1920s, has suffered a similar neglect, but qualitatively, not quantitatively: Schreker's lead roles didn't enter into the basic repertory of every singer living for three generations. We are speaking of a truly monumental fall: as if Puccini, today, suddenly lost his popularity and, ten years from now, had vanished from sight except for sporadic, generally unsuccessful revivals of *La Bohème* and *Tosca*. Moreover, Meyerbeer's were big works, spectacles doubly glorified by their concentration of great roles. *Les Huguenots* is longer than, and has more star roles than, *La Bohème* and *Tosca* combined. The disappearance of such works would have left a huge gap in the world repertory but for the fact that grand opera as such had fallen out of fashion. No wonder that Meyerbeer disappeared: his four major works for the Paris Opéra—*Robert le Diable, Les Huguenots, Le Prophète,* and *L'Africaine*—were the ultimate in grand opera.

No one did it better; this, too, was Meyerbeer's problem. His eagerness to please the Opéra's bourgeois audience did not recommend him to his more idealistic colleagues, and his transcultural résumé suggested that he had no commitment to anything but success. After all, Meyerbeer was a Berliner named Jacob Beer* who wrote German operas and failed; and who then moved to Italy as Giacomo to write Italian operas and suffered erratic success; and who then moved to France to write *Robert le Diable*, enjoy a sensation, and thus establish his metier. He was too adaptable, it seemed, an opportunist. What did he believe in, besides profits and fame? Objectionable, too, was Meyerbeer's collaboration with the librettist Eugène Scribe, so prolific he was considered not a writer but a "libretto factory."

Rossini in particular was outraged by the measly monsters that Meyerbeer and Scribe (and their imitators) raised up, for they all owed a great deal to Rossini, especially to *Guillaume Tell*. "Que voulezvous?" raged the Swan of Pesaro. "Je ne suis qu'un compositeur, moi! Eux, ils sont des *hommes d'affaires!*": I am only a composer: they are *businessmen!*

* The Meyer- was donated by a wealthy relative.

A businessman: so Meyerbeer was regarded by the art world. The ballet of defrocked nuns in *Robert le Diable* or the skating ballet in *Le Prophète;* the stodgy processions and endless set pieces; the double choruses, one side against the other in counterplay; and the insistence on treating religious problems among Christians—Meyerbeer, of course, was Jewish—seemed to some a vulgar carnival. "Effects without causes" was Wagner's judgment. The fact that much of this can be found in Wagner, including a lubricious ballet (not on skates), does not exculpate Meyerbeer, for, again, other masters used Meyerbeer's elements with a sense of rightness that he lacked himself. After *Tannhäuser*'s Bacchanale, *Robert*'s nuns lost their shock value. After *Die Meistersinger*'s exuberant parade of the guilds, Meyerbeer's processions seemed dumpy, fit for American high school graduations, not music theatre.

Actually, Meyerbeer was more than a cynical concocter. He was a careful worker—a plodder, in fact, revising and rehearsing with genuine commitment to his form. He was thought hypocritically diplomatic, trying to make a friend of everyone, and this was bound to hurt his reputation. Yet he is far more dishonored than dishonorable, the prime scapegoat of anti-Semites in the age between the ghetto and Auschwitz. Had Meyerbeer been less successful, he might have been more respected, for his narrative drive was bold and colorful. But it was thought unseemly that a Jewish composer should dominate the opera world's most influential theatre.

Meyerbeer was a victim, and his stories bear this out. The man himself is elusive—"everybody's friend" would not likely turn up in a story based on witty repartee. What we mainly see is Meyerbeer's friends and enemies assaulting him with contrary opinions—as we noted with Rossini, the one composer who had given to rather than taken from Meyerbeer and yet, like the others, his severe critic. It's a sad showing for the man who made grand opera the most successful genre of the mid-nineteenth century. There was a time when Meyerbeer was popularly ranked with Mozart: to the dismay and disgust of the entire music world.

Meyerbeer Holds a Rehearsal

A year after *Robert le Diable* took Paris by fascination, Meyerbeer came to London to reproduce the piece at Drury Lane. But the skimpy rehearsal schedule took the composer by surprise; the Opéra and its lavish weighing-in period had spoiled him.

"Excellent, genetlemen," he told the orchestra after the first runthrough. "I am quite sure that, after eight more rehearsals, you will be superb."

"I am sorry, Maestro," said the concertmaster. "This was not the first rehearsal. This was the only rehearsal."

"Is that true?" said Meyerbeer. "The only rehearsal? Well then, I won't detain you with any further remarks."

He left London the next day.

Meyerbeer Senses His Own Greatness

As Meyerbeer's guest at the Opéra for *Robert le Diable,* Rossini took delight in a particular number. "If you can write anything to surpass this," he said, "I will undertake to dance on my head."

"You had better begin practising, then," Meyerbeer replied, with a smile. "For I have just started the fourth act of *Les Huguenots.*"

"Ah? The fourth act? And what, my friend, is so special about this fourth act, may I ask?"

Meyerbeer's smile faded as he looked away thoughtfully. "Wait and see, my dear Maestro," he whispered. "Wait and see."

Mendelssohn Analyzes the Contents of Meyerbeer's Operas

"Melodies for whistling, harmony for the educated, instrumentation for the Germans, contra dances for the French, something for everybody— but there's no heart in it."

Conversation Piece

A group of *bons vivants* was sitting down to dinner, among them Ferdinand Hiller. The subject of Meyerbeer came up.

"Allons bon, mes amis," says Hiller. "Please let's not talk politics tonight."

Bribe versus Bribe

Meyerbeer couldn't work; a street musician was playing a barrel organ in the street, just outside the window of Meyerbeer's study. Worse yet, he was grinding out nothing but Rossini. Aiming a servant at the disturbance, Meyerbeer offered two francs if the nuisance would go play somewhere else. No—wait! Oh, how droll of Meyerbeer, Meyerbeer thought: *four* francs—if the nuisance would go play *Meyerbeer's* tunes in front of *Rossini's* house!

A moment later the servant returned. "I'm sorry, Monsieur. The organ grinder says no."

"No? To four francs?"

"He says Rossini gave him eight francs—to play for you!"

RICHARD WAGNER

"Bayreuth," an early visitor noted, "is almost unattainable"—uncomfortable, inhospitable, and hard to reach, a small town in Franconia that Wagner happened to choose as the site of his festival theatre. But "Bayreuth"—meaning not a place but an ideal of composition and performance—became the point opera had to reach. It was impossible yet essential, and this is the most remarkable thing about the eternally remarkable Wagner. Opera history is filled with unique authors, but how many radical reinventors?

Wagner was radical, determined to change the subject matter, ideology, musico-dramatic technique, auditorium structure, and even audience of the opera of Rossini, Cherubini, Meyerbeer, Auber. But Wagner did it in such a crass and ungrateful manner that it's hard to understand how even his genius could have broken through to success while making as many enemies as possible along the way.

Wagner could play the sycophant now and again. If Meyerbeer was the most powerful man in opera when Wagner was on the rise, then Wagner would play Meyerbeer for all the recommendation and commission he could get. He even flattered Meyerbeer's form of grand opera, writing a respectable version of it in *Rienzi*—"Meyerbeer's best opera," the wags called it. Yet, let Meyerbeer leave the room and Wagner might let loose with an anti-Semitic tirade, excoriating Meyerbeer for his success, Meyerbeer for being Jewish, and every one who was Jewish because Meyerbeer was successful and Wagner was not.

Wagner's hypocrisy is probably his overwhelming quality; it is difficult to name another great artist who was so loathsome a man. Beethoven was hard to tolerate, but Beethoven was temperamental, not treacherous. Wagner was a congenital user of people: he used the rich for money, the devoted for love, the public for support, and laughed at them all. He made his operas of saintly women and erring but redeemable men, but in the end the Wagner character who most resembles Wagner is Beckmesser, the loveless pedant of *Die Meistersinger*. Surely, Wagner intended the work's hero, Walther von Stolzing, as his vis-à-vis. Walther expounds the music of the future, though he doesn't call it that; and Wagner was never loveless or a pedant. But Walther is naturally noble, and Wagner never was. Beckmesser is petty, greedy, and a liar: this is Wagner to the nth.

The stories tend to emphasize Wagner's personality rather than his talent, making it is easy to forget that the talent was the most original and influential in opera history. But then Wagner's life was so filled with faux pas, miscalculation, fiasco, and scandal that one has to keep, forcing oneself to remember that, while he lived in vagabond chaos till he was fifty, Wagner in fact followed a very consistent artistic program. Let him be made court musical director at Dresden, and he will involve himself in revolutionary uprising and be forced into Swiss exile to escape prison—but meanwhile he has been systematically purging his style of its eclectic derivations from Marschner, Weber, and Bellini and is developing a unique autograph. Let the Paris Opéra propose to focus the attention of the greater music world upon the still provincially based Wagner and he will guarantee disaster by defying an ironclad Opéra convention—but Wagner's "music of the future" makes war on convention, so the greater his defiance, the surer his sense of self. Let Ludwig II of Bavaria champion Wagner and the composer will make himself so hated in Munich that he will again suffer expatriation in Switzerland, cut off from a nourishing culture—but the move is symbolically transitional, away from the tradition-bound court theatres where trivial art respects hierarchical social structures, onto an ideal Wagnerian stage built to present profound art to a socially unified audience. Wagner may have been his own worst enemy, but Bayreuth was attainable in the end.

Wagner was sixty when Bayreuth's foundation stone was laid, sixty-four when he gave the first festival—the first summer opera gathering in the modern style of Glyndebourne, Santa Fe, or Verona. It is fascinating to consider how much earlier in his life he might have attained Bayreuth had he been no less revolutionary an artist but much less reckless a person. What if he had given the Opéra the demanded ballet in the middle of *Tannhäuser?* Would a smash at the Opéra have given Wagner carte blanche to reform "la grande boutique" from within? Eventually, Wagner's influence grew so wide of reach that the charge of "Wagnerism" became the critic's cliché—no composer was safe from it. But what if Wagnerism had established itself not in a remote German town but in Paris, the capital city of music?

Some of the following stories will explain why this was not to be, and why, also, many of Wagnerism's most fervent admirers sooner or later conceived a violent distaste for Wagner the man—Nietzsche and King Ludwig, for prominent example. Nietzsche even became a foe of Wagnerism, of Bayreuth in all its aspects, from the sound of *Tristan* and the theme of *Parsifal* right through to the very look of the Bayreuth audience. But by that time Wagnerism was the music of the present, and an acceptable bourgeois experience. Viewing the parade of the overdressed, reactionary public at the reopening of Bayreuth in 1951, Wagnerian Ernest Newman turned to Wagner's grandson Wieland and said, "Your grandfather would never have approved of *this!*"

Wagner's Debut

Wagner's step-father (and possibly natural father) Ludwig Geyer was an actor-manager, and he gave young Richard his first taste of the theatre. The four-year-old boy was to play Wilhelm Tell's younger son in Schiller's drama with Geyer's company. Richard had but one line, spoken when Tell and his older son bid farewell to Tell's wife and the little one. According to Schiller, Richard was to cling to his mother in their dark hour and bravely declaim, "I'll stay with you, Mother." But Richard's sister Klara was playing the older son, and when Richard saw her leaving the stage, he cried out, "Klara, if you're going, I'll come along!" and raced after her.

It's a rather slight role for a farewell; but Wagner never appeared on the stage again.

The Silver Groschen Passage

When Wagner was rehearsing for the premiere of *Rienzi* in Dresden, he and his wife Minna were living on very little. It happened that the Rienzi, Joseph Tichatschek, thought his "Jungfrauen weinet, ihr Weiber klaget" solo and the succeeding ensemble in the Act Three finale was so beautiful that they all ought to pay for the privilege of singing it. Good as his word, Tichatschek produced a silver groschen and the other principals did the same. Thereafter, every time they approached the section, someone would say, "Here comes the silver groschen passage," and out came the pocketbooks.

Wilhelmine Schröder-Devrient, the Adriano, was perhaps a bit slow getting hers open; eventually she complained that rehearsing *Rienzi* would bankrupt her, and the game was disbanded.

So endeth the joke, though Wagner had the last word in noting, years later, that all those pennies nicely supplemented his and Minna's eating allowance. Little did the singers realize that their quaint gesture was in fact helping to keep Wagner alive.

Good Intentions

Visiting Dresden not long after the rebellion of 1848, journalist Henry Chorley commented to a local Wagnerian on Wagner's disloyalty to the king of Saxony, who, after all, had made Wagner his Kapellmeister and permitted the production of *Rienzi* at the court theatre. First Wagner exploits a state appointment, then he rises up against the state!

"But Wagner meant well," said the Dresdner. "He was really very fond of his King. He would have made him President of the Republic!"

Tannhäuser at the Opéra

Wagner came to Paris in the fall of 1859 with the idea of promoting a performance of *Tristan und Isolde*—an ideal one, perfectly cast and staged. The opera was, for a Wagner opus, uniquely practicable: three simple sets, five principals, scarcely any chorus to speak of, and (again, for Wagner) an orchestra of almost reasonable size.

Not only did the *Tristan* project fail, but three concerts of orchestral and choral selections from the operas failed badly. There was enthusiasm, yes; but small houses. Once more, as so often in the past, Wagner was ruined. Then he learned that Napoleon II had ordered that the Opéra present *Tannhäuser*.

Wagner was shocked, bewildered, and delirious with hope, all at once. He was given the authority to stage one of his works at the most important theatre in Europe—exactly why he had come to Paris in the first place! At that, the *Tristan* he had had in mind would never have been workable; *Tannhäuser* would be vastly more accessible to the general public in any case. Perhaps his luck had finally reached its upward turn. Like a child, he began to envision one triumph after another—*Tristan* in this theatre, *Die Meistersinger* in that, his *Ring* completed and ready to produce, perhaps *Parsifal* . . . "Never in my life," he wrote to Franz Liszt, "have the means for a first-rate performance been placed at my command so completely and unconditionally."

Most wonderful was the surprise itself: Wagner had not been aware that any opera of his had been up for consideration by the Opéra. In fact, none had: Princess Pauline von Metternich, wife of the Austrian ambassador and one of Wagner's earliest admirers, had brought the matter to Napoleon, and, it is suspected, pressed him with the help of highly placed French Wagnerians. In any case, all Wagner had to do now was cast the piece, approve the designs, oversee the orchestral preparation—including the augmenting of the Opéra's already oversize band with extra brass and quadruple winds—collaborate on the French translation of the libretto, and, in short, stage the piece to proclaim Wagnerism in every particular.

Except one: as every Opéra performance had to include a ballet at the very center of the evening, Wagner must add one into the contest scene in the Wartburg Hall of Song. The ballet was not an artistic convention, but a social one, for a section of debonair, well-born Opéra subscribers, the so-called "Jockey Club," were aficionados of the ballet—of the ballerinas, more precisely—and they habitually dined at leisure and arrived *comme il faut* at about ten o'clock. The ballet was for them.

Wagner resisted this nonsense, on social as well as on artistic grounds. Alphonse Royer, director of the Opéra, insisted that without the central dance interlude, no opera, *never, never,* could succeed at the Opéra. Wagner appealed to Princess Metternich and royal word came down: let Wagner have his way.

Ironically, at length the notion of a ballet began to appeal to Wagner as a way to illuminate the sensual atmosphere of the opening scene in the Venusberg, where Tannhäuser lives on love. Probably, too, he was amused at the idea that the Jockey Club would neither eat its cake nor have it: Tannhäuser *would* gain a ballet, but they would arrive too late to see it. For six months Wagner rehearsed his great entree into the most prestigious Hall of Song in the Western world, getting his way in nearly everything but choice of conductor. Wagner had wanted Wagner; Wagner had to settle for Pierre Dietsch, possibly incompetent and almost certainly unsympathetic to Wagnerism. And this time Wagner could not repair to Princess Metternich for assistance—he had run into one of the Opéra's most pointless and therefore most beloved traditions, that the orchestra never plays for the composer, not even for Meyerbeer himself.

A fiasco seemed inevitable, and not just because of Dietsch. The house claque hated Wagner because he refused to pay them off. The journalists hated him because he had failed to render the customary humble visit. And the Jockey Club hated him most, for the snub that promised them a second act without ballerinas. What if *Tannhäuser* succeeded? There would be countless nights of it, nights without a Jockey Club ballet. Worse yet, other composers might be heartened to drop ballet from their operas. *Tannhäuser* must be smashed. At the premiere, on March 13, 1861, these forces ranged themselves audibly against the performance—during the music, in true fiasco style.

Some who were present bore an honest dislike of Wagner's music— Berlioz, for instance. On the way into the theatre Berlioz ran into Théophile Gautier, and Gautier's fifteen-year-old daughter Judith was so indignant at what Berlioz said about Wagner that she piped up, "It is clear that you are speaking of a colleague—and, no doubt, of a masterpiece!" *

Many others in the house also attempted to defend Wagner; from the Royal Box itself came signals for silence. Princess Metternich argued the merits of Wagnerism during the intermissions in a fury, and many of the most distinguished musicians in France declared themselves converted to the cause. To no avail: the demonstrations were stepped up during the second act when the Jockey Club trooped in as noisily as possible. By the last act, the din was so dense that Baudelaire later claimed he had heard nothing of Tannhäuser's Rome Narration. Many of the anti-Wagnerians who had declined to take part in the demonstration were nonetheless glad it happened. On the way out, a French general told Princess Metternich, "Madame, you have cruelly

* Much later, Judith Gautier became the last of Wagner's mistresses, throwing terror into Cosima Wagner's life for the better part of a year.

repaid us for Solferino." Beat the Germans at war and they come back at you with music.

All Paris knew that the debacle was that of hostile sabotage rather than of artistic failure. "God grant me," Charles Gounod cried, "a failure like that!" Wagner had intrigued and what is more impressed a portion of the public. Swearing that they would prevail, the Jockey Club armed themselves with whistles and thoroughly destroyed the second performance. *Tannhäuser*'s only hope now lay with the third night, scheduled for a Sunday, when the Jockey Club busied themselves with other matters.

Wagner was too distressed by the first two demonstrations to hope for anything. When Royer suggested cutting the opera to allow time for a separate mid-evening ballet between the acts of *Tannhäuser,* Wagner simply shrugged, "Consider me as if I were dead, and do whatever you please!" For once in his lifetime of resolutions and demands, Wagner had lost the heart to fight. He did not even attend the third night, which, in the event, was whistled like the others. He laughed when told of this, though his hands were shaking; and the next morning he wrote to Royer requesting that *Tannhäuser* be withdrawn, noting that this would deliver the management of the Opéra from a very embarrassing position.

On the contrary, ticket sales for the *prima* had been good, for the second night impressive, and for the third more than excellent. On a run, *Tannhäuser* would likely pay its way right through the season. Had it lasted, say, sixty performances, Wagner would have made twenty-five thousand francs, a tremendous sum and more than enough to pay his debts, redeem the year he had spent getting *Tannhäuser* onstage, and put him in a position of strength for future negotiations. And, had they wished to, the Opéra directors could have ignored Wagner's request on contractual grounds. They might also have attempted to persuade Wagner to change his mind on the basis of the *Tannhäuser* furore, capped by a petition demanding that the opera be repeated and signed by eminent names in the arts and public life. Who knows? Some of the direst decisions are made by men who only wish to be talked out of them; and, in truth, *Tannhäuser* stood a good chance of becoming the basis for a general cultural attack upon the *ancien régime* in the person of the Jockey Club aristos, as disreputable an enemy as anyone with Wagner's politics could have hoped to humiliate.

But Wagner stood fast, the Opéra respected his request, and *Tannhäuser* vanished from the repertory, at a tremendous loss of money (though bits of the production were absorbed here and there into stagings of other works). One might be tempted to sum up the adventure as a typical Wagnerian crisis, just another chance for the composer to arrange to fail. But no rooted psychological problem prompted Wagner to withdraw *Tannhäuser* on the verge of success. It was the dull orchestra, and the dreadful conductor, and the uncooperative singers, and the expensively silly decor.

The odd truth of the matter is that Wagner hated the performance.

No Virtuoso

Wagner couldn't play the piano well.

When friends would tease him about it, he would say, "I play a good deal better than Berlioz."

Berlioz couldn't play the piano at all.

Rex ex Machina

In the spring of 1864, Wagner's fortunes reached their lowest ebb yet. He was deeply in debt. He was also deeply in love, but with someone else's wife, Mathilde Wesendonck. No company that he knew of had any plans to stage his operas, though he was now at work on *Die Meistersinger,* the longest and largest of the whole canon. He was in Stuttgart, but he might as well have been in China, so dismal were his prospects. To top it off, the keeper of the inn at which he was staying—hiding, really—told him that a nameless stranger was inquiring after Wagner, insisting that he had "urgent business" with him. This was no doubt one of his Viennese creditors. They had found him out, and he would soon be in jail.

The next morning, the stranger presented himself: Hofrat Franz Seraph von Pfistermeister of Munich, personal secretary to Ludwig II, the king of Bavaria. Ludwig was young, impressionable, and a passionate Wagnerian. He had sent Pfistermeister to bring Wagner to Ludwig's side, there to abide in eternal friendship, his earthly needs satisfied and his art made public.

The world had turned upside down—no, righted itself. Wagner dashed off a letter of gratitude to Ludwig in almost hysterical relief:

I send to you tears of the most heavenly emotion, to tell you that now the wonders of poetry have entered my poor, loveless life as a divine truth. And that life, with all the verses and music it contains, belongs henceforth to you, my gracious young king: Dispose of it as you will!

It is merest coincidence, but symbolic nonetheless, that, as Wagner was readying himself for his triumphal ride into Bavaria, word came that Meyerbeer—the most important author of everything in opera that Wagner had dedicated himself to destroying—had died.

The Schweinehunde Story

Another classic Wagner anecdote finds the Master, for once, tactfully silent while someone else makes unnecessary enemies with a gratuitous insult. Of all times, it happened on the eve of the premiere of *Tristan und Isolde* in the already anti-Wagnerian city of Munich, just looking for a chance to undermine the opera's success.

It was *Tristan*'s conductor, Hans von Bülow, who gave it to them. *Tristan*'s expansive orchestration called for more players than Munich was used to, and the orchestra section needed enlarging, with a concomitant loss of seats. When the theatre engineer objected, von Bülow snarled, "What does it matter if we have a few dozen *Schweinehunde* more or less?"

Schweinehunde, literally "pigdogs," sounds less offensive in the original; it's something like the German equivalent of "asses" or "jerks." Still, Munich brandished the insult as a stick with which to beat Ludwig's personal *Schweinhund* out of Bavaria. Von Bülow publicly apologized, explaining that he meant the term as a slam at Wagner's enemies only; this still took in most of Munich. For four days, the *Neuer Bayerischer Kurier* shrilled, "HANS V. BÜLOW IS STILL HERE!" in headlines of increasing size.

Not till Wagner added his own apology and begged the city for a cease-fire did Munich settle down to its real work: getting ready to loathe *Tristan und Isolde*.

Cosima Explains

It is a testament to the amazing talent that so many saw in Wagner that they were willing to forgive him almost anything. Consider Hans von Bülow: his wife Cosima was bearing Wagner's children, and still von Bülow could not turn against either of them. Perhaps he understood, somehow, that Wagner and Cosima were destined to make an extraordinary, an artistically necessary, couple; perhaps he was glad to give up the remarkable woman he had never felt equal to.

"I forgive," he told her, weeping.

Cosima said, "One must not forgive. One must understand."

Another *Rienzi* Story

In 1872, the Vienna State Opera mounted a handsome production of *Rienzi*. Vienna's intendant, Johann von Herbeck, not only spent lavishly of the season's budget but conducted the piece himself. Wagner was in town, and of course attended the performance, whereupon Herbeck dropped in on the composer's box to ask him how he liked it and receive his due praise.

"That fellow you cast as Rienzi!" Wagner crabbed. "Why, I wouldn't hire him to carry a fiddle case!"

Yet Another *Rienzi* Story

This production is in Bologna, the first Italian city to take to Wagner. During the first intermission, the mayor of Bolgna paid his respects in Wagner's box.

"You lucky fellow," cried Wagner, when the mayor rose to leave. "You are able to go, while I must remain here to the end of the fifth act listening to this vile opera!"

Definitely the Last *Rienzi* Story

Relishing Ernst von Schuch's conducting of *Rienzi* in Dresden, Wagner said, "He is the only *Schuch* (rustic patois for "shoe") that doesn't pinch me."

A Dinner in Bayreuth

To appreciate this tale, one must remember that Franz Liszt was: one, Wagner's most influential early supporter; two, a stupendous pianist; three, by this time an abbé; and, four, the father of Cosima Wagner.

Wagner and Liszt had left the dinner table while Cosima and Felix Mottl lingered over their coffee. After a bit Wagner returned, snorting and pouting.

"That old fake insists on playing me his latest Ave Maria!" Wagner complained.

Cosima bore this without condemning it. "Didn't you recently say that Father inaugurated a new era in art?"

"Yes," Wagner replied. "In fingering."

Nietzsche Begins To See Wagner Clearly

Visiting Bayreuth in 1874, Nietzsche, an amateur musician, brought with him the piano score of Brahms's *Triumphlied,* a jingoistic choral piece. Wagner took offense. One did not hold any other gods even near him; and, anyway, the *Triumphlied* was "Handel, Mendelssohn, and Schumann enveloped in leather." Wagner raged at Brahms for composing, and at Nietzsche for thinking Brahms a composer.

Nietzsche said nothing at the time. But later, to his sister, he gently observed, "Lisbeth, at that moment Wagner was not great."

What the Kaiser Said to Wagner upon Arriving at Bayreuth for the World Premiere of *Der Ring des Nibelungen*

"I never thought you'd pull it off."

The Last Meeting of Wagner and Nietzsche

Yet another important visitor to that first Bayreuth festival, tormented by headaches that were literally blinding, was Friedrich Nietzsche. He was already in the process of turning against Wagner, it appears—Cosima later averred that the Nietzsche-Wagner feud was entirely the result of Nietzsche's having attended *Ring* rehearsals and performances with his senses so debilitated.

In any case, a favorite Wagner legend finds the two taking a walk along the rocky coast of Sorrento one suggestively autumnal evening a year after the Festival. As clouds hover and stray above and the waves prank below, Wagner speaks of *Parsifal,* of its pieties and love. Nietzsche, hearing behind this the pietistic, sentimentalistic Wagner, the Wagner of numberless bigotries and disloyalties, finds himself unable to reply. Wagner the monster is at last revealed to him; Nietzsche must retreat and reclaim his sanity. Excusing himself, he marches off into the dusk.

The two never met again.

Since Ernest Newman, every major Wagner biographer has persuasively argued that the story is drivel, the romance of Elisabeth Förster-Nietzsche, Nietzsache's notoriously unreliable amanuensis and sister. Dismantling the tale has become almost as classic a Wagnerian energy as recounting it used to be. Nietzsche already knew about *Parsifal,* Cosima's diary entries for this period reveal harmony rather than a breach, and the weather was cold, grey, and bitter: these are the major points of rebuttal. However, some of Wagner's biographers are at the same time eager to heal the feud between these two great minds,

to find some way in which Nietzsche's misgivings might be appeased
and Wagner's faults forgiven. This is not to be. Whatever the sub-
stance of their last meeting, Nietzsche became convinced that Wagner
was one of the most corrupt and malign forces operating in Western
culture.

Wagner on Rossini

At *Il Barbiere di Siviglia,* Wagner turned to a friend and whispered,
"How I love Rossini! But don't tell my Wagnerians—they would never
forgive me!"

A Matter of Duty

Franz Strauss, father of Richard, first horn of the Munich court orchestra, and lover of Mozart, hated Wagner. It was Strauss alone who
remained seated when the orchestra rose to solemnize Wagner's death,
and never would he accept a summons to join the orchestra at Bayreuth in the summer. Once Wagner asked Strauss why he was willing
to play Wagner in Munich but not in Bayreuth.

"Here I am a public employee," Strauss replied. "I *have* to play
Wagner!"

It works better in the original: "Hier bin ich Staatsbeamter, hier muß
ich ja blasen!" The tale has become so much a part of Munich's musical lore that today it is retold as if it had happened last week.

Parsifal und Gretel

Preparing the premiere of *Parsifal,* Wagner learned that the scenery was
moving too slowly to accommodate the Transformation Music: he would
have to add in a few bars, or the Grail Scene would be under way before the Grail Temple was entirely in place.

"They always said my music was too long!" Wagner raged. "Now it
is too short!"

Engelbert Humperdinck, one of the live-in Bayreuth entourage, set
down a possible interpolation, though it was of course unthinkable that
Wagner would let anyone put as much as a note into *Parsifal* except
Wagner himself.

Wagner accepted it.

Don't look for that touch of Humperdinck in the *Parsifal* score; the addition was not published, and as soon as the stage machinery was speeded up, Humperdinck's contribution was dropped and forgotten.

Someone Dares To Cheer at *Parsifal*

From the first, *Parsifal* was sacred art, unclappable; one was supposed to behave as if in church. Imagine the scandal when, at the eighth performance of the first Bayreuth series, some crazy was so taken with the Flower Maidens that he shouted a "Bravo!" Of course the entire audience turned to shush him.

It was Wagner.

The Last Work

Truth to tell, the revelation of *Parsifal* left Wagner's devotees stimulated, fulfilled, rapt, and exhausted. Even Eduard Hanslick, in many ways the most decisively anti-Wagnerian music critic, was moved. Taking supper with Hanslick and Angelo Neumann, August Förster suddenly said, "Just wait—Wagner's not long for this world!"

"What makes you say such a thing?" asked Neumann, breaking the shocked silence.

"A man who is capable of producing a thing of that order *cannot* have much time left on earth. His work is finished!"

And so, indeed, it proved.

GIUSEPPE VERDI

"My long career is now over," he said on the night of *Otello*'s Scala premiere. No more operas. Yet mobs of grateful Italians cheered him at his hotel, roused by Francesco Tamagno's impromptu quotation of the Moor's opening line, "Esultate!": Exult! Verdi tolerated the noise; honor bored him. And after the first three performances, traditionally overseen by the composer since the days of *opera seria,* Verdi departed the public scene. "Till midnight I am still Maestro Verdi," he told them at the reception following *Otello*'s third night. "But then I return to being the peasant of Sant'Agata."

So Verdi loved to see himself: as the simple son of the earth, perhaps talented, who knows? But not fine, not eminent. Yet Verdi was no peasant. In background he was of the middle class—his father was a storekeeper, and his first wife the daughter of a wealthy merchant with whom Verdi himself boarded. Moreover, he was an educated and, better, a cultured man, well read in the classics. He was not cosmopolitan, however. Wherever he went, to Naples, Paris, London, Petersburg—he remained the Po Valley rustic, forthright, resolute, intolerant, and grouchy. He became the symbol of the nationalist Risorgimento movement not only because the letters of his name read out, as graffito, the acronymn for Vittorio Emmanuele, Re d'Italia, and not only because of the patriotic and democratic subjects he set, but because his music became the sound of the time and place in which Italy realized its nationhood: in which the different Italian states made a culture of what they had in common. It was a dangerous, exhilarating, and ultimately fulfilling era; Verdi supplied its anthems.

This makes the man a wonderful study in biographical history. But his personal rigidity and distaste for backstage intrigue limits his availability to anecdote. His personality comes through vividly in his letters, and, luckily, almost every major correspondent ignored his injunction to destroy them.* But of encounters with impresarios and divas, of feuds, scandal, and repartee, there is surprisingly little for an output of twenty-eight operas. Verdi delivers not anecdotes, but opinions; of his contemporaries in music, of performance practices, of audiences and critics, of politics and statesmen, of morality, customs, and the social contract. He was an inward-looking man, private because he had so much to do by himself or with a few close friends. He so hated dealing with strangers, even when they were colleagues, that, though he was the most expert theatre composer Italy ever produced, he despised the theatre all his life. Impresarios were reckless, the public restless, singers vain, and critics antagonistic.

Growing dissatisfied with the conditions in which all opera composers had to work, Verdi began to make demands for authorial privilege. As early as *Macbeth*—on which, on behalf of his beloved Shakespeare, Verdi took special care—he insisted that the all-important first production of each title satisfy him in every detail or he would withhold his work from the world. This ultimatum, along with such contemporary reforms as Wagner's erection of his own anti-social, pro-art theatre at Bayreuth, led to the autocratically idealistic regimes of Toscanini and Mahler, who institutionalized immaculate and committed presentations of the score as opera's guiding imperative. Thus, while taking the structures of Bellini, Mercadante, and Donizetti into a more elastic format, Verdi also imposed the composer—over singers and public—as opera's overwhelming authority.

Some of this comes through in the stories, also some of the grouchiness and a great deal of the rigidity. But keep in mind that Verdi to an extent revised his past in his letters, from which the stories derive, smoothing over some incidents and punching up others, to create a legend that would protect rather than irritate him. Certain classic Verdi stories—the resistance to setting *Nabucco,* the delayed revelation of *Rigoletto*'s most infectious tune, the auditioning of *Il Trovatore* for the elitist aficionado—may be revisions of the truth or wholly inven-

---

nanuele Muzio, Verdi's sole pupil and lifelong friend, was the exception. Muzio's last letto Verdi, however, survives at Sant'Agata, Verdi's estate—farm, really—at Busseto. "Renber me sometimes," Muzio wrote, "and let us meet as late as possible in the other world."

tions. Or: if Verdi had truly washed his hands of opera when offered
Nabucco, why was he still living in Milan? He had nothing to keep
him there. What if he did withhold a number from the *Rigoletto* rehearsals till the last minute? Eleventh-hour composition was routine
in the opera of Verdi's Italy. As for taking delight in the disdain of
the critic, no one was more disgusted with a bad notice than Verdi.
Remember, then, for the next few pages, that in some instances Verdi
wrote his own anecdotes.

Saved by the Bell

An oft-repeated tale reminds us how heavy the force of destiny lies on
the history of art. In 1814, the village of Le Roncole in the Po Valley
was sacked by the Austrian and Russian armies on their march against
the French. The women of the village took refuge with their children
in the church of San Michele Arcangelo, but the invaders swept inside
and killed everyone, except one mother who hid in the belfry with her
infant son.

That little boy was Giuseppe Verdi.

Most of Verdi's biographers mistrust the story, but a plaque com-
memorates the event in San Michele's presbytery, and apparently Verdi
did occasionally refer to the incident, though not in his letters. Documentary proof, then, is lacking; but not belief. As Frank Walker
pointed out in *The Man Verdi*, "no one who has had any experience
of what it means to be 'liberated' by Russians could find anything im-
probable in it." It rounds out the whole picture nicely to recall that
Verdi wrote an opera called *The Force of Destiny;* and, in *Il Trovatore,* a baby is saved from death by mere chance. By a gypsy, however, and not in a church belfry.

Fly, Thought

The most basic of Verdi tales finds the disheartened young composer
swearing off opera forever. His wife and two children have died, one
after the other; and his second opera, a farce written by application of
pure will, has suffered a terrible failure at La Scala. Though he is still
under contract to Scala's director, Bartolomeo Merelli, Verdi decides to
return to Busseto and be what, clearly, he should have been from the
start, the local maestro of nowhere.

But Merelli refuses to accept the young composer's resignation.
Chancing upon Verdi one evening in the street, Merelli suggests they
walk along together to the Scala. And, what do you know, Merelli
happens to have just the thing to revive Verdi's sense of purpose, a new

libretto on King Nebuchadnezzar by Temistocle Solera. It was written
for Otto Nicolai, but he turned it down. Imagine! That foolish German
wants to prove himself as a composer of Italian opera in its very capital
city—at the Scala, no less! Yet he doesn't know a great libretto when
he reads one. A splendid work! Superb entrances and effects, beautiful
lines! Magnificent! And that obstinate Nicolai won't have it! Here, let
Verdi take it home and read for himself.

"Why should I?" Verdi snaps.

"It won't hurt you, will it?"

Verdi will have nothing to do with it, so Merelli forces it on him and
hurries him off before Verdi can force it back on Merelli. So Verdi takes
it home. Throwing it on a table, he happens to glance at the open book
and reads the line, "Va, pensiero, sull'ali dorate": Fly, thought, on golden
wings. Intrigued, Verdi reads more, then—furious at himself for weak-
ening in his resolve—shuts the book and goes to bed.

He can't sleep. The words haunt him; the poetry has certain possibilities. Certainly Nicolai is no judge of librettos. Verdi rises and reads
through the libretto several times. The next morning, he shows up in
Merelli's office.

"Well?"

"Musicabilissimo," Verdi admits.

"Then set it to music."

"I won't have anything to do with it, I tell you!"

Merelli stuffs the book in Verdi's overcoat pocket, shoves him out of
his office, and locks the door.

"What could I do?" Verdi wrote later, much later. "One day a verse,
the next day another; this time a note, another time a melody; and little by little the opera was composed."

Nabucco. And with the success of this, Verdi's third opera, his career
was righted, encouraged, and assured.

Uninvited Audience

Readying *Nabucco* for its premiere, Verdi encountered one of those
sloppy, sullen, aimless rehearsals at which nobody is trying and nothing goes right. Worse yet, workmen were very noisily repairing the interior of the ancient building, so if there *had* been anything worth listening to, it couldn't have been heard. At "Va, pensiero," the chorus
sang sluggishly, utterly unmoved by the patriotic despair that had attracted Verdi to the piece in the first place. But, oddly, the yelling and
banging of the workmen had suddenly ground to a halt. Looking around,
Verdi saw them sitting on their ladders and scaffolds, listening. At the

number's end, they broke into an ovation, shouting, "Bravo, bravo! Viva il maestro!"

"Then I knew," says Verdi, "what the future had in store for me."

No Horn

The plot of *Ernani* turns upon a horn given to the bass as a token of the tenor's honor: if the bass sounds the horn, the tenor must take his own life. As both love the same woman, the bass does blow the horn, in the last scene, just after the tenor and soprano have wed, turning a joyful duet into a highly dramatic trio. It was an unusual way to end an opera in those days, as the soprano of the premiere at Venice's La Fenice, Sophie Loewe, petulantly pointed out to Verdi while agitating for something more conventional, such as a solo finale for Sophie Loewe.

If the soprano was miffed, the director of the Fenice was scandalized. "A horn at the Fenice!" he cried. "A *horn!* Such a thing has never been seen!"

"Well, it will be seen," said Verdi mildly.

It was, of course: seen and heard, in its shocking but very theatrical novelty; and the trio closed the opera, no showpiece for soprano. As the opera scored a great success, both Loewe and the house decided they were glad after all that Verdi had allowed them to make a little history with a trio and a horn.

The Evil Eye

In Naples for the premiere of *Luisa Miller,* Verdi was careful to avoid running into a musician named Capecelatro, a well-meaning fellow but one said to bear the Evil Eye. When in public, Verdi moved under a heavy guard of friends, and otherwise stayed at home behind locked doors. One glance of the Evil Eye and *Luisa Miller* would fail.

Actually, Verdi may have used Capecelatro as an excuse to keep to himself, for this was getting increasingly harder to accomplish as his fame spread. True, out on the street he had to tolerate his crowd of sheltering friends. But the Evil Eye gave him a wonderful excuse to appear at nothing but rehearsals.

Ruse or precaution, Verdi did evade Capecelatro. Then, on the night of the premiere, as Verdi was setting up the principals for the last act, Capecelatro broke through the lines to embrace his *egregio maestro* Verdi.

Whereupon a piece of the stage fittings immediately came crashing down where Verdi was standing, and just missed killing him.

Top of the Charts, Part I

The greatest sin a composer could commit was to repeat himself before the same audience. Let an aria from an opera heard in Naples turn up in another opera heard in Milan; that was fine—what Milanese would ever go to Naples? But woe to the man who tried to sing the same tune twice in the same place.

Thus Verdi was sometimes uneasy when rehearsing a premiere, fearful that unauthorized ears might pick up one of his catchier tunes before the first night, spread it about the town, and expose Verdi, on opening night, to the jeers of a public who thought they were being cheated of novelty.

Venice, 1851: *Rigoletto* is in rehearsal, and the tenor is lacking one of his numbers.

"There is plenty of time yet," Verdi tells him. "You'll get it."

The days go by, each one witnessing a similar conversation, till at last Verdi hands the importunate tenor a piece of paper, exacting his word of honor that he will not sing, hum, or whistle the melody. *No one must hear it!*

The tenor agrees; but Verdi is not done yet. The orchestra, the other singers, and the theatre staff must also keep the secret. All did.

And of course "La donna è mobile" was *Rigoletto*'s big hit at the premiere.

Top of the Charts, Part II

Everyone in Venice took up the aria, words and all. One heard it in *campo* and *calle,* on the bridges and in the gondolas, from Cannaregio to San Pietro di Castello.

Rigoletto's librettist, Francesco Maria Piave, found the tune useful one day when he spotted a woman he had loved and lost approaching in the street. As they passed, Piave quoted the first two lines:

> La donna è mobile
> Qual piuma al vento.
>
> Woman is fickle
> As a feather in the wind.

Piave's former mistress took up the song, improvising words on the spot:

> E Piave è un asino
> Che val' per cento.
>
> And Piave is an ass
> Who is worth nothing.

An Audition

A Great Critic visited Verdi as he was putting the finishing touches on *Il Trovatore*.

"What do you think of this?" Verdi asked him, playing the Anvil Chorus.

"Trash," announced the Great Critic, for he loved only the finest things.

"Now try this," said Verdi, offering the Miserere.

"What rubbish!" the Great Critic observed, for his nuanced sensibility could accept only the most profound art.

"One last test," said Verdi. He presented the tenor's aria, "Di quella pira."

"It's beastly," noted the Great Critic, for anything less than nobility made him shudder.

Verdi rose from the piano and embraced the Great Critic in momentous joy.

"What is the meaning of this?" asked the Great Critic.

"My dear friend," Verdi told him, "I have been writing a popular opera—an opera for the public, not for the purists and classicists and solemn judges, like you. If you liked this music, no one else would. But your distaste assures me of success. In three months, *Il Trovatore* will be sung, whistled, and played all over Italy!"

Verdi's Most Famous Letter

7 March, 1853

Dear Emanuele Muzio,

La Traviata last night a fiasco. Was the fault mine or the singers? Time will decide.

Always yours,
G. Verdi

The Man Who Didn't Like *Aida*

One Prospero Bertani wrote to Verdi from the town of Reggio, having traveled to Parma to hear *Aida* and not having enjoyed it. Others seemed to admire it—he overheard many an enthusiastic discussion of the work on the train returning to Reggio. Assuming that *Aida* required patience and a second hearing, Bertani made the trip again.

No luck. *Aida*, he concluded, was a work without a drop of genuine excitement, an empty spectacle that would vanish as soon as the publicity died down.

However, as Bertani lived on a stipend from his family, the money thrown away on the two *Aida* trips nagged at him, even disturbed his sleep. Would Verdi kindly refund the amount to him? It seemed only fair.

The bill ran as follows:

Railroad fare	5.90 lire
Theatre ticket	8 lire
Detestable dinner at railroad station	2 lire
	15.90 lire
The whole thing over again	× 2
	31.80 lire

Verdi directed his publisher to reimburse Bertani, on the condition that he would avoid all future Verdi premieres. Too many more such trips and the simple act of maintaining one's career could run into real money!

One other thing: Verdi would not pay for Bertani's two dinners. He could have eaten at home.

Verdi's Little Joke

In the late 1870s, with *Aida* behind him and apparent retirement cutting him off from the theatre, Verdi quietly began to consider writing a comic opera. Just then, an article in the *Gazzetta Musicale* quoted Rossini's opinion that Verdi had no gift for comedy.

Verdi was outraged, not least because his publisher, Ricordi, also published the *Gazzetta*.

"Just think," Verdi wrote to Ricordi. "For twenty years I've been searching for a comic-opera libretto, and now that I've practically decided on one, you've inspired the public to hiss it even before it's written! But have no fear! If by chance, in spite of this Solemn Judgment, my evil genius persuades me to write a comic opera . . . I'll let it ruin some other publisher!"

Verdi on Gambling

In Monte Carlo, Verdi visited the tables of the casino with austere determination. "I made a point of losing," he said, "so as to disgust myself once and for all with that horrible thing called gambling."

Verdi at Home

However much a public figure, Verdi guarded his privacy ever more tensely as the years passed. But here's a rare glimpse of the family scene at Sant'Agata: Giulio Ricordi has come to visit as the composition of *Otello* is drawing to a close, and Verdi plays his publisher a bit of the score as his wife, Giuseppina Strepponi, looks on.

As Verdi finishes, Peppina turns to Ricordi and says, in dialect, "L'è ancamò, el me Verdi!"

Or, roughly, "My Verdi still has it, eh?"

Verdi Says No

In 1898, La Scala prepared to reopen after a year's closure, under the new and imposingly idealistic management of Giulio Gatti-Casazza and Arturo Toscanini. Boito suggested Verdi's Sacred Music, four pieces of sublime technical mastery and interior piety, nothing like the more operatic Manzoni Requiem. Typically, Verdi not only did not encourage but actively resented any enthusiasm for the Sacred Music. He allowed Boito to have it performed in Paris, but asked him not to urge the quartet on La Scala.

Why? "First of all," Verdi said, "because I do not believe the work can be presented successfully at La Scala under present circumstances, and second, because my name is too old and boring." The most famous man in Italy went on, "It bores even me."

This was a Verdi tired of everything but the promise of his own death.

How To Run an Opera House

Boito introduced Gatti to Verdi when the Scala reopened, and the great maestro gave the young impresario some advice, mainly on ignoring the critics and attending carefully to box-office receipts. As Verdi got into his cab, he leaned out the window for a last word.

"The theatre," he told Gatti, "is intended to be full and not empty. That's something you must always remember."

Advice from an expert.

How To Write an Aria

Illica and Giacosa originally wrote the libretto of *Tosca* not for Puccini but for Alberto Franchetti, born to the nobility and of a temperament that did not understand melodrama. Franchetti feared that *Tosca* was too crude for music, and decided to bring the text to Verdi for judgment.

Illica read his treatment aloud, and for the first two acts Verdi was no more than receptive. But at "E lucevan le stelle," Verdi leaped to his feet, crying "Bellissimo! Ma bravo, Illica!"

Franchetti was gratified, but startled. The great maestro actually liked the libretto?

Verdi did—especially this last scene of the hero's farewell to life and love as dawn breaks over Rome. "What in the world do you young composers want?" he asked Franchetti. "If only I had had such an excellent libretto, I who in my youth had to be satisfied with all kinds of stuff!"

Franchetti could scarcely credit his hearing. Surely there was a catch somewhere. How would Verdi, for instance, set those verses of "E lucevan le stelle"? In recitative? *Arioso?* A full-blown *romanza?*

"My dear Franchetti," said Verdi. "I would simply make some music . . . a little music, that's all."

JULES MASSENET

Massenet stands out in this company of composers for his subservience as an artist and unctuous politesse as a man. Where his colleagues sought to stimulate the public with new forms, and stormed at everyone who got in their way, Massenet invariably obliged. Wielding a sharp eye for the picturesque, a good ear for ethnic pastiche, the moistly ravishing *phrase massenétique décadante,* and a battery of extraordinary star sopranos, he dominated turn-of-the-century opera from Petersburg to New Orleans, only to fade from the scene toward the end of his career and, after death, suffer eclipse almost immediately. A Massenet Revival is now under way, strongly supported by Richard Bonynge and Joan Sutherland, but today's critics are as irritated by the revivals as those of Massenet's time were enchanted when the operas were new. Apparently Massenet wrote too well: for his era only.

He was a careful and disciplined worker, favoring the early morning hours (so he could pass the afternoon along the boulevards and the evening checking the box-office take of whatever Massenet opera was going on that night), plenty of scratch notes, numerous revisions, and, at the last, an immaculate fair copy on luxurious paper. Then came the premiere, floated—once Massenet had established his name— by the soprano of the moment. The spectacular Californian Sibyl Sanderson created Thaïs and Esclarmonde; Europe's choice Carmen Emma Calvé took *La Navarraise* and *Sapho;* Georgette Bréjean-Silver sang Cinderella's Fairy Godmother in *Cendrillon* (and got the ultimate in job references when Massenet wrote her a new aria to interpolate into *Manon* in place of the Gavotte); Lucienne Bréval was Griselidis; Lucy Arbell played Thérèse; and *Chérubin* offered the *embarras de richesse* of Mary Garden, Marguerite Carré, and Lina Cavalieri. Massenet became so identified as a constructor of soprano vehicles that it seemed fitting that, when he composed an opera without a leading woman, *Le Jongleur de Notre-Dame,* Mary Garden should usurp the title role *en travesti.* At least, it seemed fitting to Mary Garden.

Opera's legends love the *amoureux,* and naturally Massenet was linked with at least a few of his stars in popular imagination, particularly Sanderson, his discovery and protégée. The reason that *Esclarmonde* is studded with a remarkable number of extremely high notes is that Sanderson's voice was, too; Massenet's early piano sketches of the opera call for a simple lyric soprano, not a human glockenspiel. Such collaboration between maestro and soprano, however artistic, tends to cause talk. And talk causes legend. Yet Massenet controlled the flow of rumor somewhat with his discretion and diplomacy. He was effortfully polite, at least when one was in the room. "Massenet," Mary Garden avers, "was the yes-man par excellence . . . He could say the most marvelous things to someone, pay the greatest compliments in the world. And the moment the door closed behind that someone he would turn to the others in the room and say something quite the contrary."

Léon Daudet left a more detailed impression:

> He began on the principle that people love sweets and must be filled with sugar to the bursting point. At this he never failed. When he had congratulated everyone present on his looks and work, he would throw himself into a chair and play the thirsty child who wants his drinky, or the doggy-poo who would like a bit of cake . . . Ancient music-loving women would surround him, simpering and eager, their bodily architecture devastated or shaky, of that type we euphemistically call "handsome remains." These Massenet would treat as if they were twenty, wreathing them in flowers.

A flatterer, Massenet: of those around him and those in the audience. Not a one of his many operas tested their taste for *opéra de cuisine,* spicy and served with elegance. At least Massenet held cordon bleu. Like most French composers, he maintained separate Opéra and Opéra-Comique strains, writing grand for the big house and intimate for the smaller; and sometimes remixing the elements of the one into the other.

Grand opera launched him, with the success of *Le Roi de Lahore* at the Opéra in 1877. Yet those great doors were strangely closed to him when he offered *Hérodiade,* his version of the Salome story. As the Opéra's chief Vaucourbeil explained it, the libretto was provocative (though vastly more refined than the Oscar Wilde text that Richard Strauss was to use), and there was the feeling that some of the more established composers had leagued themselves against the upstart in a kind of "understanding" with Vaucourbeil.

Hérodiade was premiered at Brussels, as trainloads of Parisians

marched out of the Belgian end of the trip chanting "Down with Vaucourbeil" and marched back into Paris out of the Gare de l'Est humming "Il est doux" and "Vision fugitive." For their glorification of
Biblical scandal, Massenet and his librettist Paul Milliet won secondary excommunication, but this only fed the growing report of the
musician whose forte lay in the presentation of sensuous women.
Manon and worldwide reclame followed, then the Sanderson and Calvé
operas—the blond enchantress, the tempestuous brunette—and by 1900
Massenet was the biggest name in opera.

One composer Massenet does resemble, perhaps: Meyerbeer. He too
obliged, served his public as if from a menu, and he too has lost his
popularity. But where Meyerbeer was a man of epochs who extended
from Metastasio, the castratos, and Rossini right into Wagner and
Verdi, Massenet simply and neatly capped his era as the last and greatest
master of opéra comique. He feels so *fin de siècle* that one is astonished to realize that his prime covered over three decades—decades in
which Wagner was assimilated into the great western mind and ear,
in which expressionism and dada erupted, in which *Dubliners* was
written. Yet, except for a touch of Wagnerian *frisson* in *Esclarmonde*'s melodic cut and orchestration, Massenet was not listening to
any of it. "He was always," Mary Garden recalled, "gushing."

A Lesson in Humility

Sapho, one of Massenet's Emma Calvé projects, tells of a wordly Parisienne who loves and gently abandons an innocent lad from Prov-
ence. Preparing the premiere in 1897, Calvé was detained in some mishap and arrived ten minutes late for the last general rehearsal, a breach
of theatre ethics that the composer could not let pass. With the entire
company standing by, Massenet vent upon Calvé all the rage and worry
built up over the weeks. Calvé was the very center of the show, the
performer upon whom *Sapho* depended. And *Calvé was late!*

"Mademoiselle Calvé," Massenet announced, biting off the words and
spitting them at her, "an artist worthy of the name would never keep
her colleagues waiting!"

Stung, Calvé turned and marched out of the hall—for all she knew,
out of *Sapho* itself forever. But Calvé was indeed an artist worthy of
the name. Turning back before she had even left the building, she re-
joined her fellows, now milling about in worried, angered, or philosophical groups, and cried, "My friends, the maître is right. I am at
fault. Forgive me! I am ready to rehearse my role, if I am permitted to
do so!"

To the company's applause, Massenet and Calvé embraced, maître
and artist reunited.

Massenet Plans a Murder

While working on *Thérèse*, Massenet decided to have a telephone installed in his Paris home, so he could confer with his librettist Jules Claretie on the spur of the moments. As Massenet was at the height of his renown he got his phone the day he asked for it, and the favor of having his number withheld from the *annuaire;* this may well have been the first unlisted number in Paris.

Handling the apparatus gingerly and speaking into it almost in disbelief, Massenet rang up Claretie to discuss their opera's final scene. *Thérèse,* set during the French Revolution, closes as the heroine's husband crosses the stage in the tumbril on his way to execution. And then . . . Well, surely the heroine must die. But how?

"Cut Thérèse's throat," Massenet advised Claretie, "and it will be all right."

Suddenly they heard a strange voice: "Oh, if I only knew who you were, you scoundrel, I would denounce you to the police! So calmly discussing this terrible crime! And who is to be the victim?"

The telephone wires had crossed. Unnerved, Massenet and Claretie simply ignored the intruder. "Once her throat is cut," Claretie remarked, "she can join her husband in the cart. I prefer that to poison."

"Oh, that's too much! Now the rogues want to poison her! I'll call the police. *I demand an inquiry!*"

As with so many good opera stories, this one strikes a false note. Thérèse isn't murdered: she simply cries out "Vive le roi!" and the mob drags her to the cart, to ride with her husband to the guillotine. It's difficult to imagine the authors even considering cutting her throat— people don't die that way in opera, especially in Massenet's. However, the composer himself told the story in his memoirs, so we'll have to take him at his word. At least the crossed wires ring a true bell: the Paris telephone system has tolerated kinks since its adoption. Jean Cocteau's play *La Voix Humaine* (The Human Voice) and Francis Poulenc's operatic setting of it get some mileage out of the alien voices that can rip into the most intimate phone calls without warning. As they say in Paris, the only thing worse than a stranger who interrupts your call is the stranger who doesn't.

Cheap Funerals Aren't Fun

Toward the end of his life, Massenet was honored with a gala at the Opéra, and a friend dropped by to express his regrets: a rich uncle had just died, naming this man as his heir. He had no choice but to observe a suitable mourning and neglect all galas. Indeed, he had just come from

the undertaker's, and bemused Massenet with the report of his preparations.

"If Monsieur wants a first-class funeral," the undertaker had said.
"Ah! Then! The church will be hung in black, the arms of the deceased
will be suitably displayed, singers and players from the Opéra will assist in the music, and the catafalque will impress even the connois-
seurs."

Monsieur hesitated.

"Well . . . there is always the second-class funeral, with musicians
from the Opéra-Comique, black armbands distributed at the door, and
a reasonably attractive catafalque."

Monsieur hesitated still, and the undertaker sighed.

"Very well: third class. But I warn you, Monsieur: it will not be *gai!*"

The Passing of Sanderson

Of all the sopranos he composed for, Sibyl Sanderson remained Massenet's favorite, as much for her beauty as for her ravishing voice. Her
chemistry was so telling as Esclarmonde that Massenet never wanted
to hear it with anyone else, an extreme act in an age when some sem-
blance of international copyright had been established and Massenet's
operas were in demand for local premiere at every major house. But
no, while Sanderson was active, Massenet wanted it considered hers
alone. Unfortunately, personal problems drove Sanderson from the stage
until, in desperation, she checked into a rest home in St. Cloud to recuperate and restudy in preparation for a comeback.

At length she sent for Massenet: would he hear her sing and judge if
she was ready to make her return? Fearful of what he might find—
gruesome stories had been making the rounds of the Paris cafés—Massenet took conductor Eduard Colonne with him. Besides giving the
composer emotional support, Colonne could sign the soprano for one
of his concerts, the best medicine possible—if, indeed, she had conquered her problems and reclaimed her shattered instrument.

When Sanderson came before them, she stretched out her hands to
Massenet and begged him, "Maître, save me from myself! Bring me
back to art and to life!" Massenet was too moved to reply. But the
brisk Colonne went right to the piano and began the audition. Fearing
to encourage the dense pathos of the Massenet-Sanderson nostalgia by
trying *Thaïs* or *Esclarmonde*—"their" operas—Colonne cued in *Manon*,
a work every French lyric soprano knows by heart.

Alas, Sanderson had forgotten it, and all else. Every so often the brilliant high notes rang out as of old; in between was the dead echo of

talent utterly spent. Noting the dreadful effect she was making, Sanderson lost control, and cried out, "Et voilà l'histoire de Manon Lescaut!": And that is the story of Manon Lescaut—the words Massenet's heroine utters as she dies.

"Come, Colonne!" said Massenet. "Or I shall go mad!" The two men fled as Sanderson fell into a chair and wept. There was no comeback. She never saw her dear maître again.

And that is the story of Sibyl Sanderson.

GIACOMO PUCCINI

Biographers have found Puccini a rich source. A colorful personality who left plenty of letters for documentary guidance, he lived an eventful life, suffering tragedy as often as enjoying triumph. As an author of opera, too, he is interesting, the classic example of the composer who entranced the public but seldom pleased the critics—vastly preferable, be it said, to vice versa. Puccini's artistic development is not as fascinating as that of Mozart, Verdi, or Wagner, for he was not an inventor or discoverer. Yet who of us doesn't enjoy learning about the composition, premiere, and performance history of *La Bohème*, *Tosca*, and *Madama Butterfly*, the great evergreen trio of the turn-of-the-century Italian wing? Aficionados have something to bite on as well in the arresting change of style that marks *La Fanciulla del West*, *Gianni Schicchi*, and *Turandot*, each of which has been cited as Puccini's unique masterpiece.

Perhaps the most arresting Puccini story is the one that has never been fully told, the story of how impresarios, musicians, and singers have taken to and quickly grown to love this music from the first while academicians kept explaining how terrible it was. Mozart's operas secured a central place in the international repertory only in the last fifty years. Some of Verdi's best works took decades to establish themselves—*Macbeth* and *Don Carlos* were a century old before they were thought essential. And Wagner is beyond the reach of many a voice (and ear). Yet here is Puccini, by no means their equal—would opera history have turned out any differently if he had not lived?—yet encompassingly and *immediately* popular among opera's people.

Excepting the questionable early works *Le Villi* and *Edgar*, Puccini's titles are mainstays in a vocalist's career. He offers scant opportunities to mezzos and basses. But what soprano wants to turn down Butterfly and Tosca, hazardous though they are to lyric instruments? Minnie's theatricality guarantees a success to the larger voices, and the hunger for a competent Turandot promises reputation to any who can scale the part's heights. Even Lauretta, a part consisting largely of one little aria, is certain delight. Tenors feel at their best as Rodolpho, Cavaradossi, Dick Johnson, Calaf; and consider the diversity of baritone parts—mellifluous Marcello, lurid Scarpia, *buffo* Schicchi.

These are perennially grateful parts, written to present a singer at his or her best. There is not all that much exploitation of the chorus in Puccini (though one thinks of Mozart's reply to Joseph II, "as much as there should be"). Puccini's opera centers on the principals. In certain acts, such as *Manon Lescaut's* fourth, *Tosca's* second, or *Fanciulla's* second, virtually the entire stage is theirs alone. Perhaps the title of this story is "Puccini Knew How To Idealize Singers." He may tire them. Manon, Butterfly, and Minnie work the voice cruelly through the passion that must be sustained at length. But these are great personality roles that draw on the performer's imagination as they give to the singer's musicianship. Many a great soprano unable to field a Mozartean technique or a Verdian (not to mention Wagnerian) voice can thrive in Puccini. And it is not only singers' enthusiasm, but the public's, that keeps these works alive.

Perhaps it is best to follow Puccini's adventures in the context of this peculiar breach of critique, so to say. Much of the Puccini we see in these tales is concerned entirely with things of the theatre, of finding the right source, the right adaptation, the right style of song, the right singers and conductor. That Puccini was a "man of the theatre" is one of opera's most tired clichés—also a foolish one: are Mozart, Verdi, or Wagner dull in the theatre? But it is notable that their anecdotes find them concerned with sociopolitical matters—Mozart seeking independence in a paternalistic society, Verdi sounding the nationalistic note from the stage to inspire the dream of patriarchal confederation, Wagner cultivating the anti-monarchical, anti-Semitic, and proto-Teutonic subcultures of his day.

Puccini, on the other hand, could pursue a contract with a Viennese publisher at a time when Italy and Austria were at war—and be amazed that anyone should object. Many did, and it cost Puccini some of that popularity that was his sine qua non. He was not an experimenter, to be reified by future generations; he had to be immediately successful or he was worthless. But then nothing succeeds in Italy like a posthumous masterwork. If *La Rondine,* tainted by "collaboration," has been regarded with loathing in Italy till recently, the pathetic picture of the composer dying (of throat cancer) before he could complete *Turandot* won public sympathy and made the last opera a legendary work, conceived in legend, perhaps to make some. Puccini's largest work, most expensive to stage and most difficult to cast, it is the exceptional piece in his output, and it too fascinated the public, immediately. Ask not when this overrated Puccini will fade from the scene. Ask when *La Fanciulla del West* will start selling out. Soon.

Another *Manon?*

In the 1700s and early 1800s, multiple operatic versions of a single source—even multiple settings of the same libretto—were commonplace. By the late 1800s, the habit was largely broken, and Puccini came under fire when he proposed setting Prévost's *Manon Lescaut* only a few years after the premiere of Massenet's adaptation (not, by the way, the first—Auber set it in 1856, under the same title as Puccini).

Aside from his rudeness in implying a "correction" of Massenet, Puccini risked unfavorable comparison with an established master. But in the matter of sources for opera, Puccini was an open-market man first and always. "Why shouldn't there be two operas about her?" he asked. "A woman like Manon must have more than one lover!"

Neighborly Competitors

While Puccini embarked on the composition of *Manon Lescaut*, Ruggero Leoncavallo similarly began to score what was to be *his* first hit, *Pagliacci*. Finding Milan too hot for work, Leoncavallo took a cottage at Vacallo, far north in the Italian Tyrol, and advised Puccini to do the same; Leoncavallo would even arrange lodgings for the Puccinis.

The Puccinis duly arrived. Their place was just across from Leoncavallo's, and they were greeted by the painting of a clown (in Italian, *pagliaccio*) hanging in Leoncavallo's window. Puccini promptly countered with a towel bearing a hand *(mano)*.

So the two composers celebrated their friendly rivalry. And friends they remained till Leoncavallo came up with a wonderful idea for his next opera, an adaptation of an old novel about life among the garret artists of Paris's Left Bank. What a novel!—comic episodes, violence, bizarrerie, and *two* love plots. Who knows? This one might become even more popular than *Pagliacci*.

And if Leoncavallo had not told Puccini about his plans, his opera might well have swept the Continent. But Puccini liked the idea so much, he decided to use it himself. His version came out a year before Leoncavallo's, and bore the same title.

La Bohème.

Hard at Work

Puccini's wife Elvira resented the composer's love of hunting. Instead of boating around on Lake Massaciuccoli with his vagabond friends, gunning for water fowl, he should be at his piano, working on *La Boheme*.

Puccini fixed it. He hired a village lad to come in, early in the morning before Elvira got up, and play "Che gelida manina" and "Mi chiamano Mimì" in a pensive, questing manner. Elvira was happy. Puccini was putting the time to good use after all. Puccini was happy—and he *was* putting his time to good use.

Just not on *La Bohème*.

A Lesson from Sardou

We have already seen Alberto Franchetti expressing doubts about the musical possibilities in Sardou's *La Tosca*, even when Verdi gave it his recommendation. Oddly, after having taken the libretto away from Franchetti (through their publisher Ricordi, who played on Franchetti's doubts), Puccini himself suffered doubts.

He revealed them to Sardou in Paris. Perhaps a Frenchman should set it; perhaps *Tosca* is too forceful to suit Puccini's kind of heroine; perhaps Franchetti's fear of it is a warning that others should fear.

Sardou couldn't have disagreed more. *Tosca* was not for a Frenchman—it is a Roman work, and needs Italian *canto*. Moreover, there is no such thing as a "kind of heroine"—women in love are all the same. As for Franchetti, the very fact that someone else had shown interest in *Tosca* proves its viability.

Still Puccini hesitated. Even if *Tosca* is right for opera, is it right for Puccini? Sardou is tense, direct, violent, but Puccini's music is gentle, delicate. Puccini writes in a different style.

"There are no styles, Monsieur Puccini," Sardou thundered. "There is only talent!"

The First Night of *Madama Butterfly*

No ultimately popular opera had a fiasco on its premiere to compare with that of *Madama Butterfly*. The Paris *Tannhäuser* comes to mind; but this was only the premiere of a new version. *Carmen* did not impress on its first night; but *Carmen* was not jeered off the stage. Boito's *Mefistofele* had as bad a time as *Butterfly*, and at the same theatre; but *Mefistofele* is not the core repertory favorite that *Butterfly* is, so its difficulties are less astonishing. *Il Barbiere di Siviglia* was jeered in Rome, but everyone knew it was going to be, in defense of Paisiello's version. The closest instance of comparison is *La Traviata*'s failure at La Fenice; but even there we encounter the qualifying explanation of an inferior cast. When *Madama Butterfly* held its first night at La Scala on February 17, 1904, it offered Rosina Storchio, Giovanni Zenatello, and Giuseppe de Luca, under Cleofonte Campanini, a sterling lineup. What went wrong?

The curtain rose to Puccini's swirling Oriental string figures, Zenatello delivered the lovely "Amore or grillo," De Luca joined him in the duet that offers the work's first musical climax . . . nothing. An eerily silent house just sat there. One can imagine what the authors were thinking—Puccini had even, for the first time, brought along his family. Italian audiences of Puccini's day did not simply listen to an opera, especially a new one: they praised or damned it, very loudly. Even Storchio, waiting backstage for her entrance, could feel it. There was something terribly wrong.

The storm broke just after she came on. *"Bohème!"* screamed voices high in the gallery, as if recognizing a tune. "That is *Bohème!"* The wedding ceremony won a temporary reprive—no hisses, though no bravos either, and not a single call for a *bis,* not even during the Love Duet, which brought on more yells of *"Bohème!"* and ended in the hollow ring of about forty hands clapping.

Backstage during the one intermission, everyone was stunned, angry, or in tears. But Puccini's publisher, Tito Ricordi, remained calm, if icily so. He knew the opera was first-rate; Italians love first-rate operas. "In the second act," he said to Storchio, presumably thinking of "Un bel dì," "Che tua madre," and "Piccolo Iddio," "the reception will change. I swear to you that it will be a success!"

In the second act, the reception did change: from casually hostile to contemptibly vicious. When a sudden draft of air from the wings inflated Storchio's kimono, someone cried out, "Butterfly is pregnant!" and another answered, "Yes, with Toscanini's child!," an allusion to her liaison with the conductor. Ironic cries of *bis* rang out when Butterfly brought out her little boy, Trouble; and the bird calls during the night-to-dawn intermezzo inspired a hail of animal imitations. In his staging of the original play, David Belasco devised one of his impressionistic tableaus in suggesting the shifting lights and sounds of a Nagasaki nighttime, and Puccini wanted to use this in the opera. Much of Belasco's effects Puccini left to the orchestra and a small men's chorus, but he retained the bird calls that greet the sunrise, and the audience chimed in with cock-a-doodle-dos, mooing, braying, groans, and shrieks. Storchio likened it to Noah's Ark. The suicide silenced them, but the curtain fell on more laughter, and no one dared take a curtain call.

Why did this happen? It is often suggested that the opera's unusual length annoyed the spectators. As first presented, the first act carried some eight minutes more than it does at present, most of it in the wedding scene, where Butterfly's Uncle Yakusidè gets sozzled on saki. Then, too, the second act comprised the present Acts Two and Three; they were at first connected, without a break, by the intermezzo. Everyone had warned Puccini that this was dangerous. The great Verdi, who knew more about the relationship between opera production and the public than the Italian people themselves, had set it into code that forty minutes was the most an act should last.

However, none of this entered into the public's behavior at *Butterfly*'s premiere, for the ominous silence began when the music did. Clearly, a cabal had intrigued to smash Puccini, most likely with the help of a claque sent into the gallery—it was there that most of the disturbances broke out. In this, then, *Butterfly*'s fiasco reminds one of the terrible first night of *Norma,* again at the same theatre, for Bellini, too, was harassed by a cabal. The dismal truth is that much of Italy's music world was antagonistic to Puccini because of the Ricordis' championship of his music. First Giulio, then son Tito, treated Puccini as if he and no other would have the success that Verdi, another Ricordi client, had had. Controlling the rights to Verdi's operas allowed the Ricordis to recommend other Ricordi composers to impresarios: strongly recommend. Flout the Ricordis and a theatre might lose access to the cream of the repertory. Thus, other Ricordi composers not as well favored, and composers writing for rival publishers, found themselves passed over while this Puccini got the plums. By 1904, they were ready to strike, vindictively and thoroughly.

Oddly, it was one of Puccini's most intent competitors who had the last word that night—an encouraging one. "Your opera has fallen," said Pietro Mascagni. "But it will rise again."

Elvira Puccini's Persecution of Doria Manfredi

This unique and terrible story offers no sparring divas or cutting conductors, no hectic premieres or opera house wars. There is scarcely any opera in it at all, but for the difficulty Puccini had in working on *La Fanciulla del West* because of the mental anguish he suffered. His wife Elvira suffered also, but she is the villain of the piece. Doria Manfredi suffered most, and Doria was innocent, and Doria died.

It began when Elvira conceived a suspicion that Puccini was carrying on an affair with their maid Doria, a girl of the nearby village, Torre del Lago. Whether or not Elvira's accusations were well founded has never been known; but she, at least, was certain. Like one obsessed she swore a vendetta, driving Doria from the house, denouncing her to her family and the local priest, following her about the village screaming invective, and threatening to drown her in Lake Massaciuccoli. The Torre townspeople did not like Elvira; relations between them and the Puccinis were nothing like the proprietary adulation the folk of Bussetto felt for Verdi and Giuseppina. But Elvira's insistence at length began to persuade them. Surely the world-famous composer was used to sei-gneurial rights; surely no wife would so pursue such a scandal without grounds. As the village began to turn against her, the helpless Doria poisoned herself clumsily and died after days of torture. The Manfredis then instituted a suit against Elvira. Crucial in the case were the results of an autopsy conducted on Doria's body.

She had died a virgin.

Elvira treated the approach of the court case as she had treated Doria, with hysterical outbursts, threats, and unproved assertions. She was found guilty, fined, and sentenced to five months and five days in prison. As well, her domestic situation had deteriorated drastically; she had virtually lost her husband and badly troubled her children. On appeal, the case was settled out of court, and eventually Puccini and Elvira were reconciled. Theirs must have been a powerful bond to survive such an ordeal; indeed, they had lived for years out of wedlock, because Elvira had already been married, and were not able to legitimize their son Tonio till he was almost a man. Doria was not spoken of again. But Puccini— struck by the girl's resemblance to the gentle, doomed "Puccini hero-ine"—sometimes visited her grave to leave flowers for his "povera But-terfly."

Class War

The world premiere of *La Fanciulla del West,* at the Met on December 10, 1910, offered Emmy Destinn, Enrico Caruso, and Pasquale Amato, staging by David Belasco, and conducting by Arturo Toscanini. Yet by far the most significant celebrity involved was the composer. Puccini had been in New York once before, to assist in the Met premiere of *Madama Butterfly.* At that time, he was one of the notable composers; since then, he had become Verdi's heir, the most famous composer liv-ing.

Naturally, New York's important hostesses vied to make Puccini the guest of honor at a hundred fêtes. No sooner had he stepped off the boat with Tito Ricordi than the two found themselves surrounded by a ransom's worth of Knickerbocker aristocrats, chattering over their teacups. And no sooner had they entered the room than Tito suddenly grabbed Puccini's arm and dragged him away, insisting that the com-poser had important work to do.

Bemused at Tito's rudeness, Puccini asked for an explanation.

"I just couldn't resist the chance," said Tito, "to slap a million dol-lars in the face."

Cancel That Present!

During one of his occasional wars with Toscanini, Puccini forgot to strike
the conductor's name from the Puccinis' Christmas pannetone (fruit-
cake) list. Realizing his error, he wired Toscanini: PANNETONE SENT BY
MISTAKE PUCCINI. Came the answer: PANNETONE EATEN BY MISTAKE
TOSCANINI.

Strauss at His Best

Puccini visited Vienna during Franz Schalk's tenure as director of the
Vienna State Opera, and Schalk took the opportunity to show Puccini
the score of Richard Strauss's most complex stage work, *Die Frau Ohne
Schatten.* The Italian took a fast look and pushed the music aside: "It's
all logarithms!"

What Exactly Did Toscanini Say at the Premiere of *Turandot?*

Despite their on-and-off battles, Toscanini and Puccini managed to end
as friends, Toscanini because he did truly admire Puccini's talent, and
Puccini because he knew that no one could prepare and conduct his
operas as well as Toscanini. When Puccini went off to Brussels for
treatment of what was to be revealed as throat cancer, Toscanini was
among those who saw him off at the station in Milan. There Puccini
begged him to take care of his "beloved princess"—*Turandot,* his yet
incomplete and, he believed, greatest opera.

Not long after, Toscanini was rehearsing the Scala orchestra when
one of *Turandot's* co-librettists, Giuseppe Adami, approached him—
ordinarily an unforgiveable breach of discipline, but the solemnity of
the news demanded it. "Dead?" Toscanini asked, without preamble.

"Dead," Adami replied. Throwing down his baton, Toscanini ran to
his dressing room, dropped onto his sofa, and wept.

Naturally it was Toscanini who led the Scala players at Puccini's funeral in Milan's Duomo, in Anna's death march from Puccini's first opera, *Le Villi.* The conductor's major task lay in overseeing the premiere
of *Turandot* under the best possible auspices for its future health. Not
only must the performance be superb: someone must finish the work,
whose decisive confrontation of prince and princess Puccini had no more
than sketched.

Toscanini thought first of Riccardo Zandonai, Tito Ricordi's choice
as successor to Puccini just as Puccini was to be Verdi's successor. But
was not Zandonai too successful himself to take on so thankless a task?

Would Puccini have completed anything by Zandonai, had their positions been reversed? Never. Eventually Toscanini entrusted the job to Franco Alfano, who of all Italian composers best matched Puccini's style. Alfano's early success, *Resurrezione*, from Tolstoy's *Resurrection*, might have been the work of Puccini but for a certain lack of melodic ingenuity. Moreover, in *La Leggenda di Sakùntala*, Alfano had experimented with a percussively Oriental instrumentation comparable to Puccini's in *Turandot*. The choice was apt.

However, Toscanini was not pleased with Alfano's completion of the score. He felt there was too little Puccini in it, too much Alfano. The young composer felt he had been scrupulously *pucciniano*, treating every scribbled notation as holy writ and offering only as much of his own as was needed to piece the sketches together. As Alfano recounts it, Toscanini demanded more, thinking the completion too skimpy—and Alfano then had no choice but to write his own tunes into the piece. He had exhausted the sketches, and more meant . . . more Alfano. It was catch-22.

With the opera world eager to hear *Turandot*, Toscanini put the piece into rehearsal with an ending rich in Alfano, and even allowed Ricordi to proceed with the printing of the score. After the premiere, there would be revision and deletion; for now, the Beloved Princess must be heard.

Casting the opera proved touchy, because every star wanted a shot at what promised to be one of the era's most distinguished first nights. Whom would Puccini have wanted? Perhaps Maria Jeritza as the Princess—he had adored her Tosca in Vienna. Doubtless, Giacomo Lauri-Volpi as Calif; the part might have been written around the ring of his high notes. And definitely Gilda dalla Rizza as Liù (the "Doria role," so to speak), Puccini's "cara dolce Gildina," his personal favorite as Minnie of the Golden West.

Toscanini had his own ideas. He gave Turandot to Rosa Raisa, Calaf to Miguel Fleta (Toscanini was feuding with Lauri-Volpi at the time) and Liù to Maria Zamboni. A sound cast, potentially excellent. News leaked out from rehearsals to greater Milan that *Turandot* might be Puccini's greatest opera, that the three leads were inspired, and that Toscanini was superintending his greatest production, to rank with the spectacular, similarly posthumous completion and mounting of Boito's *Nerone* two years earlier. Only Alfano was without glory; the task proved thankless after all. Milanese wits dined out on the tale that, after the dress rehearsal, Alfano asked Toscanini what he thought of the whole work with Alfano's ending. The words he used were, "What have you to say, Maestro?" And Toscanini replied, "I have to say that I saw Puccini coming from the back of the stage to smack me."

The premiere, on April 25, 1926, was a memorial event—Toscanini saw to that. When he reached the close of Liù's death music, the point at which authoritative score gives out and Alfano's reconstruction of the sketches begins, Toscanini stopped the performance and the audience left the theatre in silence.

What, exactly, did Toscanini say? There are several versions, most popularly "Here the Maestro put down his pen." But Enrico Minetti, concertmaster of the Scala pit on the night in question, insists—from a vantage of mere inches, remember—that Toscanini turned slightly to the public and said, "Qui finisce l'opera, rimasta incompiuta per la morte del Maestro": Here ends the opera, which remains incomplete because of the composer's death.

RICHARD STRAUSS

An anecdotal guide through opera is a tour of personalities. Suddenly, talent matters less than temperament, and genius can come off as flawed, selfish, vicious. We admire recklessness in an artist, for thus are made the great revolutions in art. But recklessness in a person?

Strauss's legends are disappointing. As with Wagner, the man is much less inspiring than his music. But Wagner at least offers a demonology of political activism, adultery, and murderous bigotry, from fiasco and enthusiastic public neglect to musical sainthood. Strauss stories reveal the Bavarian equivalent of H. L. Mencken's boobois: uncultured, insensitive, henpecked, a card-playing businessman who happened to choose music as a career.

It's hard to square this image with the compositions. Among the orchestral works, the gallant, ecstatic *Don Juan,* the lithely bumptious *Till Eulenspiegel,* and the rhapsodic nature-painting *An Alpine Symphony* suggest a poetic sensualist, not the composer who accepted a conducting engagement in Wanamaker's department store in Philadelphia, not the yokel from the south who could scandalize northern Germans with his slovenly speech and unbuttoned formality, not the gambler who was never happy till the skat table was manned and the cards ready to shuffle. In song Strauss proved himself a colleague of Schubert and Schumann; doesn't the intimate, compressed world of the Lied call for the greatest sensitivity? And in opera, was not Strauss an adventurer? His titles cover a far wider range than those of Wagner or Mozart, Strauss's two major sources of command. *Feuersnot* is a medieval romantic farce, *Salome* Biblical *guignol, Intermezzo* a modern-dress comedy of manners. *Elektra* and *Die Frau Ohne Schatten* are great frenzies of sound, *Daphne* and *Capriccio* intimately measured. *Der Rosenkavalier* is worldly, *Ariadne auf Naxos* both worldly and prim, *Arabella* sensually chaste.* One might take Strauss for a

---

* *Arabella* has come under fire for being *Der Rosenkavalier*'s second helping, but apart from the Viennese setting and the nostalgic grip of the waltzes, the two have little in common.

seeker in opera, not among the first of his tradition but among the best—until one reflects that this was the composer who set lines so casually that more than once he mistook stage directions for verse and wrote them into the score.

Perhaps the worst aspect of Strauss was his casual willingness to retain honors as Germany's greatest composer under any regime, from monarchy through Weimar democracy to Nazism. Strauss was apolitical; but lending one's greatness to the causes of a fascist state is a political act, however intended, and Strauss has earned the disappointment of a later generation for such stunts as taking over Toscanini's Bayreuth *Tristan* when the Italian began his political boycott of Germany. One of the Nazis' notable points of vulnerability lay in the dilution of Germany's cultural compounds, at first through Hitler's racial laws, then through the forced defection of people like Thomas Mann and Paul Hindemith, and at last through foreign strikes like Toscanini's. All this proved especially damaging to opera-house personnel. Toscanini's refusal to make music in Germany made international headlines, and sorely embarrassed the regime—Hitler actually wrote to ask Toscanini to reconsider. By substituting for Toscanini, Strauss was covering a disgrace that should have been allowed to stand as a naked accusation.

On the other hand, Strauss was vulnerable himself: his son had married a Jewish woman, so Strauss's daughter-in-law and grandchildren lived as hostages to Strauss's promise of good behavior. Why did he not leave when he could have, when Fritz Busch abandoned Dresden, when Lotte Lehmann laughed at Goering and booked passage to London, when Kurt Weill fled to Paris? The idea of leaving his homeland never occurred to Strauss. He was a German; Germans live in Germany. Besides, he thought, his eminence was a shield, his music too infiltrated into Germany's musical life to permit any harassment. Strauss was a man without a policy, it seems, in any field. When *Don Juan* was new, they called him a rebel; he just shrugged. When *Salome* was new, they called him an expressionist; another shrug. And his conducting, not surprisingly, was the opposite of the Romantic *Sturmleiden* approach, with its athletically dramatized direction. Strauss simply sat and beat time.

One aspect of his life is as colorful as anything in opera: his wife. Pauline de Ahna was an opera singer when Strauss met her, she soprano and he conductor at Weimar. Pushy, rude, thoughtless, and snobbish, an oaf without the slightest inhibitions of loyalty or compassion, Pauline became one of opera's great curiosities, Strauss's severest critic but his only, and lifelong, love. "She gets horribly angry a lot," Strauss admitted to Gustav Mahler, "but that's what I need." She made him work. The most famous illustration of how the two functioned together finds Strauss about to set a poem by Otto Julius Bierbaum when Pauksel—Strauss's nickname for Pauline—announced that she wanted to take a ramble on his arm. So he's working, is he? Well, that's all right for now. She'll go upstairs to change, and in twenty minutes she will come down and they will go out, whether he has finished or not. Rather than break his concentration, Strauss hastened to finish his song, and in twenty minutes had completed a gem, "Traum durch die Dämmerung."

Some of Pauline's acts were less productive, such as the time she threw her score at him during rehearsals for *Guntram,* Strauss's first opera, produced during their Weimar period. She missed Strauss but hit two string players; and it was a big score. Pauline was even more critical of some of Strauss's later operas, the first to inform Strauss that he was losing his touch. "See, I *told* you *Die Ägyptische Helena* was garbage," she said. "Now that Jeritza is in America, you can't give the tickets away!"

Did Strauss decline after his six operas to librettos by Hugo von Hofmannsthal? One virtually hears Strauss's muse giving up about halfway through *Arabella,* the last Strauss–von Hofmannsthal collaboration and the end of opera's most bizarre pairing, the poet so cultivated and the composer so ordinary. Somehow this chemistry ignited Strauss as no other librettist did, though most of the later operas have their partisans. And in their defense, we must note that *Die Schweigsame Frau, Daphne, Friedenstag, Capriccio,* and *Die Liebe der Danae* were all first given during the Nazi era, when Strauss was cut off from the international exposure that helped launch *Elektra, Salome,* and *Der Rosenkavalier.* Worse yet, the Nazis closed two of the later works by state power, cutting them off even from Strauss's fellow Germans. *Die Schweigsame Frau* offended them because its librettist Stefan Zweig was Jewish, and *Die Liebe der Danae* was shut down after the dress rehearsal for Hitler's Total War. No composer deserved it more, for not till he realized that war meant the bombing of opera houses and the depletion of paying audiences did Strauss even care about Hitler's plan for the world.

Yet we listen to *Elektra*'s Recognition Scene, the Marschallin's monologue, *Ariadne*'s comic quintets, Helen's Awakening Scene, *Arabella*'s Betrothal Duet, *Danae*'s finale . . . is this the music of a boor? Perhaps it's best to remember, as we read these tales, that art is nobler than artists.

Von Bülow on Strauss

The acerbic, brilliant pianist and conductor Hans von Bülow died the year Strauss produced his first opera, and of the major tone poems could have known only *Don Juan* and *Tod und Verklärung.* But he had an opinion ready, as usual a negative one. "When it comes to Richard, I prefer Wagner," he said. "And when it comes to Strauss, I prefer Johann."

The Strausses in America

On tour in 1904, the two Strausses gave a Lieder recital in Philadelphia, during which Pauline suddenly felt weak and seemed about to faint.

Strauss leaned over to her and whispered something, she revived, and the recital continued. Naturally, everyone wanted to know what Strauss had said: "Wiener schnitzel with spaghetti after the concert!"

Pauksel's favorite dish.

Great Volume

Elektra calls for an orchestra of 111 players, and for much of the evening the pit is so noisy that it became a joke. During rehearsals for the Dresden premiere in 1909, at the scene between Elektra (Annie Krull) and Klytemnestra (Ernestine Schumann-Heink), Strauss called out to conductor Ernst von Schuch, "Louder, louder the orchestra! I can still hear the Heink!"

> In a similar vein, Thomas Beecham mustered his crew just before the dress rehearsal of *Elektra*'s London premiere: "Those singers up there on the stage think they are going to be heard. It's up to you and me to take damned good care that they are not."

Great Silence

Came the day for *Elektra*'s final dress rehearsal, a horde of the music world's great and near-great in attendance. At the curtain's fall, nobody cheered; there were not two hands clapping. No doubt everyone was simply too awed by the piece to react with any outward show— but Strauss mistook the silence for disapproval.

"Well, *I* liked it!" he roared.

Now How About a Little Something for the Mayor?

This seldom-told story pointedly illustrates Strauss's lack of sensitivity. The occasion was the premiere of Mahler's Sixth Symphony, in Essen, with Mahler himself on the podium. The Sixth is of course an overpoweringly sorrowful work, and its impact on those hearing it for the first time was formidable.

By chance, the Mayor of Essen had died that day. After the concert, Strauss bounded into the green room and said, "Mahler, you'll have to conduct something [in memoriam] for the Mayor"—as if the Sixth were not memorial enough! Then Strauss looked around the room and noticed the generally tragical atmosphere. "Well, what's wrong with you people?" Strauss asked. "You all look so depressed!"

Caution

Strauss was almost as famous for his conducting as for his composing, especially for his conducting of Strauss. The critic Neville Cardus, who had heard Strauss conduct *Elektra, Salome,* and *Die Frau Ohne Schatten,* thought it odd that he so seldom tackled *Der Rosenkavalier.*

In due course Cardus met Strauss and asked what the problem was. Did he love the opera too much to want to minister to it as technician? Did he prefer to sit in the audience and enjoy it? Was he too perfectionist for most singers' comfort?

Nothing like. "It is very difficult to conduct," Strauss told Cardus. "Especially the last act."

Once More, With Feeling

Like Beecham, Knappertsbusch, and some other giants of the podium, Strauss was not a dedicated rehearser. He would often disconcert orchestras by reading through one of his own works—even the most complex—without a stop and without comment. In England on a guest jaunt, he rehearsed in exactly this way, and, to his players' bewilderment, said nothing afterward, either.

Finally the concertmaster approached to ask, "Maestro, is there anything you would like to suggest to us?"

Strauss considered this. "Yes," he replied. "Bar 336, violins: up bow."

Empty House

During the great inflation after World War I, few Germans had the money to attend the opera, and an impresario complained to Strauss that *Tristan und Isolde* in particular was drawing so poorly that it might have to be put by for the duration. "You must play this opera," Strauss told him, "even if a single person sits in the theatre to hear it: for that person would be the last German alive!"

Strauss on Hindemith

Though Strauss was an efficient worker (especially once Pauline shooed him into his study), he regarded the extremely prolific Hindemith with suspicion. Where did all this music come from? The man simply overflowed with it—but was it *good*? There was too much *Gebrauchsmusik* in his file to suit Strauss—"useful music," like a sonata for bassoon students who would otewise have had nothing to play but scales.

Once Strauss walked up to Hindemith after the playing of his umpteenth piece and asked him how long it had taken to write it.

"About three days."

"Yes," said Strauss, thoughtfully. "Yes. That's *just what I thought!*"

Strauss Loses a Librettist

The mismatching of Richard Strauss and Hugo von Hofmannsthal as artists is one of opera's most arguable clichés; but their lack of genuine friendship is not open to debate. They were cordial and respectful, but not amicable. They scarcely ever met, preferring to collaborate by mail, and when they did come face to face, Strauss's easy Bavarian ways (and Frau Pauline's temper) irritated the tensely correct von Hofmannsthal.

Thus, when Strauss didn't come to his librettist's funeral it was taken by some as a proof of the two men's lack of sympathy. Von Hofmannsthal had just completed his revision of the *Arabella* text when his son committed suicide, devastating the poet. The timing was uncanny: Strauss's telegram congratulating his partner on his beautiful work joined the pile of wires condoling with his loss. He never read them. While waiting to be taken to the cemetery for his son's burial, von Hofmannsthal suffered a stroke and died.

Friends they may not have been, yet Strauss suffered a terrible sense of loss. When the news first broke at the Strausses' home in Garmisch, Pauline invented a terrific series of tantrums to keep Strauss's mind occupied, and he was unable to mention his collaborator's name without sinking into blank despondency. This is why he did not attend the funeral: he couldn't bear to. Reining in his emotions was the only way he could survive this implausible, brilliant teamwork.

No, there was another way: he could immerse himself in the composition of *Arabella*. After a while, he felt well enough to visit his neighbor Elisabeth Schumann, with the intention of reading her the wonderful, last libretto of Hugo von Hofmannsthal. By hap, Schumann was entertaining a houseful of guests, much too large an audience for the intimate celebration of talent that Strauss had in mind. But some of the party were close friends, and they stayed behind to listen while Schumann took the others off on a walk.

And it was then, while reading *Arabella* to Schumann's husband Carl Alwin and Baron Clemens Franckenstein and his wife, that Strauss at last broke down and wept for the man who was his most sage adviser, most dependable inspiration, and in some indefinable way perhaps Strauss's best friend after all.

Strauss Stands Up to The Bureaucracy

Apparently not even Richard Strauss was exempt from the Nazis' petty paper work. A form asked him for two references as to his professional capability. Strauss put down *Wolfgang Amadeus Mozart and Richard Wagner.*

Strauss Stands Up to the Nazis

Strauss's eleventh opera, *Die Schweigsame Frau* (The Silent Woman), marked the beginning of his post-Hofmannsthal period, and his only collaboration with the interesting Stefan Zweig. A resident of London and an Austrian citizen, Zweig was not technically subject to the Nazi regime at the time, but he was a non-Aryan all the same, and his libretto had to be approved by the authorities. It was, and Hitler himself proposed to attend the Dresden premiere, set for June 1935.

A few days before the opening, Strauss asked to see the proof sheets for the program and found that Zweig's name had been eliminated. The text was "adapted from the English of Ben Jonson"—no more than this. In cool fury, Strauss wrote Zweig's name into its proper place, to the consternation of the Dresden intendant. "Do what you want," said Strauss, "but tomorrow early I'm leaving and the performance can take place without me."

Hitler never showed up, the intendant was fired, and Strauss's relations with the Nazis remained difficult thereafter.

Concerning the Parentage of Fanto

Strauss was not above cracking jokes about the Nazi racial hatreds, despite his son's family. Once, at a skat session, someone questioned the ancestry of Leonhard Fanto, set designer at Dresden and a collaborator on a number of Strauss premieres. Fanto, everyone was sure, was Jewish. Yet he went about his business unmolested right through the 1930s with their Nuremberg Laws and pogroms.

"Fanto handled that one neatly," said Strauss. "He simply told them he was a foundling—so now they can't do a thing to him!"

Complimenting Hotter

Friedenstag (Day of Peace), Strauss's least popular opera, covers the last few hours of the Thirty Years War in a besieged German fortress, to end with a spectacularly coarse imitation of the finale of *Fidelio*. There is not even a decent soprano lead, an unusual lack for a Strauss opera. The role of the Commandant of the fortress, however, offers excellent opportunities to a bass-baritone, and young Hans Hotter was seizing the day, first at the Munich premiere in 1938, then in Vienna a year later. At the latter stand Hotter was suffering from hay fever, and, on conductor Clemens Krauss's advice, decided to mime his way through the part at the dress rehearsal to save his voice for the next day's performance.

After the rehearsal, Strauss stopped in at Hotter's dressing room and said, "It sounded gorgeous."

Was this a joke? "Doctor," Hotter replied, "I didn't sing a note."

"I know. But I heard in my head how it will sound tomorrow."

Pauline Shocks Elsa Respighi

At least one person thought Strauss well-mannered and thoughtful: Elsa Respighi, the highly educated wife of composer Ottorino Respighi. It was Pauline who startled Elsa, with her brusque ways and self-righteous opinions. Was this the wife of a great composer, chattering about all the diplomats and generals she should have married? At one point, Frau Strauss suddenly rose and toured the Respighis' apartment, touching the tables and windowsills.

"You are a perfect hausfrau," she announced. "Not a spot of dust anywhere!"

Pauline Stands Up to the Nazis

Pauline gave Hitler's people what she gave everyone else she ever met: a piece of her mind. In 1941, when the Strauss family moved to Vienna, Strauss warned Pauline that they would be moving among some high-ranking Nazis; she must guard her tongue as she didn't have to in the country at Garmisch. One might as well warn Vesuvius to be nice to Pompeii.

At a gala reception, Pauline found herself talking to the Gauleiter of Vienna, Baldur von Schirach, and asked him if she dared tell him something or ought she to guard her silence.

"What have you to say, gnädige Frau?" he asked, somewhat condescendingly.

"Well then: when the war is lost and over, then, Herr Schirach, I'll save a little place for you at Garmisch, when you're on the run. But as for that other trash . . ."

Schirach was equal to the situation. "Many thanks for your friendly warning," he replied. "But I don't believe that I'll need your help."

Strauss was not equal to the situation. Pearls of sweat (as they put it in German: *Schweissperlen*) decorated his forehead. For the room was filled with that other trash. And Pauline the fearless, daughter of a Bavarian general who served an army that had stood for something, would make her rounds . . .

Last Words

In the summer of 1949, Strauss, just turned eighty-five, took to his bed at his home in Garmisch, and word went out that the season for the paying of last respects had arrived. Rudolf Hartmann, a stage director closely connected to Strauss, found his man in bed, pale and weary, an oxygen apparatus at the ready. "Death has dealt me the first blow," said Strauss, "given me the first sign."

They spoke of the bombing of the theatres and their reconstruction, of the old repertory and the new singers. They spoke of Strauss's work. "So much for me still to do," the composer sadly remarked.

Both men were silent for a long time. Then Strauss said, "Grüss' mir die Welt": Greet everyone for me. Beautiful words; what are they from? Hartmann recalled something similar in *Die Walküre,* in the Todesverkündigung scene. No, said Strauss: it's these exact words. "Grüss' mir die Welt," he said again, thoughtfully. The line is from *Tristan und Isolde*'s first act, when Isolde prepares to drink a death draught with Tristan:

> Nun leb' wohl, Brangäne!
> Grüss' mir die Welt,
> Grüsse mir Vater und Mutter!
>
> Now farewell, Brangäne!
> Greet everyone for me,
> Greet my Father and Mother!

Last words, indeed.

ARNOLD SCHOENBERG

One doesn't expect Schoenberg anecdotes—is this not the most austere character in music?—remote, complex, patriarchal, silently disapproving? Schoenberg is like Moses, bringing a new code of behavior to his people—twelve-tone composition—and raging when they prove unworthy. This a favorite historian's romance, for Schoenberg's opera *Moses und Aron* feels rather like his dialogue with himself on the problems of eloquence—or simple communication—in art. Moreover, Schoenberg found himself mysteriously unable to complete the work, reaffirming the metaphor of inarticulate genius.

Schoenberg was in fact a lively personality, something of a grim jester. (One would have to be to spend several decades in Los Angeles after Vienna and Berlin.) Like other elite creators, he fussed at reviews and blamed his publishers for not pushing harder; but he was the elite of the elite, the founder of the century's essential compositional revolution, the Freud of modern music. When these stories begin, in the first hours of Nazi Germany, Schoenberg was known mainly among musicians. A refugee in America, he becomes even more obscure, cut off from most of his colleagues and his culture (thus the dropped umlaut in his name, an Americanization of the original Schönberg). Relish, as the tales proceed, the ponderously gradual expansion of Schoenberg's fame, and realize that, some time after his death, he began to be perceived as one of the century's most influential composers. Schoenberg was inevitable—and reluctant, the conflicted messiah. "Are you Arnold Schoenberg, the composer?" he was asked once. He nodded, but explained: "No one else wanted the job, so I had to take it on."

Schoenberg Departs Germany

On January 30, 1933, Hitler came to power. Nine days later, at a concert of student compositions at the Berlin Hochschüle für Musik, composer Paul Graener took exception to a string quartet, somewhat advanced and dissonant in the Weimar manner. Loudly breaking into the applause, Graener called the piece "a lamentable excuse for German art," resented its performance "as a German artist," and stormed out, followed by a half-dozen other conservatives.

Shortly after this, the Senate of the Prussian Academy of the Arts discussed the matter. Some, including Schoenberg, wanted to lodge a protest, but President Max von Schillings announced that the "Jewish influence" in music must be broken.

"You don't have to say that to me twice," said Schoenberg, on his way out.

Two months later he, his wife Gertrud, and their infant daughter Nuria were in Paris. There, in solemn resistance to the Paul Graeners and Max von Schillingses, Schoenberg reconverted to the Jewish faith he had abandoned many years before. By Hallowe'en the Schoenbergs were in America.

Schoenberg's Ear

It is music history's happiest quirk that many of the middle-European refugees from Nazism gathered in Los Angeles, socially, climatically, and geographically as unlike their accustomed environs as any place in the West. There was the language problem as well, for if many émigrés spoke English, few Angelenos do.

For Schoenberg, there was an acute music problem. He was able to earn a living as a teacher, but opportunities for hearing the music he found stimulating—much less his own, most stimulating of all—were limited. A typical local concert opened with Beethoven's Third Symphony but went on to an arrangement of themes from Franz Waxman's *Rebecca* soundtrack.

"I never heard anyone less interested in the Eroica!" was Schoenberg's comment on the conducting. Had he by chance heard the *Rebecca* suite?"

"I *started* to!" he said dangerously.

His First Autograph

Summering in Chautauqua in 1940, Schoenberg and Gertrud were out strolling when a little boy came up to ask for an autograph. Imagine! The neglected Arnold Schoenberg is finally breaking through to fame! Pulling out his pen, Schoenberg was about to present his signature when the boy said, "Naw, not you. I want *hers!*"

Gertrud had won a ping-pong tournament the day before.

He's Difficult, But Fun

Schoenberg's music *is* difficult, but one of his works stands out for its tunefulness—only the tunes are Brahms's. The piece is Schoenberg's transcription of Brahms's g minor piano quartet, made at Otto Klemperer's suggestion, and Klemperer gave the premiere with the Los Angeles Philharmonic in 1938. After the concert, the orchestra manager told Klemperer, "I don't know why people say that Schoenberg has no melodies. That was very melodic."

G. Schirmer Goes to Heaven

Gertrud Schoenberg's blessing was marriage to the man she regarded as the greatest composer of the twentieth century; her curse was that few others shared her opinion, especially music publishers.

As a widow she took an active hand in the various Schoenberg accounts, most particularly with a German firm that published *Moses und Aron*—so difficult that despite maintaining a fascinating reputation for twenty years it had never been performed. Hamburg Radio offered to give it in concert in 1954 under Hans Rosbaud, and Gertrud demanded a fee so tremendous the publisher feared it would prove prohibitive. *Moses und Aron* is so hard to perform that anyone opposed to giving it would have a persuasive economic reason handed right to him. Gertrud stood her ground—and Hamburg paid.

Her most inspired encounter was with G. Schirmer, who published Schoenberg after he came to America. In 1951 she appeared in the New York office, where she denounced the firm's neglect of her husband's music. Was such-and-such score available at the Los Angeles Schirmer's outlet? No. Did the orchestra parts for the Violin Concerto arrive in time for a concert in Helsinki? Barely, and in tatters. What did Schirmer's flagship store in New York feature in its window? The music of Arnold Schoenberg, creator of the twelve-tone row and other wondrous happenings? No. What did the window feature? Song sheets from *The King and I* and "similar waste-paper of tomorrow"! What has Mr. G. Schirmer to say?

Schirmer was nearing the end of a long, prestigious, sometimes triumphant, and often disappointing career. Even in youth he didn't like meetings with composers' outraged widows and he especially didn't like them now. "Madame," he replied, "we have done a great deal for your husband and are still heavily in the red."

True, but beside Gertrud's point. "Mr. Schirmer, one day you will be dead," she began. "You will go up to heaven and knock at the gate. And Petrus will come out and ask who you are and what you want."

She took on the manner of a corporate boss. " 'I am the great G. Schirmer. I have a big publishing house and many music stores and a huge printing plant and I made a lot of money.' And Petrus will look at you and say, 'Down to hell you go!' " She pointed the direction as St. Peter might point it, with an Austrian index finger as straight as St. Stephen's spire.

"And then you will say, 'But I also published Schoenberg and lost money on him.' " Her face now broke into a smile as sweet as Lehár as Peter stepped aside to say, "Come right in."

And with a grand wave of her hand, Gertrud Schoenberg admitted G. Schirmer to Paradise.

INTERMISSION I
Operas

DON GIOVANNI

Spitting Distance

Madame Henriette Méric-Lalande, singing Donna Anna, was uneasy at her Don Ottavio's habit of throwing off phlegm when he sang—especially as she was wearing her own costly gown rather than theatre trunk material. Anxiety over her costume threatened to ruin her performance, until at last, during the Mask Trio, she whispered to him, "Voyons, mon cher ami, ne pourriez-vous pas, une foi par hasard, cracher sur la robe de Donna Elvira?": My dear friend, do you suppose you could spit on Donna Elvira for a while?

Good News

An overweight Giovanni became stuck in the trap door on his way to the nether regions in the banquet scene. Though he squirmed and ooched and puffed at the galop, he could not squeeze through. Nor, by then, could he pull himself up. He was trapped at the waist, neatly and permanently.

"Hurrah, boys!" cried a voice from the gallery. "Hell's full!"

FIDELIO

What Admiration!

Ferdinando Paër set, as *Leonore,* virtually the same libretto that would later serve Beethoven as *Fidelio.* What, one wonders, were Paër's thoughts when Beethoven paid him this thorny compliment?: "I have just seen your piece. I think I'll set it to music."

IL PIRATA

Golden-Age Master Class

Il Pirata, Bellini's third opera, was his breakaway piece, the one that inaugurated the Bellinian style rather than answered to the Rossinian. Preparing the Scala premiere, Bellini found himself in great difficulty trying to communicate his novel ideas on interpretation, though Giovanni Battista Rubini already seemed likely to become the essential Bellinian tenor, much as Giuditta Pasta would be the essential Bellinian soprano. Everything, Bellini knew, rested on the singers: they would have to make his history for him.

Rubini's wonderful sound had never been the kind that projects character, and that he *must* do in Bellini's new style of declamatory song. Exhausted by the apparently useless struggle, Bellini at last exploded.

"You beast!" he cried. "You are singing with half a soul! You could revolutionize opera, but you're languid, cold! Show me passion! This is a love duet—have you never been in love?"

Rubini said nothing.

Calming himself, Bellini went on, "Come, my friend, do you want to be Rubini or play the character of Gualtiero, desperate and furious as he is? Don't you know that your voice is like a gold mine that has been barely explored? You are one of the greatest artists I know of. But that isn't enough."

"I understand what you want," said Rubini. "Of that I am sure. But I cannot become Gualtiero simply through my own imagination."

"Come, admit it: the real problem is you don't like my music because it makes you work harder than you like to—than you're used to working. But consider this: if I have it in my head to find a new form of musical expression that renders the sense of the words, that makes a unique thing of opera—if I will it so, must I fail in this wonderful project because you won't help me? I know you can. Just forget who you are. Put yourself entirely into my impetuous, brilliant Gualtiero. Now, my friend . . . let us try again . . ."

LA FILLE DU RÉGIMENT

Praise from the Master

In London over a century ago, opera buffs were happily ripping Donizetti's martial comedy to shreds. The company included composers who were to Donizetti as the paper napkin is to the lace handkerchief. But Felix Mendelssohn was there, too. At length he spoke.

"Well, I don't know. I am afraid I like it. I think it very pretty . . . Do you know, I should like to have written it myself!"

That was the end of the Donizetti-baiting for the evening.

TANNHÄUSER

Strange Music in My Ears

Luigi Arditi was playing through *Tannhäuser* at the piano, scouting highlights for a selection he wanted to arrange. In the next room, his little daughter Giulietta asked her mother, "Who is playing the piano?"

"Your father, dear, of course."

"Oh. I thought it was the tuner."

Strained Greetings

Running the Bayreuth Festival on strictly traditional lines after Wagner's death, Cosima often shackled independent singers. One Elisabeth wished to open *Tannhäuser*'s second act by running into the Hall of Song with her arms upraised as if overcome with joy.

Cosima said no. But word got out that the singer was planning to do it her way at the performance.

Came the night, as she raised her arms, they stopped dead short at the waist: Cosima had sewed up the sleeves of her dress.

IL TROVATORE

Azucena Will Not Sing Tonight

In the dangerous days of Colonel Mapleson, the exigencies of getting the curtain up regardless of the crisis at hand made for some questionable performances. Today, if a company found itself without any Azucena hours before a *Trovatore,* it would put on a different opera or cancel the performance. The good Colonel simply gave *Il Trovatore* without Azucena.

This happened in 1862, on one of Mapleson's many tours of the British provinces, with a small ensemble that afforded only one voice in the then quite narrow repertory of contralto parts. When Mapleson's Azucena, Mlle. Borchardt, came down with la grippe, Mapleson decided to try to talk a comprimaria into walking through the role with the help of rather slashing cuts in the music.

Mapleson calmly told his conductor to begin the opera, and spent the first act—in which Azucena doesn't appear—exhorting the comprimaria to save the show. Finally she gave in, under Mapleson's instruction to look so and stand thus; posture, profile, tableau. Mapleson had wisely warned his Leonora, Manrico, and di Luna to outdo themselves in the trio that closes the first act; they did; and it was only then that the impresario dared come before the public to beg their indulgence for his substitution.

Mapleson went on to present what must be the shortest *Trovatore* in the annals. Act Two, scene one, with the Anvil Chorus and a long scene between Manrico and Azucena, ended after the Anvil Chorus. Act

Three, scene one, which treats di Luna's interrogation and arrest of Azucena, found Azucena abruptly arrested the moment she appeared. Act Four, scene two, set in the prison where Manrico soothes the troubled Azucena, found her sleeping comfortably throughout the "duet." Moreover, she slept right through Manrico's execution, waking up only to deliver her famous final lines, "Sei vendicata, o madre!" (Mother, you are avenged!) and "Egli era il tuo fratello!" (He was your brother!).

"Thus treated," Mapleson urbanely notes in his memoirs, "the part of Azucena is not a difficult one to play."

AIDA

The Two Illustrious Rivals

Not long ago, a Met *Aida* offered two quite celebrated sopranos who were somewhat less than the best of friends. In the first scene of Act Two, wherein the Egyptian princess confronts the Ethiopian princess, rival to rival, there is a moment in which Aida falls to the floor in supplication to Amneris. When the moment came, those sitting in the first rows of the orchestra heard the Amneris whisper to the Aida, "On your knees, bitch!"

The two never shared a stage again.

CARMEN

The White Meat

The very young Pablo Casals, playing 'cello in the orchestra at the Barcelona Liceo, was discussing *Carmen* with a double-bass player during intermission. Which part, the bassist asked, did Casals think the most beautiful?

Perhaps the prelude to the third act, that serenely naive melody for flute in E Flat Major, a calm within the storm?

"No," said the double-bass. "That's not the most beautiful part."

Perhaps the Flower Song?

"Nor that," said the double-bass. "The most beautiful part of *Carmen* is when the tenor sings, 'Vous pouvez m'arrêter. C'est moi qui l'ai tuée!' "

Casals agreed that this, the tenor's final line and the very climax of the opera's tragic realism, was very beautiful.

"That is beautiful," the double-bass insisted, "because when I hear that I know I will be going home in a few minutes."

Casals told the story to Plácido Domingo, concluding, "After more than eighty years, I cannot forgive that man for what he said that evening."

BORIS GODUNOF

Boris Christoff's Clock Scene

Back in the days after World War II, when a reformed Covent Garden was building up a musical style under Karl Rankl and a production style under enfant terrible Peter Brook, Boris Christoff came to Covent Garden to sing Boris Godunof. Just on the brink of international celebrity, Christoff had a compelling musicality and a grandly Chalyapinesque approach to characterization; but Brook was somewhat less than delighted to give way to Christoff's scene-stealing.

They locked horns on the Clock Scene. Brook wanted to play it before a gigantic nightmare of a clock—after all, this is a mad scene. Christoff wanted to play it before a more naturally scaled piece. After all, this is one of his big solos, and he had no desire to be upstaged by the decor.

Brook refused to budge: big clock.

Christoff refused to budge: small clock.

They appealed to Covent Garden's manager David Webster, putting him in a tight place. There, on one hand, was his tautly inner-directed Director of Productions, impatient to get back to the perilously avant-garde *Salome* he was staging to Salvador Dali's designs with the amazing Ljuba Welitsch. There, on the other hand, was the intense and monumental Christoff, who would surely prove extremely useful to the house in coming seasons.

Big clock or small clock?

Blandly gazing just over Christoff's left ear, Webster says, "Why not have both?"

Michael Langdon's Opera Debut

In this same production, bass Michael Langdon was assigned the part of a grotesquely crippled peasant in the Revolution Scene, a complex surge of choristers and small principals. Brook had no time to give detailed instructions. "Can you crawl on," he asked Langdon, "using perhaps your left elbow and your right knee?" This was all Langdon had to work with.

He threw himself into it, nonetheless, dragging and heaving about the dusty stage while trying to avoid the other singers' feet. After a bit Langdon found himself utterly lost in the vicinity of a rock upon which was mounted an imperious contralto singing "Death to Boris!" Thinking he might trouble her for further instructions on the playing of the scene, Langdon tugged at her skirt.

Whereupon she immediately hefted a great big stick and whacked him on the head.

OTELLO

The Moor Goes Commercial

Many decades ago, the opera programs in Houston, Texas, sold advertising space more or less at the advertiser's whim, and Crisco decided to intersperse its proclamations of quality between the lines of the plot synopsis. Thus, Houstonians making their first visit to Verdi's great Shakespearean tragedy learned that, in the first scene,

Othello arrives and greets the people with the words:

USE CRISCO, THE BEST SHORTENING

"Rejoice! The Turk is vanquished and drowned in the sea."

CRISCO IS UNSURPASSED

Iago, jealous of Cassio, who enjoys Othello's confidence, tries to get Cassio drunk. A drinking song

CRISCO HAS NO RIVAL

is heard and Cassio, by now intoxicated, attacks Montano. Othello rushes in and calls out:

CRISCO IS ECONOMICAL

The program's blend of synopsis and consumerist initiation reached its apex in the last paragraph . . .

After Othello has strangled Desdemona, he plunges his dagger into his breast and sings the touching phrase:

ASK ONLY FOR CRISCO,
THE WORLD'S FAVORITE SHORTENING

LORELEY

A Tough House

The Parma opera public is notorious for its expertise and fierce opinions. During a performance of Catalani's *Loreley*, the soprano singing Anna cracked on the big high B Flat at the end of "Gorgheggiate usignoli" (Warbling nightingales), eliciting a storm of hisses. As she stood on stage, waiting for the noise to break so she could continue, the entire audience began to sing the aria in unison for her, from beginning to end, all of them perfectly in pitch.

SALAMMBÒ

The Trials of an Impresario

Ernest Reyer's *Salammbò*, from Gustave Flaubert's novel about a queen of old Carthage, was given an expensive production at the Met in the 1900–1901 season, at a time when French opera was in vogue. Or was it? Taking his place in his box just before the first performance began, general manager Maurice Grau remarked to a companion, "Encouraging, isn't it? Some say the public want novelties."

The house was half empty.

MADAMA BUTTERFLY

Joan Hammond Wigs Out

Born in New Zealand of English parents, Joan Hammond got her start when the Williamson Grand Opera Company made a visit down under in 1932. Italian pros had the lead roles, but locals were hired for the chorus, Hammond among them. Playing one of the wedding party in *Butterfly*, Hammond suddenly realized that her Japanese wig had become impaled on the twig of a cherry tree, leaving her looking distinctly less Oriental than she needed to be.

Could she retrieve the wig, perhaps? No—discretion before valor. Fanning herself vigorously, Hammond bowed here and there and shuffled offstage. Actually, this was smart thinking; most of the audience probably took it for a bit of human interest in the staging.

The stage manager didn't. "Gor blimey, Hammond," he remarked. "Can't you keep your ruddy roof on?"

ELEKTRA

Command Non-performance

When Thomas Beecham gave the British premiere of *Elektra* at Covent
Garden in 1910, the press whipped the public into agonies of antici-
pation, and the first night enjoyed a grand success. George Bernard Shaw
was partly impressed. Mr. Beecham conducts *Elektra* extremely well,"
he wrote, though "he certainly does occasionally make the score sound
like a concerto for six drums."

Other ears noted in particular the advanced quality of Strauss's music, including those of King George V. When Bandmaster Williams of
the Grenadier Guards led his men in an *Elektra* potpourri in the court-
yard of Buckingham Palace, a page echoed forth from the Royal listening room bearing a note for Williams: "His Majesty does not know
what the Band has just played, but it is *never* to be played again."

DER ROSENKAVALIER

Stravinsky's Night at the Opera

As Stravinsky takes his seat in the third row of the Vienna Staatsoper
just before the start of this most Viennese of operas, he is recognized
and cheered. He acknowledges his applause with a dignified bow, but
as he sits he tells his neighbor, "It is only because everybody is very
happy to see me obliged to sit through four hours without syncopa-
tion."

THE RAKE'S PROGRESS

Save Your Tears

Stravinsky is always good for a one-liner. When playwright and librettist Ronald Duncan commiserated with him over the bad reviews accorded *The Rake* on its premiere, Stravinsky took out a check—his
payment for conducting the performance. "This," said Stravinsky, "is
the only review I read."

Singers

"I enquired throughout Italy at what place boys were chiefly qualified for singing by castration, but could get no certain intelligence. I was told at Milan that it was at Venice; at Venice that it was at Bologna; but at Bologna the fact was denied, and I was referred to Florence; from Florence to Rome; and from Rome I was sent to Naples. The operation is most certainly against the law in all these places, as well as against nature; and all the Italians are so much ashamed of it, that in every province they transfer it to some other."

So writes Charles Burney, the first English-language writer to leave an extensive eye-witness report on the European music world and therefore a much-quoted authority. What an infamous practice for an art to be famous for! Burney almost goes on to say. But he wants to be scientific, wants to learn why the art would need such a sacrifice. There truly were places where boys were qualified for singing by castration—Burney heard that there were gelding parlors in Naples bearing the sign "Qui si castrono ragazzi."

Actually, by the 1770s, when Burney wrote, the castrato was on the verge of his eclipse. The "male soprano," as English writers liked to term the beast, would last into the 1800s; Rossini and Meyerbeer wrote castrato parts in their earliest operas, and one of the last of the line left a few recordings. But in major particulars the castrato as the essential star of Italian opera knew his glory in the first half of the eighteenth century. By the time of Gluck and Mozart, in the transition from Classicism into Romanticism, the gifted composers avoided casting castratos in their more important operas. In Handel's day, back in the 1710s and 1720s, the castrato gathered unto himself all that was wonderful in opera: the surprise and the swagger of it, the precision, the energy, the intensity. Later on, when Gluck's sense of realism was offended by the dancing of chaconnes in Greek tragedies, or when Mozart could set a farce about the class war—then the castrato seemed to embody all that was objectionable in opera: the sheer vanity of it, the artifice and flattery, the reckless cultivating of star personalities at the cost of everything that is admirable, honest, poetic. The essence had become the excrescence.

The very fact that a castrated man should ever have been the essence of music theatre tells us how unnatural early opera must have seemed. The French thought the practice abominable, but in Italy and at court theatres dominated by the Italian style, such as Vienna, Dresden, and Berlin, the castrato was opera's certain principal. "One God! One Farinelli!" screamed an overwrought Lady of Fashion in London when that perhaps greatest of castratos made his greatness manifest. It was apparently a stupendously special sound, the vivaciously reedy brightness of the adolescent trumpeted forth by the lung power of an adult. Farinelli and his like could amaze in bravura display or soothe in the seamless outpouring of golden song. Not all castratos were great, of course, and the worst of it was that some thus ruined males never developed an important instrument and had to live out their lives having paid the price without earning the reward. The operation was performed in youth, but the castrato voice did not break till puberty, as other voices do, and not till then did anyone know what sort of voice the singer had to work with. "Indeed the *musici* in the churches at present," Burney remarks, "are made up of the refuse of the opera houses, and it is a very rare thing to meet with a tolerable voice upon the establishment of any church in Italy."

What sort of people would hand over sons to the knife? Who performed the operation? Who thought up this grotesque sacrifice in the first place? The answers are cloudy, because legal prohibitions made the practice secretive. Historically, the castratos, or eviratos (literally "unmanned"), sang in church in place of woman, forbidden to raise the voice in holy places by one of St. Paul's misogynistic instructions. The less reverent and more sensual arena of opera naturally made use of a practice already centuries old, and when Italian opera extended its territory to cover the European map, the castratos duly roamed. Heroic opera *(opera seria)* used them far more than comic *(opera buffa)*, for their vigorous radiance marked them to play noble characters, kings and princes. Talk of internal contradictions!

Were they men at all? Casanova noted their atmosphere of androgynous allure, a polymorphous perverse of the Baroque:

> He had the waist of a nymph, and, what was almost incredible, his breast was in no way inferior, either in form or in beauty, to any woman's; and it was above all by this means that the monster made such ravages . . . You were madly in love before you realized it. To resist the temptation, or not to feel it, one would have had to be cold and earthbound as a German. When he walked about the stage during the *ritornello* of the aria he was to sing, his step was majestic and at the same time voluptuous; and when he favored the boxes with his glances, the tender and modest rolling of his black eyes brought a ravishment to the heart.

Yet they were men, complete ones. We learn of amorous intrigues, jealous husbands, duels, and hired bravos lurking in an alley. Who but a eunuch can tell us what exactly a eunuch can and cannot do? English audiences in particular found it amusing that castratos played romantic heroes and sang love songs, but then the English could not enjoy opera till it was given in their own tongue in the 1800s, when the castratos had virtually vanished from all but Italian theatres.

Who were they? For the most part they were of obscure or humble origins, sold to the knife in hard times or through their own or their parents' ambition. Taking a code title for the stage—few important castratos bore a whole name—they became favorites of this or that court, tamed peacocks who had the run of the palace. They were famous without a past—Caffarelli, for instance, originally Gaetano Majorano; or Farinelli (Carlo Broschi). Some of these stage names betokened a character quality, or paid homage to the castrato's teacher, or borrowed the name of the most promising role—as if, say, Maria Callas might have billed herself as Furibonda, or Hidalga, or Norma.

The castratos' anecdotes favor illustrations of their surpassing artistry or belligerent egotism, but Farinelli actually became a grandee of some power at the Spanish court, to which he was brought to cheer the despondent Philip V with music. Every evening, the legend runs, Farinelli sang the same four songs, and such was his talent that the monotony of the program never irritated the king. On the contrary, he did cheer up, and Farinelli survived Philip's death to extend a musician's influence—no! a courtier's—under Ferdinand VI, and to found an opera company.

How can we of today perceive the castrato? The sound is quite dead—even those discs that the last one left are the work of a church singer, not an opera personality, and piety and taste are not marks of the great castratos. We do have the counter-tenor, but he is simply a man with a very high voice, not a castrato. Moreover, opera uses the counter-tenor not for the romantic roles the castratos sang, but for exotic parts, like Oberon in Britten's *A Midsummer Night's Dream,* or to fill in for the castrato parts in ancient opera, which is exotic by rules of archaeology.

So we cannot perceive the castrato. Nor can we, perhaps, experience the opera of his time, even in revival: too many revolutions in stagecraft have changed the nature of theatregoing, and the most faithful revivals reinterpret, cannot reproduce. The following anecdotes, then— more than any others in this book—recall a lost corner of opera's history, one without issue, continuity, or influence. These may not be opera's proudest stories; they are surely its unique ones.

A Basic Course of Study

A classic anecdote of the *opera seria* era finds teacher Nicola Porpora teaching the castrato Caffarelli to sing on a course consisting of one sheet of vocal exercises—and nothing else—for five years. In the sixth year Porpora branched out a bit into the pronunciation of language, this naturally being Italian, which, Caffarelli couldn't help noticing, he already spoke.

Caffarelli submitted to Porpora's approach, though he must have been wondering when his maestro would let him try an aria or two. Suddenly, one day, Porpora rose from the keyboard and told Caffarelli, "Go, young man. You have nothing more to learn. You are now the greatest singer of Italy and the World."

A Novel Cast

In the 1750s Caffarelli extended his fame to Paris, where Louis XV sent him the gift of a gold snuffbox. Caffarelli was not impressed; he already had two dozen snuffboxes, each a gift of some noble or other and each far more finely decorated than Louis's. See the jewels here, the dearly spun fastenings there, the inlaid cameos, the pearls, the diamond webbing. What's gold to Caffarelli?

"But Monsieur," the king's emissary protested. "Such gifts as those are fit for the most noble ambassadors of state!"

"Then let the noble ambassadors sing for His Majesty!" replied the divo. "Caffarelli will be silent!"

When this was repeated to His Majesty, Louis sent Caffarelli another present: a passport to take the bearer back to Italy, to be used within three days.

Caffarelli Pays a Compliment

Castrato Gioacchino Conti was one of those who took his stage name from his teacher. Conti's maestro was named Gizzi, so Conti sang as Gizziello. His debut in Rome in 1730 won such reclame that Caffarelli journeyed from Naples to hear him, unrecognized in a cloak. After Gizziello's first solo, Caffarelli cried out, "Bravo! Bravissimo, Giziello!" Then, to put the stamp of authority upon this praise, Caffarelli threw off his disguise and cried out, "È Caffarelli che ti lo dice!": *Caffarelli says so!*

Caffarelli's imprimatur made Gizziello the talk of the boot, and, nearly two decades later, they appeared together in *Achille in Sciro,* maestro to maestro.

Sensitive Orchestra

Some castratos were known for brilliance, others for power. Gasparo Pacchierotti, a star of the late 1770s, was known for expressive plangency above all. In Rome performing Bertoni's *Artaserse,* Pacchierotti came to the great line, "Eppur sono innocente!" (Yet I am innocent!), which is followed by an orchestral peroration. But nothing came forth from the players, and Pacchierotti turned in surprise to the concertmaster.

"What is happening?" the singer asked.

"We are crying," was the reply.

Force Majeure

Giovanni Battista Velluti was the last of the great opera castratos, outlasting the heyday of his type to sing a depleted repertory and a few contemporary works by composers who quickly found they liked the sound of a tenor better. Velluti must have sensed that he was living beyond his age, for he sang with Malibran, one of the exponents of opera's newly discovered yen for the romantic semi-realism that would finally drive the castrato out of opera. Still, Velluti made the most of it, for if he was the last of the line, that only added to his fame.

One evening in Milan, a man encountered an acquaintance he had heard was watching by the deathbed of a wealthy uncle.

"Where are you going, my friend?"

"To La Scala."

"But I thought your uncle—"

"Yes. Poor soul. They say he may expire at any moment."

"And you're going to the *opera?*"

"Absolutely. Velluti sings tonight."

SOPHIE ARNOULD

Arnould was a born star of anecdote, for she was not only a vivacious prima donna but a witty woman who was on intimate terms with many great men of her time and place, Paris between the *Encyclopédie* and the Revolution. She was as well a born performer, to her prim mother's despair. Madame Pompadour predicted a great career for Arnould when she was still a child, and Arnould is supposed to have said with a shrug, "To go to the opera is to go to the devil. But so what? It is my destiny!" Madame Arnould had the girl shut up in a covent, but on Pompadour's urging, the King had Sophie released and sent to study singing with Madame Fel and acting with the great tragedienne Clairon (who appears as a character in Richard Strauss's *Capriccio*).

Clairon's teaching proved notably apt: Arnould was one of the few singers of her day celebrated for her characterizations as well as musicianship. As French opera was taken seriously as theatre, this made Arnould a very focus of social and artistic life. She became Gluck's favorite soprano when he came to Paris to put forth his reform of music theatre, and sang the title role in the premiere of *Iphigénie en Aulide* and Euridice in the Paris version of *Orfeo ed Euridice*. Rosalie Levasseur sang Amour in that production, and, when Arnould and Gluck quarrelled, Gluck began composing his heroines for Levasseur. Arnould lost what had become the foundation of her career as singer and celebrity.

Still, she held the stage thereafter, and continued to sharpen her tongue on the throngs of the soirees. When she retired, she bought and redecorated a former monastery near Luzarches, some twenty miles outside Paris, and—typical Arnould—had the words *Ite missa est** inscribed over the portal.

Ite missa est is the dismissal of the Latin mass.

Sophie Coquette

The poet Bernard seemed distracted.
"What are you thinking of so deeply?" Arnould asked.
"Nothing. I was talking to myself."
"Careful! You gossip with a flatterer!"

Sophie Philosophe

A Capuchin monk was eaten by wolves.
"Poor beasts!" cried Arnould. "Hunger must be a dreadful thing!"

Sophie at the Ballet

Madeleine Guimard was thin even for a ballerina. Watching her dance
a *pas de trois* as a nymph pursued by satyrs, Arnould remarked, "It
makes me think of two dogs fighting for a bone!"

Sophie Critique

At the height of the Gluck-Piccinni war, both men set *Iphigénie en
Tauride* (to different librettos), and while Piccinni's version was heard
two years after Gluck's, still all Paris was present to seethe and compare. Piccinni's deft style was naturally overshadowed by Gluck's dynamic austerity; worse yet, Piccinni's heroine, Mlle. Laguerre, appeared
on stage noticeably drunk.

So Sophie pipes up, *"Iphigénie en Tauride?* This is *Iphigénie en
Champagne!"*

Taking Laguerre's condition as a personal affront, the King had her
imprisoned in For l'Evèque, but certain nobles and Piccinni himself
interceded for her. When she was released, Laguerre sadly repeated
the first two lines of her role:

> O jour fatal, que je voulais en vain
> Ne pas compter parmi ceux de ma vie!

> O fatal day, that I had vainly hoped
> Not to count among those of my life!

One reason why we don't have kings anymore is that the music critics
are worse than the prisons.

Sophie Discharges Her Debts

When it came time to break with her jealous but surprisingly long-term lover, the Count de Lauragais, Arnould acted with her customary eclat. She sent a carriage to his home containing everything he had given her: jewelery, fine lace, bundles of letters . . . and two children.

The Countess de Lauragais nobly accepted the children and returned the rest to Arnould.

Sophie Makes Warning

Despite their rupture, Arnould and the Count remained friends, to the point that he spoke to her of his succeeding passions. Pursuing a dancer in the Opéra ballet, the Count was making slow headway, and he complained to Arnould that, whenever he visited the young woman, she would be entertaining a certain Knight of Malta.

"You had better take care," Arnould advised him. "Il est là pour chasser les infidèles!"

I quote the original to catch Sophie's pun on *infidèle*, meaning both "heathen" and "unfaithful": "He is there to hunt the _____!"

Sophie Trades Mots with Voltaire

Says Voltaire to Arnould, "I am eighty-four years old, and I have committed a thousand follies."

"A mere trifle," counters Arnould. "I am not yet forty—and I have committed more than a thousand!"

Sophie Nears Retirement

It is difficult to give up the stage, especially while you are still the rage of Paris. Perhaps Arnould stayed at it a bit longer than she ought to have done. Eventually, the Abbé Galiani remarked of her singing, "That is the finest asthma I have ever heard!"

Sophie Politique

During the early years of the Revolution, a gang of *sans-culottes* invaded Arnould's retirement home and, irritated by her mordant reception, were about to drag her off when she pointed to a bust of Gluck.

"There!" she cried. "See! Would I keep a marble of our great Marat if I were not a true citoyenne of the Revolution?"

Satisfied, even thrilled, they left.

ANGELICA CATALANI

Billed as "La prima Cantatrice del Mondo," Catalani swept through the opera world in the first two decades of the nineteenth century, ever on tour in search of higher and higher fees. If she was indeed "The First Singer of the World," it was at least in part because her financial demands were the first (and most). If Sophie Arnould typifies French *tragédie lyrique* in her thespian grounding and nationalist career devoted to the local arena in Paris, Catalani typifies the Italian imperialist, carrying the intentions of Italian vocal supremacy everywhere and rewriting her roles to suit the free-wheeling "singer take all" mentality of *opera seria*. She embellished vocal lines beyond understanding, interpolated her specialties into any piece without a thought for dramatic coherence, and ruthlessly checked the slightest display of talent from her colleagues.

Ironically enough, Catalani capped her vagabond career as a resident in Paris, where she and her husband, diplomat Paul Valabrègue, ran the Théâtre-Italien, treating the Parisians of Arnould, Gluck, and Vestris to the Catalani style in opera. Angelica did not conceive the notion of the heedless *diva assoluta*, but she lent it some of its definitive outlines—in such colorful escapades as the time a court official offended her in Munich. Catalani not only departed the city swearing never to set foot in it again: she refused to set foot there while she was leaving, and had her servants cover the ground with rugs so she could mount her carriage on neutral territory. She dared even defy Napoleon, who ordered her to stay in France despite a contract with the King's Theatre in London. Catalani sneaked out of the country rather than miss her London debut. Other Catalani stories reveal a woman of no great education, as when, *au salon* at Weimar, she noted how deferentially her fellow guests were treating a dignified old man. Renown being one of the few things Catalani understood, she asked who this venerable gentleman might be.

"That is Goethe, Madame."

"Ah. The famed violinist."

"No, no—"

"Of course, how silly of me. His ravishing keyboard sonatas . . ."

"Goethe is not a musician, Madame. Goethe is . . . Goethe."

At length the name rang a bell, and Catalani went over to Weimar's genius-of-the-place to congratulate him on his early success, *Werther*. "What a superb farce that was," she told him. "A comic delight."

Goethe was taken aback. *The Sorrows of the Young Werther* a farce? "Madame—"

"I almost fell to pieces laughing!"

It seems that Catalani had attended a burlesque version at one of Paris's *maisons de vaudeville,* and had no idea that the authentic *Werther* is a sad and sentimental novel. But there was a lot Catalani didn't understand. To compare her with any star singer of today is to comprehend the difference between the disconnected egomania of the good old days and the collaborative instincts—and disciplines—of contemporary opera production.

Recipe for Success

Impresarios continually balked at the fees Catalani's husband demanded on her behalf. Once the theatre paid the prima donna, there would be nothing left for the other singers.

Why should there be? "You want an opera company?" said Valabrègue. "My wife and four or five puppets—that's all you need."

Shocking in its happy cynicism, the comment became a classic quotation, cited by horrified historians long after the threat of perfect star power had faded.

Imperfect Pitch

While she was running the Théâtre-Italien, Catalani sometimes gave encores between the acts of an opera, accompanied only on piano. Once she found the instrument too exalted in pitch for her taste; rather than ask the accompanist to transpose downward, she asked her husband to have the piano lowered.

That night, after the first act of the announced piece, Catalani came out to give her little entr'acte; to her annoyance, she realized as soon as she started singing that the piano was still pitched too high. But it was too late to withdraw and she gamely sang it through. When she reached the wings and her husband, however, she sang a vastly different tune.

"I demanded that you lower that cursed piano!" she said. "And it has *not* been!"

"Is it possible?" said Valabrègue. "I myself stood by while your order was carried out."

"I tell you it has not been lowered!"

Whereupon Charles the *machiniste* was called for. "Charles," said Valabrègue, while the great soprano fumed imposingly, "did you or did you not lower the piano for Madame?"

"You saw me do it yourself, Monsieur."

"Then you *did* lower the piano?" Valabrègue pursued, watching for his wife's reaction.

"Oh, yes, Monsieur. By two inches, at least."
They hadn't retuned it, *corbleu:* they had shortened its legs!

A Strange Visitor

Having enjoyed the most successful career of the age, Catalani retired to a villa in Florence. A cholera epidemic drove her to Paris, and there she was to end her days. One odd event marked this quiet retirement, the visit of a young woman who refused to give her name. Or so the servants reported.

Curious, Catalani went to meet the stranger, who bowed and said, "I have come to render homage to the most noble of women, and the most celebrated soprano of our time. Bless me, Madame, if you will. I am Jenny Lind."

LUIGI LABLACHE

The greatest bass of the early-middle nineteenth century, Lablache summons up a time when opera was a stream of lore-laden names. Malibran, Pasta, Lind, Viardot, Grisi, Rubini, Mario, and Tamburini were Lablache's colleagues. Bellini, Donizetti, and Verdi wrote roles for him. Princess Victoria of England studied singing with him, Sigismond Thalberg was his son-in-law, and, at the funerals of Beethoven and Chopin, it was Lablache who sang the bass line of the Mozart Requiem.

Lablache didn't borrow personality from his coevals; he lent it. He claimed three cultures—French from his father, Irish from his mother, and Italian from his birthplace, Naples. Tall and, for much of his career, immensely fat, Lablache brought grandeur to noble roles like Massimiliano Moor in Verdi's *I Masnadieri* and Lord George Walton in Bellini's *I Puritani*, a bizarre vitality to comic roles. As Donizetti's Don Pasquale he set a tradition with his costume of pantaloons and dressing gown, topped by a black silk nightcap and shrewdly trimmed with a camellia in his buttonhole. As Mozart's Leporello, Lablache would pick up Masetto bodily and carry him offstage under his arm.

This ability to leap naturally from *seria* to *commedia* and back marked Lablache particularly, for the great singers of his Romantic age counted on pathos and tragedy more than on wit, and comedy was regarded as second-class art. It may well be that Lablache, by his support, kept it going, for after his death in 1858 comedy went into a decline, or at any rate suffered a neglect, that lasted till the turn of the century. Lablache may also have helped to popularize the bass line of the musical ensemble, for till his sound inspired composers to make use of the deeper male voice, high voices were the major instruments of operatic narration except in France and Germany. When Lablache sang Oroveso, *Norma* became more than a triangle of two sopranos and a tenor; the shadow of the tribal patriarch fell over the entire action.

Critic Henry Chorley noted Lablache's force as singer and actor in a concert of the music of Palestrina, rarely heard in those days:

> Lablache's perfect acquaintance with the great Roman style, his marvellous voice and, little less marvelous, his power of sustaining and animating his comrades without bearing them down, afforded a distinct idea of how such music might be sung, and how (when well sung) it might move, impress, and exalt those who heard it as a portion of a rite.

"Animating his comrades"! How seldom could that have been noted of the singers of this star-oriented time. Even in the spoken drama, principles of partnership and cohesion had not yet been evolved. To find a sharp performer who was also one of the most gifted singers, then, was startling; all the more so that Lablache was so versatile. "No music was strange to him," Chorley tells us. Wilhelmine Schröder-Devrient, Maria Malibran, and Pauline Viardot were tragediennes, mainly or wholly; Lablache was everybody.

Weber Is Impressed

Having run away from home in his eagerness to wed the theatre, Lablache could not wait the years for his voice to develop, and launched himself as a double-bass player in opera-house orchestras. He seems to have kept his ears open, for one day a singer fell ill and Lablache simply left the *sinfonia,* walked onto the stage, and took over the part.

After some consideration he decided he liked singing better than playing, and stayed with it. It was not long before the voice had developed: into luxurious dark velvet. The first time Carl Maria von Weber heard him, the composer said, "My God! He is a double-bass *still!*"

Lablache Sententioso

Despite his quite literally towering prominence, Lablache often had to make do with parts of smallish importance in between his Leporellos and Pasquales, for the repertory offered few genuine leads for basses. When a colleague commiserated on Lablache's being wasted as Don Basilio in *Il Barbiere di Siviglia,* Lablache said, "My friend, to a great singer there are no small parts. And to a small singer there are no great ones."

Lablache Furibondo

Lablache storms into the theatre to berate another of those scurvy impresarios. What is it this time? Back salary still outstanding after three weeks' patience? Lablache's name a bit too discreetly placed on the posters? Whatever the cause, the bass is in thunder—and, remember, that's six feet and some two hundred pounds of it.

But the impresario knows his man. "My dear Lablache," he says, "You're too good-natured to feel this way by yourself, so your wife has loyally puffed you up and sent you to me to do business from a position of strength."

"Unfair!" cries Lablache. "I come here to have a row, and you disarm me with a pleasantry!"

"My dear fellow, you were not made to have rows. Go home and tell your wife I said so."

They shake hands on it, and Lablache starts out. At the door, he pauses: "No . . . I think I'll tell her you weren't in."

Stretch Marks

Once, Lablache was staying in the same hotel as P. T. Barnum's attraction General Tom Thumb, "the smallest man in the world." One of the General's fans, an Englishman, sought an audience with this curious celebrity, and made the mistake of asking Berlioz for assistance. Offended that the Briton assumed there was some sort of confraternity of musicians and freaks, Berlioz gave the man the address of Lablache's hotel suite. When the giant Lablache opened the door, his visitor was so startled he could scarcely speak.

"I . . . I was calling on . . . well, on General Tom Thumb. Monsieur Berlioz sent me here."

"Yes," said Lablache. "Yes, I am Tom Thumb."

"But . . . excuse me . . . Tom Thumb is the smallest man in the world!"

"Yes," agreed Lablache, "in public, of course. But when I'm at home, I make myself comfortable."

DIVAS OF THE GOLDEN AGE

The early-middle nineteenth century marks the start of our knowledge of opera as a theatrical experience. We can say little of performance practices in Monteverdi's day; we can only imagine how the castratos sounded; we wonder what the backstage of Rameau's Opéra was like, or how it felt to sit on the premiere of *Die Zauberflöte* at the Theater auf der Wieden. But Giuditta Pasta, Wilhelmine Schröder-Devrient, Henriette Sontag, Giulia Grisi, Pauline Viardot, Jenny Lind, and Thérèse Tietjens call up a world of lore and conventions that integrates them into our sense of opera. With this generation, music comes near to us as theatre. We know this music; we have trustworthy reports from those who heard it when new. The sopranos speak to us, almost sing.

It is significant that this generation of divas invented or definitely changed the elements of mission in their profession. These were the years in which star turns began to give way to ensemble collaboration, in which the Italian monopoly began to break up into French, German, and other national schools, in which composers made new attempts to instill a respect for compositional integrity, in which librettists began to balance convention with experimental novelty, in which the tenor entered into his heyday as the castrato's replacement. We leave behind an antiquity of *dei ex machina,* da capo arias, and wigs; we proceed to the era of electric light, cycloramas, and orchestra pits.*

This is the opera as we accept it, and is probably the main reason why we call this a golden age: because now they're singing opera to our taste. More important, they're enlightening it. Before Pasta and Schröder-Devrient, sopranos merely displayed; these two enacted, and in their wake all sopranos had to. Before Lind, sopranos were creatures of the demimonde by their very sharing of themselves so publicly; but Lind celebrated the singer's respectability. Before Viardot, sopranos were musical dolls, not known for their education; but Viardot was sage, the adviser of writers and composers. The woman who takes Turgyenyef for her lover—as Viardot did—is going to have plenty of soul.

Perhaps these divas were most important in their inspiration of a more characterful repertory. Through their theatricality and musicianship, they prompted composers to reach beyond the set forms and persons. Pasta created Norma, Amina, and Anna Bolena; Schröder-Devrient Adriano (in *Rienzi*), Senta, and Venus; Sontag Euryanthe and Miranda (in *L'Éclair,* Halévy's adaptation of Shakespeare's *The Tempest*); Grisi Adalgisa, Elvira (in *I Puritani*), and Norina (in *L'Elisir d'Amore*); Viardot Meyerbeer's Fidès and Gounod's Sapho; Lind Verdi's Amalia (in *I Masnadieri*).†

Would opera have taken its course through these years if the stars had all been forms of Catalani? Remember, composers seldom wrote

*Till about 1900, the orchestra sat on the ground floor along with the audience, their instruments blocking eye view and the acoustic obstacle sorely trying singers as the orchestra grew in volume. American theatres pioneered the sunken pit; and, at Bayreuth, Wagner offered the "mystical abyss" of the somewhat covered and unseen orchestra. Not till the present century, however, did a vertical delimitation of the players become standard.

†Meyerbeer wrote Vielka in *Ein Feldlager in Schlesien* for Lind, but at the Berlin premiere a local prima donna took the role under official pressure. Lind stepped in shortly after and took the piece everywhere, identifying it with herself till the French revision, *L'Étoile du Nord,* came along.

for an ideal cast in those days: they wrote for available talents. The talent had to grow before opera could. Similarly, the talent had to travel, luring the discrete styles across each other's borders. Norma. Senta. Valentine. Axes upon which turn the three great strains of opera, Italian, German, and French. Three distinct heroines: but their parts would blend soon enough, into Hélène, Gioconda, Sulamith. In the eighteenth century, Frederick the Great could say, "What? Hear a German singer? I should as soon expect to derive pleasure from the neighing of my horse!" But note that of these eight divas only Pasta and Grisi were Italian. Opera's culture expanded beyond the traditional national boundaries—another sign that the day of the Catalanis, immutably Italian, was over. The diverse arts of the vocally resonant Italian, orchestrally powerful German, and theatrically ingenious French schools became more widely known to each other, as if bound together by a belief in the diva as opera's central icon. This is the time of the Romantic heroine: it is Norma who fascinates, not Pollione. True, Wagner gives us *Lohengrin,* not *Elsa;* but Wagner is always exceptional. Throughout Europe, composers have sensed that their wisest allegiance binds them to the sopranos, poetic, fierce, dedicated, and astonishing.

Jenny Lind Sings for Garcia

In the summer of 1841, Lind arrived in Paris; armed with letters of introduction, she went to Manuel Garcia the Younger. He heard her sing without betraying an opinion of any kind, and, when she had finished, said, "My dear child, you have no voice."

She was stunned, of course. Her career had scarcely begun; she had not even sung in public outside of Scandinavia. "Or you have *had* a voice," Garcia went on, "and are just about to lose it. Probably you have been singing too much or too early, for your instrument is worn and rugged. I cannot give you any instruction at present. Do not sing a note for three months and then call on me again."

Poor Jenny waited out the time in despair, alone and friendless in a strange country. Surely few foreigners have gotten as little out of a first trip to Paris as Jenny Lind did. "I was living on my tears and the agony of homesickness," she said. To busy herself, she studied French and Italian. When the time was up, Lind returned to Garcia. Once more he heard her, his expression unreadable. When she had sung he rose, dismissed her accompanist, and sat at the piano.

"Now we begin," said Garcia.

Jenny Readies Herself For Glory

Preparing for her debut as Agathe in *Der Freischütz*, Jenny decided to thrill her teacher, Madame Erikson, by putting her utmost power into the singing and interpretation. When she had finished, Erikson said nothing, just sat there.

"Dear me," Jenny thought. "Am I so incapable and stupid?" Then she saw tears streaming down Erikson's face.

"My child," said Erikson, "I have nothing to teach you. Go now, and do as nature bids you!"

Jenny Explains Why She Retired

After dedicating herself to music, after even submitting to the lavishly crass management of Phineas T. Barnum, Lind left music in her prime, to general surprise.

A friend asked her why. "Each day when I was singing," Jenny explained, "I thought less and less of this"—the Bible. "And nothing of that"—the sun. "Nothing at all of that." Jenny collected her thoughts, her nostalgia, regrets, souvenirs, everything. "Well," she concluded. "Well . . . what else could I do?"

Schröder-Devrient Breaks Character

Schröder-Devrient was the choice of the age in *Fidelio,* the most intense of Leonores, yet even her monumental concentration could shatter—as, for instance, when a tenor was slow to receive the crust of bread that Leonore gives Florestan in the dungeon scene. *"Take it,* will you?" she whispered. "What are you waiting for, butter?"

Contra Sontag

A Sontag devoté argued that she was superior to any Italian singer. An Italian detractor, who had never heard her, thought this unlikely; even Germans generally accorded with Frederick the Great's dismissal of northern vocal technique. So the debate raged till the pair went to the opera to let Sontag settle the argument herself from the stage.

Scarcely five minutes after Sontag began, the Italian rose to leave.

"No," urged his friend. "You haven't given her a chance. Stay and you will be conquered."

"I know. That's why I'm going."

If Giulia Grisi Married Mario,
What Would Their Children Be Called?

Grisi did marry Mario, one of the great tenors of Bellini-era opera, and when the two sang together at an embassy in London, their host asked Grisi, "And how are the little Grisettes?"

"Nay, Milord," replied Grisi. "You mean the little Marionettes."

Viardot Views the Ruin of Pasta

Pasta attempted a comeback concert in London in 1850. "Her voice," Chorley tells us, "had been long ago given up by her. Its state of utter ruin . . . passes description." Not only was Pasta now beyond her powers: she looked it. "Her hairdresser had done some tremendous thing or other with her head—or, rather, had left everything undone. A more painful and disastrous spectacle could hardly be looked on."

Pauline Viardot was present, listening through the decrepit sound to comprehend the artist within. To think of it: Pasta created Norma! Others that night in Her Majesty's Theatre listened and laughed, but Viardot listened. "It is like the *Cenacolo* of da Vinci at Milan," she said. "A wreck of a picture, but the picture is the greatest picture in the world!"

Thérèse Tietjens's Last Lucrezia

Suffering from cancer, Tietjens faced an operation in the spring of 1877, and decided that a Lucrezia Borgia at Her Majesty's would be her last performance before undergoing surgery. At that, she was already too ill to sing, and her doctors opposed her going on. But Tietjens didn't like cancelling. And who knew when she might sing again?

She must have been as great an actress as is claimed, for though she sang in agony, she never showed it. She fainted with exhaustion after each scene, but dragged herself to her feet and pursued the piece right through to the end, when Lucrezia's scream of terror over the body of her son sounded shockingly realistic even for the redoubtable Tietjens. Equally persuasive was her swoon at the curtain's fall—and this was not realistic, but real. Nor did Tietjens regain consciousness, though the curtain rose and fell several times.

A week later the operation was performed, unsuccessfully. She died later that year.

Rossini Introduces the Next Section

Rossini lived all the way through this golden age, but he also had preceded it, and thus had the chance to view it in perspective. Truth to tell, he thought standards of singing had declined in these latter years, but, at one soiree, when asked to name the greatest soprano he knew of, he had a timely answer. Gallantly, Rossini cited Isabella Colbran, the Spanish mezzo who left both the king of Naples and the impresario of Naples's San Carlo for Rossini, becoming his first wife and creating the Rossinian coloratura mezzo in *Elisabetta, Regina d'Inghilterra, Otello, Armida, La Donna del Lago, Mosè, Semiramide,* and *Maometto II.* Colbran, however, was not the only name Rossini mentioned.

"The greatest was Colbran," was how he put it—"but the unique was Malibran."

MARIA MALIBRAN

"There was something feverish . . . both in her nature and her art," wrote Henry Chorley, "which dazzled while it delighted." In her nature *and* her art: the singer as personality, the impersonator who reveals herself as well as her characters. Malibran held the center of this golden age of divas, as the most special talent with the most spectacular biography. All her great colleagues gave some reading of the personal mystique that enlarges prominence into legend, as when Wilhelmine Schröder-Devrient's Leonore heartened young Richard Wagner's conception of music theatre,* or when Jenny Lind allowed Phineas T. Barnum to boast her forth as if she were not merely a marvel but a freak. But it was Malibran above all who developed the notion of a compulsive performer, not husbanding her talent but spending it, and so intensely that she consumed herself. She died, at the age of twenty-eight, in a horseback-riding accident. Yet such was her restless magnetism as a performer and personality that her public preferred to believe that she had died of enthusiasm: of boundless commitment to music.

A sound mythology needs a birth of entitlement, and Malibran had it, as the daughter of Manuel Garcia, master of the most authoritative course in vocal instruction and the father as well of Pauline Viardot and Manuel, Jr., who took over the family vocation of imparting highest professional standards to the next generation of opera's postulants. As impresario, composer, and tenor, Garcia senior had a virtual opera company in residence, and he made sure that young Maria learned the

---

* Scholars have corrected this legend: apparently Wagner saw Schröder-Devrient in some other, less exalted, role, but claimed it was Leonore in order to emphasize his lineage as Beethoven's heir.

trade well. "Papa's glance," she said, "has such an influence upon me that I am sure it would make me fling myself from the roof into the street without doing myself any harm." Garcia's approach offered more incentive to the imperfect student than an inspiring glance. In a classic tale, two men hear terrible screams echoing out of the Garcia house.

"Good heavens," says one. "Shall we call the police?"

"Have no fear," says the other, gesturing for them to move on. "It's only old Garcia beating cadenzas into his daughter."

Maria took the name Malibran from an early, unhappy marriage to a middle-aged merchant she met in New York, all happily put by when she married violinist Charles de Beriot. In those days singers trained their voices, learned the repertory, and marched onto the stage in a major role; there was none of the eccentric vocal apprenticeship, conservatory stalling, and slow rise through small parts to leads that we favor today. You had it or you didn't. What Malibran had, besides a generous heart and a breathless *joie de vivre,* was a mezzo-soprano, drilled by Papa to encompass by strategy all the standard leading roles. The voice, then, was not precisely equal to all the demands that her career might make on her. Add to this a born actress's extrovert panache, and one ends with a controversial figure, the kind to be proclaimed supreme by some aficionados and damned as mannered by others. So it was with Callas, later; and, as with Callas, the sudden death did much to silence the opposition. Not to listen to the myth shows a lack of wisdom. So all subscribe to the legend, and the age then seems framed by the materialization and passing of this one singer.

Whether or not Malibran was the greatest singer of the day is not important: opera needs these personalities to create a sense of epoch come and gone, a style. And the style was that of the Romantic heroine, to provide in Norma, Maria Stuarda, Amina, and Desdemona a challenge to what Manfred and Faust and Don Juan provided in literature. "She never produced a single type in opera for other women to adopt," Chorley records. "She passed over the stage like a meteor, as an apparition of wonder, rather than as one who . . . left her mantle behind her for others to take up and wear." Nay, that was the point: to propose an inimitable immortality with which all other reputations must be compared unfavorably. Malibran did not set a standard of excellence; she made a magic, showed a once-in-history brilliance, effected an enlightenment of the nobility of the diva. She was, onstage and off, a living experience of what beauty means.

Death and Love

Emma Calvé liked to tell the story of the night Malibran sang Rossini's Desdemona to her father's Otello. Garcia would warn his daughter that she'd catch it if she blundered, and this of course made her nervous, which in turn made her blunder. By the last scene, Garcia was enraged and Malibran terrified. As "Otello" approached "Desdemona" to strangle her, the look of the ferocious pedagogue and implacable Papa urged Malibran to flee in earnest.

"Help!" she cried, and "Murder!" as she raced about the stage, Garcia in pursuit. "He's after me!" she remarked, a touch superfluously. "He's going to kill me!"

She leaped into the orchestra, landing in the arms of a first violinist named Charles de Beriot: who became her second husband.

Calvé embroidered a bit. It was backstage history that Malibran took *Otello* so seriously that she would attempt to evade the Moor as if her life were truly in danger—but surely she never leaped into the orchestra. And de Beriot did not play in opera orchestras; he was a soloist. Sweet tale, though.

Realism

A benefit at Paris' Théâtre-Italien found Malibran offering scenes from *Il Barbiere di Siviglia* and *Otello,* Rossini comic and tragic, Malibran soubrette and romantic. Despite a ban on demonstrations, the public went wild, filling the stage with floral tributes. By evening's end, the *Otello* murder scene, the entire theatre was fairly transported with the intensity of Malibran's projection of doomed innocence. As the Otello, Domenico Donzelli, prepared to drop the dead Desdemona to the floor, the public was hushed in pity and terror.

And Malibran piped up, "Mind where you put me! Don't crush my flowers!"

Generosity

Another flower story finds Malibran and Henriette Sontag taking calls for a joint concert in Paris. As Malibran picks up a wreath that has fallen at her feet, a voice calls out, "Leave it alone! That's not for you!"

"I would not deprive Mademoiselle Sontag of the wreath," Malibran tells this brute. "I would rather place it on her myself."

Determination

About to go on stage as Arsace in *Semiramide,* Malibran suddenly fainted. The curtain was held and various treatments tried, including a draught of what was supposed to be vinegar. Whatever it was, it raised a few unsightly blisters on Malibran's lips. She revived; but could not appear so deformed.

But what power on earth could keep Malibran from the stage when she was in voice? Picking up a pair of scissors and marching up to a mirror, she calmly cut the blisters off.

"Now for Rossini," she said; and on she went.

Greed

In 1835, a year before her death, Malibran gave a concert in London for an Italian professor of music, by hap to very poor attendance. When the musician called on Malibran to pay her, he asked if she would consider taking a portion of the twenty guineas they had agreed upon.

Malibran refused, and the ruined professor slowly counted out the coins. At twenty pounds he paused—would she at least forgo the last sovereign?

"My terms," Malibran insisted, "are twenty guineas, not twenty pounds."

"My poor wife and children," the man sighed as he handed over the last coin.

"I demanded my full terms," Malibran then said, "because I wanted the sum the larger when I gave it back to you." Handing the coins to the stunned musician, she fled in tears from the room.

ADELINA PATTI

Did Patti really have a parrot trained to scream "Cash! Cash!" whenever Patti's manager Colonel Mapleson entered the room? Was she truly the Queen of Song, as she was dubbed? And did she actually build a private theatre in her Welsh castle so she could take curtain calls to an audience of neighbors long after her collapsed voice had driven her into retirement?

The answers appear to run to the affirmative; yes, the parrot, the Queen, the private theatre. No doubt the parrot was not aware that Patti was by far the highest paid singer of the day. But by simple proximity it must have noticed that she was the most punctually paid singer—because no cash, no Patti. She disdained rehearsals as damaging to the voice, sending her manager, agent, or even maid to attend as go-between, and this may be why she held the stage for nearly forty years of stardom, though she had been singing even before she could read, as the child wonder Little Florinda. "Rehearsals," she declared, "tire the voice."

Her fees alone made her the Queen of Song. Comparing amounts proportionately from her day to ours, she was the highest-paid singer of all time. Her colleagues were amazed, her managers grumbled—but the Song of Patti, they say, was extraordinary. It was a golden voice with perfect bravura, aptly suited to the repertory of the time—Lucia, Amina, Marguerite, Juliette, Violetta, even Aida. She was not, supposedly, a great interpreter of character; yet she had the gift.

She had inherited it, for both her parents sang opera. They were playing Pollione and Norma in Madrid on the night Patti was born— her mother collapsed during the performance and had to be rushed to her childbed, so Adelina might be said to have been summoned into opera, called to greatness. Friends asked the Pattis why they didn't name their daughter Adalgisa, to complete Bellini's triangle.

It was a fine age for opera—not for music theatre, surely, but for Song and those who would be Queen of it. It was the age of Garcia, of the sound training that encouraged the graduate to make the most of her individual musicianship. There was only one technique—Garcia's. But once one mastered it, one could make each role one's own by variations in tempo, accent, coloring, embellishment. "Her style is Italian," the London *Times* trumpeted, "her pronunciation of the words Italian, her delivery of the voice Italian, her method of execution Italian, and, in short, her whole performance, from first to last, Italian of the purest." They say her sense of involvement was strongest in recitative. In aria, she concentrated on a metallically sentimental bel canto, the voice bright and forward, and the line plangent and loving, but tending to the perky, with fast tempos and aimless flair. George Bernard Shaw, for one, thought her too much the diva and too little the artist:

> Madame Patti's offenses against artistic propriety are mighty ones and millions. She seldom even pretends to play any other part than that of Adelina, the spoiled child with the adorable voice; and I believe she would be rather hurt than otherwise if you for a moment lost sight of Patti in your preoccupation with Zerlina, or Aida, or Caterina. [Christine] Nilsson, a far greater dramatic artist, so far stood on her dignity that she never came out before the curtain to bow until there had been applause enough to bring out [Patti] at least six times. (Patti will get up and bow to you in the very agony of stage death if you only drop your stick accidentally.)

Still, Patti's day was not noted for great singing actresses. Earlier in her century, Julie Scio, Wilhelmine Schröder-Devrient, and Maria Malibran had pointed the way to the diva of drama, one in whom song was a poetry of character. But all three were dead before Patti was twenty, and Patti's day was the day of Patti, content to delight in song without portrayal. An early Patti biographer, D. M. Dalmazzo, thought her "almost always exquisite and always animated by the tone and confidence of genius." If Patti did not herself act, she let the roles act for her: not just another pretty voice, but a great singer.

The greatness never faltered. Thanks to the solid training, the essentially lyrical approach to an already light repertory, and of course the cavalier approach to rehearsals, Patti never really had to retire, and somehow never quite did, going on and on at that little theatre in Craig-

y-nos ("Rock of Night"), her Welsh home. She gave more than curtain calls—a *Traviata*, say, more or less fully staged with her husband,
Ernesto Nicolini (or was it her butler?; reports vary), as Alfredo and
a chorus of local enthusiasts. (What better place to pick up a chorus
off the street than in Wales?) The house staff rained flowers on Patti
after each scene, and the weekend guests, having supped well, expressed gratitude with ovations. And, it is told, when Patti was indisposed, her fans were not disappointed: the diva was simply propelled
back and forth across the stage in a flower-strewn gondola. The homage was ferocious.

All this suggests an extravagantly vain woman, and most Patti stories confirm this profile. Yet another Patti occasionally suggests herself, one of admirable traits—the Patti, for instance, who hied herself
from Craig-y-nos to Covent Garden to hear Luisa Tetrazzini, "the new
Patti," and took a seat down front and smiled welcome to the debutante. Or the Patti who emerged from old age to taste a dangerous
immortality by making some of the first gramophone records. Perhaps
"emerged" is not quite the word, as Patti insisted on receiving the recording technicians and their equipment at Craig-y-nos: the new age
must catch the old, golden one *in situ*. Nor did the acoustic horn truly
catch Patti in any fair sense, for by then the tone was dusty and the
breathing labored. Only the famous Patti trill was intact. Still, the
blessing of Tetrazzini and the late recording sessions testify to a rather
likable prima donna, one lost in legend but dimly glimpsed in those
sad but fascinating old discs. How can we dislike anyone game enough
to gamble her legend on an uncertain technology? Read these stories
knowing that Patti was regarded by many as the greatest opera singer
who ever lived—and remember that nine-tenths of an opera legend is
a raconteur's hearsay.

The Celebrated Tale of Patti's Shoe

Patti was appearing with Colonel Mapleson's company, and on the day
of a Boston *Traviata* sent her agent to the Colonel to collect her fee,
invariably payable on the afternoon of each performance.

The colonal habitually amassed Patti's fee out of the house receipts,
but on this trip he had tried Boston at an unusual time on little notice,
and the box office stood at less than par. All Mapleson could offer Patti
of her £1,000* was £800. Would the agent accept this much on account and pick up the outstanding £200 later?

He would not. Nay, he immediately cancelled Patti's contract. The
Colonel consoled himself with the thought that, at Patti's salary, a poor
house would ruin him, anyway. Then Patti's agent returned with news.

"You are a marvellous man, and a fortunate one, too," he tells Ma-

* Roughly $5,000. I quote the figures in pounds to retain the Maplesonian flavor of the original.

pleson. "Madame Patti does not wish to break her engagement with you, as she certainly would have done with anyone else under the circumstances. Give me the £800, and she will make every preparation for going on to the stage. She empowers me to tell you that she will be at the theatre in good time for the beginning of the opera, and that she will be ready, dressed in the costume of Violetta, with the exception only of the shoes. You can let her have the balance when the doors open and the money comes in from the outside public, and directly she receives it she will put her shoes on and at the proper moment make her appearance on the stage."

Mapleson decided to chance it. But the walk-in business yielded only £160, £40 short of the goal. Patti's agent took it and returned with the joyful announcement that Patti had got one shoe on. "Send her the £40 and she will put on the other."

The last £40 dribbled in, and Patti, face wreathed in the glow of noblesse oblige, came forth to donate her Violetta to Mapleson's *Traviata*. That she would not trust Mapleson for the smallest fraction of the whole says as much about the questionable ethics of nineteenth-century impresarios as about the iron will of prima donnas. But let us grasp the context of these figures by realizing that the going rate for Mapleson's other stars, including such notables as Thérèse Tietjens and the tenor Mario, was £50 a night.

Grounds for Divorce

In 1876 Patti went to Petersburg, Russia, for a short season of some of her great roles. By the third *Traviata* the Russian climate had caught up with the Italians; the scheduled Alfredo was replaced, and Patti herself wasn't feeling much like a Queen of Song that day. Her husband, the Marquis de Caux, begged her to cancel. She decided to sing.

After the first act, she asked the Marquis, "Haven't I sung well, after all?"

"Yes," he replied. "But"—how to put this diplomatically?—"I have heard you more advantageously in the same act on former occasions."

That was not diplomatic enough. Suddenly irate, Patti threw off her costume and wig, told her husband off, and fainted. Somehow, she pulled herself together and finished the opera. But she could not forgive her husband's disloyalty: a few days later her lawyer in Paris presented her petition for separation from the Marquis de Caux.

Patti's Taste in Royalty

"Which crowned head," she was asked, "do you like best?"

After some thought, Patti chose Alexander II of Russia. "He gives the best jewellery," she explained.

Patti Helps a Colleague Prepare Her Toilette

In Patti's day, the more glamorous divas affected false eyebrows, shaving off the natural ones and donning creations more suitable to greatness. Patti thought this rubbish; as Rossini said, opera was voice, voice, and more voice—not costume. One time, a rival prima donna was enjoying her false eyebrows, her claque's ovations, and herself far too much for Patti's comfort. Patti started to stare at the upstart's face in a kind of fascinated horror.

"What's the matter?" the rival whispered.

"Your right eyebrow has fallen off!"

In dismay, the rival turned her back to the public and deftly removed her left eyebrow. In fact, there had been nothing wrong with the right one—and the rival played the rest of the act with part of her face missing.

To which we may append the moral: Never try to out-diva the diva.

Patti and the Evil Eye

Because they had similar voices and sang the same roles, Patti and Etelka Gerster became fierce rivals, not least when both sang for Mapleson in his American seasons. Let one enjoy a triumph as Lucia and the other would refuse to sing Lucia ever again, or any Donizetti, or any opera. Let there be too profuse an array of flower baskets handed up to the one, and the other would storm back to her hotel, pack, and board the first train for New York.

Mapleson's star tenor Ernesto Nicolini enjoyed the feud. As Patti's second husband, he could not resist taking sides, and encouraged Patti's belief that Gerster was hexing Patti with an evil eye. Everything, from a rough scale to a late train connection, was put down to Gerster's black magic. While Mapleson's troupe was in San Francisco in the spring of 1884, a minor earthquake struck, shocking—as San Francisco's earthquakes love to do—all visitors almost into panic. Not Patti: for she knew this was no Act of God.

"Gerster!" she muttered.

Gerster Replies

Patti admirers during the San Francisco tour included the governor of Missouri, who was so moved by her "Home, Sweet Home," that he bestowed a kiss upon her.

Patti was philosophical. "When a gentleman, and such a nice old gentleman, and a governor of a great state, kisses one so quick that one has not time to see and no time to object, what can one do?"

Gerster, pressed by reporters for her view, thought the event received far too much attention. After all, she pointed out, "There is nothing wrong in a man kissing a woman old enough to be his mother."

Celebrating the Reign of Patti

After this western tour, Patti returned to New York to sing Lucia at the Academy of Music, twenty-five years after her debut at the same house in the same part with the same Edgardo, Pasquale Brignoli. Alas, Brignoli died shortly before Patti's arrival, and the opera had to be changed, a routine occurrence chez Mapleson. On November 26, two days after the exact anniversary, Patti sang Martha, complete with ovations and a torchlight parade up the avenue to Patti's hotel, her carriage of course dragged by a team of delirious fans. Unfortunately, Mapleson had decided to rent the ovations and parade rather than trust to chance, and something of true delirium was lacking. The critic Henry Krehbiel was so disgruntled by this insult to the Queen of Song that he proposed a gala banquet at the Hotel Brunswick. But this, too, was a disappointment, for some of the women who were to grace the table with social *ton* refused to sit with Patti, who had scandalized society when she left the Marquis de Caux. Krehbiel had to content himself with a stag dinner, as the husbands did not object to taking banquet with a divorced woman. At that, Krehbiel was upstaged by the resourceful Mapleson, who arrived late in splendid kit, sailed through the room to his diva, fell to his knees, and touched her hand to his lips.

Actually, the height of the festivities was neither parade nor banquet, not anything, indeed, in the matter of Patti tribute. Rather, it was Patti's tribute to her own nostalgia: for at *Martha*'s end, the curtain rose on a marching band before a dropcloth bearing the American Eagle and the inscription, "Patti, 1859–1884," all this to a march tune expressly composed in Patti's honor by the bandmaster back in 1859. That gentleman was again present to lead the march, and at its close the Queen of Song told him, "I thank you for your kindness from the bottom of my heart."

For once, her voice was shaking.

Another Attempt To Out-diva Patti

This time Patti's challenger is a singer of highest rank. Patti had been entertaining at a soiree, and an aged woman came up to compliment her on her command of technical matters. However, she thought Patti's Mozart lacked spirit, heart, *Innigkeit*. Why is Patti sailing through "Batti, batti" at such a fast tempo? She makes it sound like the Bell Song from *Lakmé*. And, lest Patti think her critic knew nothing of music, she gave her name: Jenny Lind.

"I know you were a famous singer once," Patti snapped back. "I recall my grandfather speaking of you."

Bargaining with Patti

Invited to assist at a special week of concerts in the British hinterland, Patti quoted the usual quite sizable figure, and the management asked her to come down somewhat in her terms. After all, this wasn't just a Patti recital. This was a music festival.

Replied the diva, "Patti *is* a music festival!"

The Diva Hears the Diva

Not only did the technicians of the Gramophone Company have to journey to Craig-y-nos to record her: they had to wait around until she felt the time was precisely right. To help the time pass, she accorded them champagne with their dinner, and at last she dared, and sang, and— for the first time in her life—heard Patti.

Playing her discs back to her was a hazardous courtesy, for after all the voice was sixty-one years old, and might not meet the diva's expectations. When the records were released, on a unique pink label to the fanfare of store posters reading, "Patti is singing here today," many listeners were disappointed.

Not Patti. Blowing kisses into the playback horn, she cried, "Ah, mon Dieu! Maintenant je comprends pourquoi je suis Patti! Oh, oui! Quelle voix! Quelle artiste! Je comprends tout!": Now I know who Patti was! What a voice! What an artist! I understand everything!

MINNIE HAUK

"She is justly considered the representative American prima donna," the *New York World* declared, partly out of local pride. Minnie Hauk, a native New Yorker, was an exemplar of the golden age in the days when the Patti type of stardom was ceding to the Farrar type: when the simple accomplishment of singing well began to seem simple, compared with singing with flair.

Hauk was a performer as well as a singer. Typically, she was America's first (and, in her day, the world's most successful) Carmen—what great Carmen ever made it on voice alone? It was a remarkable voice, capable of doing justice to Gounod's Juliette and Bellini's Amina as well. Granted, Hauk was a soprano, not a mezzo, and probably sang the higher alternatives still used today when a soprano sings Carmen—may have sung yet others, in that arrogant era. But Hauk was versatile, no question, especially in her ability to bring theatrical commitment to any part, from little sisters to *femmes fatales*, gamines to princesses. Manon, Elsa, Rosina, Sélika, Marguerite, Violetta, Senta, Mignon, Aida, Santuzza—her gallery of roles impresses as much for the diversity of person as for that of style or tessitura.

Strangely, her memory lodges entirely in Carmen; those who have heard of her imagine her as a mezzo. This limited typing had begun even in her prime. When she sang with Colonel Mapleson, he locked her into her famous role despite her request for a more stimulating program—*L'Africaine*, perhaps, one of her favorite works for its tragic grandeur and exploitation of her mezzo depths and soprano heights. "*Carmen* fills the house," Mapleson told her. "You ought to be satisfied with your triumph in it." Let us sample Hauk on her terms. . .

A Chance Meeting

In her apprentice days in Paris in the late 1860s, Hauk had the opportunity to attend an important soiree at Théophile Gautier's. A goodly fraction of "all Paris" would be there, and Hauk's manager Maurice Strakosch had arranged for her to sing. It was quite a turnout: Dumas *fils*, Daudet, Renan, and some highly influential musicians, including Mathilde Marchesi and Auber. One of the guests kindly accompanied her at the piano, and Hauk proceeded to sing her way into renown; not long after, she became the first American to sing at the Paris Opéra.

Some years after all this, Hauk was thinking how sad it was that she, the most famous Carmen of her day, should never have met Bizet. It was sadder yet that he had died so soon after *Carmen*'s unsuccessful premiere; if only he had lived a bit more, he would have seen his masterpiece prosper.

Hauk voiced these musings to Strakosch, who reminded her of Gautier's soiree. "Remember the man who played for you?" he said. "That was Bizet."

The Chatterbox

In the 1873–74 season, Hauk shone as a star of the Austro-Hungarian opera circuit, commuting between Vienna and Budapest. Her parties attracted many a celebrity. The most useful of these was the Abbé Liszt, who would play; the least useful was the painter Hans Makart, the most unsociable man in Vienna.

At one dinner, Makart, to Hauk's left, never uttered a word, despite an animated group of guests and the earnest efforts of his hostess to draw him out. Finally, she turned to him and said, "Now, Herr Makart, really *do* let us speak of something else!"

Command Performance

A royal favorite in Berlin, Hauk at times seemed to be singing directly to Their Majesties—just as well, for when the Imperial Box was occupied, no one clapped till the Emperor did.

In those days it was incumbent upon anyone singing Rosina in *Il Barbiere di Siviglia* to interpolate an encore favorite into the Lesson Scene; Hauk usually sang something in English to underline the novelty of an American's reigning in a German opera house. After several nights of "Kathleen Mavourneen," she thought Their Majesties might enjoy a change, and chose "Swanee River."

No sooner had she begun playing the introduction than she sensed a commotion in the Imperial Box; shortly after, she saw Berlin's intendant von Hülsen speaking to Her Majesty; and after *that* she heard von Hülsen in the wings calling to her: "Fräulein Hauk must sing 'Kathleen Mavourneen' by Her Majesty's command."

The Lesson Scene had ended by then, and the opera was speeding on through its story. But the Bartolo improvised a cue in the recitative just before the end of the act. "Well, Rosinchen," he bubbled, "as I have been so good as to give way to you in everything, you must sing me your favorite song, 'Kathleen Mavourneen.' " He turned to imaginary servants in the wings. "Hey, there! Let the spinet be brought out!" Thus Hauk accommodated Rossini (somewhat) and the Imperial taste (excellently).

Her Majesty was amused.

Beware of Don José

On tour with Colonel Mapleson, Hauk was singing Carmen to the José of Luigi Ravelli, who could not accustom himself to her realistic interpretation—especially in Act Three, during the duel between José and Escamillo, when Hauk would rush up to Ravelli, grab him, and cling. Ravelli preferred to stand apart and make a smashing effect with a high note at this juncture, and wanted no sopranos crowding his act.

In Philadelphia, at the Academy of Music one night, Hauk's grab-and-cling disconnected Ravelli's throat from Bizet's music with more than her usual emphasis, and he resolved to hurl her into the orchestra. This only made her cling the harder.

"Laissez-moi! Laissez-moi!" he screamed, as the buttons came popping off his costume.

Finally Hauk did let go, and briskly got herself to a remote part of the stage, whereupon the distraught Ravelli turned to the audience and cried, "Regardez! Elle a déchiré mon gilet!": Look, she has torn my waistcoat! Thinking this part of *Carmen*, the house exploded in cheers.

Backstage during the intermission, Hauk locked herself in her dressing room while Ravelli charged around the stage area shouting, "Je la tuerai!": I will kill her! As Bizet's last act affords him a splendid chance to do just that, everyone warned her not to go on. She did, however, and Ravelli gave her no trouble—"to the disappointment," she dryly remarks in her memoirs, "of everybody."

A Private Farewell

Though America's unrivaled Carmen and a native New Yorker, Hauk impulsively decided to make her farewell in her hometown in that very role without making any public announcement. Still, the event charged her with a tensely nostalgic sorrow. At her entrance she was as vital as ever, but she was weeping; and when she tossed the rose to José she felt as if she were throwing a fond memento to herself.

During the first intermission she saw the rose lying on the stage, seized it, and—passing her bouquets to the choristers—kept that dusty, broken flower as a souvenir of all she had been.

The next day, while cleaning up, the maid threw the flower out the window.

SINGERS OF THE AGE OF THE GRAMOPHONE

If Malibran and her contemporaries inaugurate opera's most vivid legends, the singers active around the turn of the present century form the first generation of opera's vocal archives in the recordings they left behind. Some contributed no more than quaint souvenirs, dim glimpses around a corner; others left an illustrative repertory, virtually a concert of all they did best. In either case, they made themselves tremendous, and pushed their predecessors into a kind of honorable mention, a mute history. "Jenny Lind is only a memory," observed a Victor ad of the day, "but the voice of Melba can never die." And there is Melba as Gounod's Marguerite, vital, touching, and in color—while Lind, in a ghostly concert gown, merely hovers.

Though the recording machine was at first regarded as little more than an amusement, today's historians cannot praise it enough. It preserved a taste of Verdi's first Otello and Iago, Puccini's first Mimì and Manon Lescaut, Mascagni's first Santuzza, Strauss's first Marschallin, Octavian, and Sophie, Massenet's first Werther, Debussy's first Mélisande, Chaikofsky's first Lisa—and these in the arias they introduced—among countless fascinating documents. True, many of these are at best curiosities, as veteran voices try to recall a theatre experience in a little room where "Thou shalt not simulate theatre volume" was the first commandment. Under such conditions, Francesco Tamagno can scarcely be said to have "committed" Otello's "Esultate!" to disc; the primitive technology and his advanced age sapped his energy. Worse yet, Cesira Ferrani's "Mi chiamano Mimì" is simply drab, not possibly representative of a Mimì who coached the premiere with the composer or of the soprano whom Toscanini chose to sing the first Italian Mélisande.

Still, all the lore and legend in a thousand books does not give the immediacy of contact we experience in a single record, so from here on each singer's personality registers with greater concentration: through the voice that lies behind the stories. It is one thing to learn, say, that Emma Eames cut a fine figure on stage but lacked characterological oomph, quite another to hear the sound of this cold beauty, to sense her come to her bit of life, so austere, so proper. We begin to understand why critic James Huneker said, of Eames's Aida, "last night there was skating on the Nile."

Similarly, we read that Emma Calvé was impetuous, curious, daring, the perfect Carmen. This is interesting; but doesn't the soprano come more truly forward in her scattershot encounters with recording apparatus, some of which were released as was? "Am I not in good voice?" she crowed to her accompanist—right in the middle of the Habañera. Later, she decided she had to dance as she did on stage—again, right in the middle of a take. At another session, she hit a rancid note at the end of the Séguedille and murmured, "Ah, mon dieu!" This very spontaneity, surely, is what made Calvé's Carmen perfect.

Spontaneity is a sometime thing on records, but by about 1908 they did begin to approximate a sensitivity in picking up (certain) voices, and the installation in 1925 of the electrical microphone in place of the acoustical horn at last gave fidelity and a broad range of sound, especially grateful to Wagnerian-size orchestras. Still, the great talents spanned the two eras without reference to breakthroughs in machine technique: talent is talent. Rosa Ponselle's flawlessly composed vocal structure comes through better on her later records than on her earlier, but on them all one is aware of a uniquely magnificent instrument. Fyodor Chalyapin and Antonio Scotti brought a performer's vitality to the recording studio (not to mention Chalyapin's Boris Godunof, captured onstage at Covent Garden), and come through with personality intact even on their earliest discs.

Further technical developments of course followed the electrical recording process—the long-playing disc in 1948, stereo separation in 1955. But the essential wonder of all this science is the invention of recording itself, the intimacy with which it grasps history. Lotte Lehmann's Sieglinde and Marschallin, two of the century's great portrayals, would be merely statistics now, famous yet unsung, but for Lehmann's having had the chance to record them.* It may well be that some singers approach us more personally on records than they did in the theatre—Richard Tauber, for instance: He was not a very textured thespian, and his somewhat stiff figure might have detracted from his characterizations. But on records Tauber is nothing but voice, style, and musicianship, here biting off a phrase with *accento*, there caressing it *pianissimo*, now putting *Schwung* into opera, then making operetta sound like Mozart. Tauber's art *is* personality, so he lacks nothing as a disembodied voice.

We have come to the 1900s, to epochs of the not-too-distant past that some of today's operagoers can remember. Many of the traditions Pasta and Grisi were used to—the encore, for example, or the directionless mise-en-scène—have collapsed, and opera's cultural status is shifting from the elitist to the populist. The star remains a constant. But the star is becoming familiar in a personal way, more surely perceived.

Listening to the gramophone/phonograph/stereo/CD player tells us why.

Otello's Lunch

Francesco Tamagno was as famed for his eccentric penny-pinching as for his trumpeting tenor. When Luigi Mancinelli gave a lunch for some singers at an Italian restaurant, Tamagno took note of some leftover

---

* We should note a classic quirk of recording history: of the Marschallin's many memorable phrases, her final utterance, "Ja, ja," is outstanding, a key element in the individuation of portrayal. Yet, when recording *Der Rosenkavalier* for HMV, Lehmann apparently left the studio after the trio in Act Three—before the famous last words. Elisabeth Schumann, HMV's Sophie, stepped in for Lehmann, imitating her delivery.

veal cutlets and asked Mancinelli what he intended to do with them.

"Do with them?" asked Mancinelli. "Nothing. What would one do with a veal cutlet?"

Ordering some newspaper from the waiter, Tamagno wrapped up the cutlets, explaining that his little dog adored them.

The next day Mancinelli showed up at Tamagno's hotel suite at noon. The tenor and his daughter were dining: on veal cutlets.

Aggressive Elsa

Emma Eames, the cool beauty whose Aida skated on the Nile, shocked a Met audience during the second act of *Lohengrin* by turning around and giving the Ortrud a terrific slap in the face. Eames felt that her rival's prideful demeanor was attracting undue attention.

Had Eames been singing Tosca, the act might have fit in as a sort of correct improvisation. But Elsa is no Tosca; nor was Eames. The press picked it up with pleasure, and asked the Ortrud for her view of it. She was forgiving: "I was really surprised and delighted to see *any* evidence of emotion in Madame Eames."

Calvé Records

Landon Ronald's oft-quoted recollection of the day Calvé was to have made her first discs finds the young Ronald, Gramophone Company's accompanist, picking up Calvé at her hotel and riding with her to the studio in Maiden Lane. The record industry, barely hours old, tended to offices befitting firms that could prove fly-by-night at any moment—Gramophone itself incorporated a typewriter subsidiary as a hedge against the collapse of the record craze. One look at Gramophone's headquarters and Calvé said, "Mon Dieu, but never in my life will I enter such a place. It is a tavern, not a manufactury! I shall be robbed there!"

In vain did Ronald reason. What Calvé saw of the Gramophone and Typewriter Company, Limited, looked like a thieves' den. Begging her to wait, Ronald dashed upstairs, grabbed a presentable young clerk, and told him to race down to Calvé, look handsome, and give her her fee in advance.

Minutes later, Calvé was sweeping into the office: thanking, beaming, gracious, and ready to make some history.

Calvé in Utah

In the old days of the Old Met, the spring tour was a transcontinental journey that took in virtually every town that had a good-sized theatre. Passing through Utah, the company made a rest stop and Calvé visited a Mormon family that included three wives and quite a few children. Admiring one, Calvé asked one wife if it was hers. The Mormon turned to her, Calvé reported, "with the quiet dignity of a woman of the Old Testament."

"*We* are the mothers," the woman explained.

Chalyapin Conducts

The Russian bass was not only a formidable performer, but a giant of a man with a will to match. When he didn't like a conductor's tempo he would take over himself from the stage, stamping out the rhythm he wanted and leading the players himself. Rehearsing Rimsky-Korsakof's short piece *Mozart and Salieri*, Chalyapin pulled this stunt, at which the maestro stopped the music and said, "Kindly remember that I am the conductor."

"In a garden where there are no birds," Chalyapin observed, "a croaking toad is a nightingale."

The Creative Interpreter

Chalyapin's colleagues repeated Chalyapin stories so often that virtually every one has become a classic. The most popular finds the bass arriving in America in 1921 for his first postwar concert tour. Besieged by reporters at Ellis Island and armed with impresario Sol Hurok as interpreter, Chalyapin launches into a spectacular speech—in Russian—about poverty and hunger in the Russia of his childhood. And remember Chalyapin doesn't just speak: he gestures, he dances, he mimes, he whispers, he poses, he roars, he lunges, he thunders. All in the world is hungry! Chalyapin's uncles are hungry! Chalyapin's father is hungry! Chalyapin, God in heaven!, is hungry! Dancing, posing, lunging. The humiliation, the agony, of Russian hunger!

At last Chalyapin finishes, and the reporters scream, "What'd he say?" at Hurok.

Replies Hurok, "He says he thinks America's great!"

Chalyapin in Trouble

About to make his New York return on this tour, Chalyapin was stricken
with laryngitis. He had cancelled two concerts, and now, on the third
date, he was in its grip and despair. "Bozhe moy!" he moaned: *God!
God of all the Russias and the world! What have I done to deserve
this?* He threw himself about the room as his manager begged him to
find a way. One more cancellation would jeopardize the entire American tour. Chalyapin *must* sing!

"God, why should I be so punished?"

Chalyapin's valet Nicolai remained calm. "Fyodor Ivanovich, go to
the concert. God will give you your voice when the moment comes."

Chalyapin shot his valet a look mixed of incredulity, torment, and
anger. "What has God," he shouted, "got to do with my *voice?*"

You Have It or You Don't

Antonio Scotti enjoyed one of the longest careers in opera—forty-four
years, thirty-three of them at the Met. When he retired, he did not turn
to teaching. "Why I give lessons?" he asked. "Always old singers open
studios. No. Scotti not opening studios. Scotti not *learn* to feel—Scotti
born to feel . . . nothing to teach."

Praise

Hearing of Toscanini's perfectionist rages, Lotte Lehmann avoided
working with him as long as she could. But they were doomed to meet
in a Salzburg Festival *Fidelio*: no one sang a greater Leonore than Lehmann and no one conducted a greater *Fidelio* than Toscanini, and of
such greatness festivals are made.

Lehmann took the chance, then—but she trembled. That Toscanini
was capable of anything. If he didn't like the way you hit a note, he
would stop the orchestra and rate you with words Dante never used. If
he didn't like your phrasing he would scream that you had *no right to
music*. Even your acting was subject to his editing rages.

Sure enough, early in rehearsals, Toscanini stopped the orchestra and
looked hard at Lehmann. "Mein Gott," she thought. "Was kommt
jetzt?": What happens now?

"You," said Toscanini, "are an *artist!*"

Lehmann nearly fainted.

Not Tonight, Mademoiselle

Richard Tauber spent his twenties at the Dresden Opera, logging his experience and building up his repertory. Narraboth in *Salome* was one of his favorite parts, for the curtain is not long up before the officer kills himself—freeing the young tenor for a night out with his light of love instead of sending him home late (and exhausted), as Don Ottavio or Rodolpho did. Tauber used to tease the four men who played Herod's soldiers, for after they carried his corpse offstage, they had to march back on and stand at attention for the rest of the opera while Tauber went off a-Maying.

One night they took revenge. As usual, Narraboth stabbed himself and fell, Herod made his entrance, saw the body, and ordered it taken away. Instead of carrying Tauber into the wings, the soldiers dumped him upstage, in full view of the audience. Tauber tried curses, pleas, and threats, but they left him there for the entire show.

Amazing How Potent Cheap Music Is

When Tauber abandoned the opera house for the operetta stage, people often reproached him for his lapse of taste. His voice and musicality, they pointed out, were too good for operetta. "I don't sing operetta," Tauber would say. "I sing Lehár."

Fast Thinking

Fleeing Hitler's Europe as a non-Aryan, Tauber settled in England and, like many performers, carried on right through the Blitz as though London were as safe as Reykjavik. He did have some near misses, and friends warned him to be more prudent. "Hitler has stopped me from singing in Germany and Austria," he said, "I'm not going to let him stop me now!"

Once, in a packed theatre, a bomb fell with a terrible report in the street outside, and the audience seemed about to panic. Tauber stopped singing, calmly stepped to the footlights, and told them, "I think that last bomb was a bit off-key."

He took up again where he left off. Nobody moved.

A Sad Coincidence

An Englishwoman serving with the Polish army near the end of World War II was billeted in a farmhouse in northwest Germany. Seeing the farmer's wife preparing an unappetizing old bed for her, she stepped over to a sofa, announced that she would sleep there instead, and promptly sat down on it as the woman cried out, "Please! *No!*"

Too late: a ghastly cracking noise echoed out of the cushions. When they were pulled up, the Englishwoman discovered a cache of Tauber records that the farmer couple had hidden from the Nazis. All were broken.

The Englishwoman was Diana Napier—Tauber's wife.

More Ponselle

Rosa Ponselle sang rarely outside of America—only at Covent Garden and once, in *La Vestale*, at the Maggio Musicale Fiorentino. Her singing of "O nume tutelar" in Florence roused the audience to insist on an encore, though conductor Vittorio Gui opposed the practice. Anyway, isn't the role of Giulia tiring enough as written? Holding firm, Gui decided to wait out the public's cries of *bis!*—till he heard a woman behind him say, "When shall we ever hear such perfection again?"

She had a point. Signaling to Ponselle, Gui raised his baton and launched the encore.

NELLIE MELBA

By unanimous consent, Melba was not only one of the golden age's greatest singers but also one of its greatest personalities. Quick-witted, outspoken, and unpredictable, she held her ground at stage center, against rival sopranos and male colleagues as well as conductors. The public adored her; musicians tended not to—but they praised her. "You sing my music," Puccini noted. "You don't sing Melba-Puccini." Mary Garden said, of Melba's final high C in the first act of *La Bohème*, that "it came over like a star . . . and went out into the infinite . . . My God, how beautiful it was!"

The silvery quality of Melba's instrument was a legend of the era, roughly fifteen years on both sides of the turn of the century. Also legendary was her tongue. When conductor Eugene Goossens dropped in on her Covent Garden dressing room just before *Faust* to ask if she varied the usual tempos, she replied, "I sing it exactly as Gounod wrote it. And I hope you conduct it that way!" Later that night, during the Garden Scene, when the Mephistophélès began to pull his line about during the Quartet, Melba shot him a look that would have stopped an assassin.

Why was Melba so brusque, so contentious, so unbending? Shouldn't power make one generous? Apparently, Melba felt that resolve encrusted in rude gall was the only way to rise to the summit and hold that position. Melba had no intention of standing among the great names; she wanted hers to be the greatest. Like Patti, she would be Queen of Song. Acts of generosity would compromise that eminence, ruin the thrill of being the ultimate star. "When she addressed one," her record producer Fred Gaisberg recalled, "she made no attempt to clothe her speech with sweetened words." She let Gaisberg's Gramophone Company woo her with perquisites no other diva asked for—but that was how Melba knew she was still Melba.

As with Patti, the staff and equipment had to come to Melba's house, in Kensington. Patti had only a piano to support her; Melba had an orchestra of fifty. Not to mention a special Melba label for the discs, to be hers and hers alone. And of course Melba retained the final decision on whether or not the discs would ever be marketed. Typically, she dawdled on this, though she had recorded quite well and the company was dying to put the results into the stores.

It took a stratagem to win her over. Gramophone's sales manager Sydney Dixon visited Melba in Monte Carlo, to ply her with flowers, dinners, and groveling. Camille Saint-Saëns was also in Monte Carlo, and also, by hap, a Gramophone artist; best of all, he was a Melba confidant. Dixon maneuvered Melba and Saint-Saëns into a room, played a Caruso record, and asked Saint-Saëns for his opinion. More *politique* than Melba, Saint-Saëns registered a fine impression—and Melba immediately consented to the release of her discs. How does one get what one wants from a Queen of Song? By playing on her jealousy.

It goes without saying that Melba made enemies easily. "Do you have many cats in your lovely hotel?" the normally even-tempered Luisa Tetrazzini asked an official at the Savoy, passing Melba's room during Practice Time and doubtless smarting from the vindictive fury with which Melba greeted Tetrazzini's London triumph. Co-workers had it even tougher. "No! No!" Melba advised John McCormack while rehearsing *Roméo et Juliette*. "Jean [de Reszke] sang it like this . . ." "I'm John McCormack," the tenor insisted, "and I sing it like *this*!" Presumably he was thinking back to his Covent Garden debut, when Melba thrust him back as he started out to share a curtain call with her. "In this house," she informed him, "nobody takes bows with Melba."

In this house, indeed. Melba sang at the Met, at Oscar Hammerstein's Manhattan Opera, all over America, in Berlin, in Petersburg, in Paris, in her native Australia: yet Covent Garden only was The Official Place of Melba. A pupil of Pietro Cecchi in Australia and then of Mathilde Marchesi in Paris and a cohort of Gounod, Delibes, Massenet, and others, Melba made a stir on her debut at the Monnaie in Brussels but won little more than polite applause at her Covent Garden debut as Lucia on May 24, 1888. It sounds like the beginning of a rather Continental career, with a French accent. Moreover, Melba's beautifully placed and technically proficient voice was ideally suited to the heroines of post-Meyerbeer French opera. But Melba won the admiration of some influential people, led by Gladys, Countess de Grey, one of those who guaranteed the season's bills at Covent Garden. Lady de Grey heard Melba in Brussels and spoke firmly to the management on her behalf. Thus under the support of the nobility, Melba at last broke through to triumph in her house of choice, in a *Rigoletto* with the de Reszke brothers.

From then on her rise was fleet and steady, and the "Melba night" became one of Covent Garden's most special if constant events, promising an audience as pretty as the talent. Now Melba reigned supreme at Covent Garden. "Powerful invisible spirits were hard at work," one soprano noted of the house during the Melba years, "to eliminate artists who might easily have settled in the heart of the public."

Of Melba's singing there can be no reservations. The voice was as beautiful as everyone says, the intonation faultless, the emotional commitment fetching, the style secure. At first primarily a coloratura specializing in the Patti roles, Melba graduated herself to the less embellished lyric parts and even tried Wagner (the *Siegfried* Brünnhilde) for one disastrous night at the Met. She was not a great actress. In her music theatre, music did all the work. But then her personality, well known to the public in anecdote and scandal, made up for her stiff aplomb in costume. She was one of the last of the Gilded Divas, who manifested themselves in private railway cars, gala feuds, fancy menus, and—in Melba's case—a personal order of knighthood for service to Melba, solemnized in the presentation of jeweled tiepins ranked by rock.

The scandals enlarged Melba's persona as much as the wit and hauteur did. Her liaison with the heir to the French throne, though it ended sadly, seemed suitable for the queen of divas. Her advice to Clara Butt, planning an Australian tour—"Sing 'em muck! It's all they can understand!"—also fitted the dossier, though it fired national outrage in Melba's homeland. One false note was struck in the legend that Melba cancelled a concert in Launceston, Tasmania, because she was drunk— a legend devised by the scurrilous newspaper tycoon John Norton, who, according to journalist Cyril Pearl, "had been publicly denounced many times as a thief, a blackmailer, a wife-beater, and an obscene drunkard, without ever refuting the charges." Melba had cancelled her concert because of an extremely rough crossing of Bass Strait, the strip of ocean between Melbourne and Tasmania. Norton routinely savaged the reputation of public figures, apparently for the fun of it, but this attack held, vilifying not only the reputation but the memory of Melba. Even more shocking was *Evensong*, a novel by Melba's lifelong friend Beverley Nichols, which told of a ruthless and aging prima donna, using the details of Melba's life. Worse yet, Nichols published *Evensong* in 1932, less than a year after Melba had died. The soprano was unable to defend herself; but would she have wanted to? She showed, at times, a fierce sense of humor about herself.

She might well have laughed at her defeats, for in all hers was an inspiring tale of talent and determination winning the greatest success. Helen Porter Mitchell, married Armstrong, born in a Melbourne suburb, adapted her hometown into a fanciful "Italian" surname, mated

it with her nickname, forgot her married name (and her husband), and
became one of the most famous people in the world on her terms:
Melba, the Imperious, yes—but also Nellie, the kid from down under
who took over Covent Garden. Now, fifty years after her death, the
repartee and headlines have receded into a dim folklore. What survives vitally, on Melba's many records, is the sound of Melba. "My
God, how beautiful it was!"

The Greatness Shows

Though she had mastered the instrumentation of her voice in Australia,
Melba applied to the celebrated Mathilde Marchesi in Paris for polishing. Immediately, Marchesi sensed a great voice in the making—no, the
finishing. Crossing the floor and throwing open the double doors, she
called to her husband in the next room. "Salvatore, n'est-ce pas, j'ai
enfin une étoile?": I have a star at last, don't I?

Marchesi then returned to her find. "Mrs. Armstrong," she asked, "are
you serious?" Nellie said yes. "Then," Marchesi decided, "I will make
something extraordinary of you."

Stage Fright

Melba was singing Gounod's Juliet to Jean de Reszke's Romeo in Chicago in 1896. Near the beginning of the Balcony Scene, during Romeo's aria, "Ah! lève-toi, soleil!," an unknown man rushed through the
house, climbed onstage, and said, "Put down your arm, Romeo. I want
to make a speech."

De Reszke just looked at him. "You may think I'm crazy," the man
told the audience, putting it mildly. He had been Converted at a YMCA
meeting, and believed himself a Messiah. De Reszke, however, was
skeptical. Without missing a note, he ordered the curtain pulled, calmly
witnessed the arrest of the intruder, then, curtain up again, went on
with his apostrophe to Juliet's beauty as the audience buzzed in marvel
at his composure.

His Juliet was not so composed. Behind the shutters of her balcony,
she could clearly be heard shouting, "Ring down the curtain! My voice
is gone!"

Finally Romeo lost his temper. "For God's sake, be quiet, Melba!"
he thundered. "Open the window and come out!"

Probably to his great surprise, she did just that, and the performance
continued as if nothing had happened.

The story expanded over the years, and by the time Mary Garden came to Chicago decades later, the common tellings had it that the man had taken a gun onstage with him and threatened de Reszke with it. In one version, the tenor pinned him to the wall with Romeo's sword. I tell it above as I believe it actually happened. It's less exciting, but just as silly.

Melba Cancels a *Bohème*

Melba was singing Mimì at Covent Garden to the Musetta of the young Fritzi Scheff, one of the many singers who could challenge Melba in temperamental display. Annoyed at the fuss the audience was making over the upstart Scheff, Melba impulsively joined in at the climax of the Waltz Song, "Quando m'en vo." The piece is Musetta's one big solo, and while Puccini wrote in subsidiary lines for Alcindoro, Marcello, and Mimì, Musetta takes the final line absolutely *sola*: high B, falling E Major scale, then shooting up to a second very gala high B culminating in an ovation. But on this night Melba did not cut out, as the score demands, but sailed happily on with Scheff right through the last line, of course utterly overwhelming Scheff's high notes with the Glory of Melba.

Scheff strongly disapproved of Melba's intrusion, and went over to claw her face to pieces. But suddenly she fell into hysterics, raced off stage, and refused to go on, not only with the act, but with the opera. Scheff downed, Melba graciously consented to sing Lucia's Mad Scene to fill out the evening—and to remind the house that it was and shall remain Melba Garden.

Scheff left the business immediately after this to become a prima donna of American operetta, especially memorable for her creation of the title role in Victor Herbert's *Mlle. Modiste*, which she toured in and revived for years. Later, when her voice failed, she turned to the spoken stage. Her colleagues recall her as being a difficult proposition. Why not? She had expert instruction.

Melba Rates a Comprimaria

At the Met one day, a rehearsal of *Tristan und Isolde* was called on the afternoon of the performance. One of the minor singers went up to Lillian Nordica, the Isolde, and said, "Why don't you refuse to attend, dear?" Ignoring the stormclouds gathering o'er the brow of Melba, who had been talking to Nordica, the two-bit artiste went on, "Nothing on earth would induce me to rehearse Isolde the day I sang it."

"Don't worry," says Melba. "*You'll never be asked to do it!*"

The Insult That Backfired

Melba was trying her luck at the tables of the Monte Carlo Casino with Lady de Grey, the two of them separated by a fat, bearded Frenchman. They were doing well; he was losing. For some reason he thought it their fault. At every play, he would glare and snort at the two women, until at last he rose, shouting, "What can I expect sitting between two *cocottes?*"

Before Melba could make reply, Lady de Grey whispered, "Don't say a word! I have never been so flattered in my life!"

And Rhodes Should Know

"Tell me, Madame," said the Right Honorable Cecil Rhodes, prophet of Empire in Africa, "is it the art or the applause you like?"

"How dare you ask me such a question?" Melba fumed.

He was silent for a moment, as if rethinking the concept. "I was wrong," he then said. "It is the power we like, isn't it?"

No Interviews!

Melba had a fear and suspicion of the press unusual in so public a figure as she became. Once, a journalist accosted her aboard a steamer and threatened to publish an interview whether she liked it or not: if she wouldn't answer his questions, he'd fake the entire piece. "Then fake!" Melba cried.

Another time, a woman reporter caught Melba taking the air outside her train at a depot in Wichita. These questions Melba did answer, but so evasively that the woman was getting absolutely nothing. Finally, she tried the simplest and least threatening question possible, to break the ice. "Where do you live when not on the road?"

Melba thought it over. "In a house," she said.

No story was filed.

Melba Evens the Score

In her early days as an unknown in Australia, Melba had auditioned for the impresario Luscombe Searelle, who thought her voice good but her musicianship lacking. No doubt it was, for this was before Melba had met up with Marchesi, Gounod, and the other cosmopolitans who polished her as her Australian teacher Cecchi seems not to have.

But Melba never forgives. Years later, in her London greatness, she was passing through the lobby of the Savoy Hotel when she spotted Searelle and beckoned him over.

"My name is Melba," she said. "I am the girl you would not engage in Melbourne because my voice was only passable and wanted training. Good morning."

She swept off in a gale of laughter.

Charity

In Chicago, at winter's height, Melba saw a very young and much too lightly dressed newsboy at work on a railroad platform. How long, she asked him, had he to stand there?

"Until I sell these fifty papers."

"Well, I'll buy the fifty," said Melba.

And the shivering boy, torn between relief and doubt, asked "But have you got enough money?"

How To Woo a Diva

Oscar Hammerstein had a devil of a time trying to talk Melba into singing in his new opera house, the Manhattan. She was secure at Covent Garden, admired in Paris, and for travel there was the occasional Australian tour to busy her. Besides, she had already done New York, at the Met. Hammerstein needed Melba, but Melba could not use Hammerstein at all.

The wily impresario would not admit defeat. He visited, he phoned, he wrote. Fifteen hundred a night, two thousand, three. Still Melba said no. "Three thousand dollars a night," Hammerstein insisted, "and you open in *Traviata*." Then he pulled out a roll of thousand-franc notes, tossed them into the air to rain over Melba, bowed, and left. Melba, for once, was speechless.

And Melba signed with Hammerstein.

Melba Makes Mary Garden Feel at Home

In 1906, already famous but still quite young, Mary Garden was on holiday in Rome when she was flattered with a command performance at Windsor Castle in honor of the king of Greece: meaning that she was invited to travel to England at her expense to perform for nothing but fancy congratulations, and was sincerely expected not to say no.

Garden said yes, and did not regret it. The sight of so many royal personages in their splendid uniforms and gowns, the women's diamonds glittering in the table crystal, the very tension of so much self-possession and grandeur in one room—all this, Garden felt, was worth the trip. What further excitement, then, when she learned that she would meet Melba, along with a young violinist. Melba sang "Caro nome" and "Mi chiamano Mimì," Garden "Depuis le jour" and "Vissi d'arte." After accepting regal thanks, the musicians went downstairs to their supper. No sooner had an official introduced the two divas than Melba piped up, "What a dreadful concert this would have been if I hadn't come!"

> Garden wasn't in the least upset. Apparently she had heard something of Melba's bite and was amused to suffer it personally. In the train returning to London that night, the two struck up a bit of *amitié*. Garden even gave Melba pointers in the singing of *Tosca*, at Melba's request, though they both knew that Melba was vocally and temperamentally unsuited to it and would never dare the part. Garden believed that their disparate repertory was what enabled Melba to befriend her—or perhaps Melba did not think Garden's unusual vocal style truly competitive. She actually offered Garden a place in her troupe on one of her Australian tours. In any case, they became fast friends. Garden would come over to Melba's for a late-night sing at the piano, and Melba visited Garden at her villa in Monte Carlo. There Melba introduced Garden to gambling, and, Garden recalled, when Melba won a few francs, she got so excited "you'd have thought it was a million dollars."

Hoist With Her Owne Petar

Louis-Philippe, the Duke of Orléans and the Bourbon pretender to the defunct throne of France, was a great love of Melba's life. They could not wed. The disparity in their ages (Melba was older) and social backgrounds mattered greatly in those days; anyway, Melba was still married (however long separated from her husband) and the Duke was a Roman Catholic. As it was, their liaison became public gossip, and Melba's husband filed for divorce, breaking the tale into full-scale scandal. Melba and the Duke parted.

Some years later, it was put to Melba to have lunch with the famed café singer Yvette Guilbert while both were appearing, in their distinct arenas, in New York.

"With that chanteuse?" Melba sneered. "At the most, she might be invited to come for dessert, for a fee, to sing one of her *couplets*."

"I quite understand," said Guilbert, when told of this. "I am of humble birth—but Madame Melba of course belongs to the royal family of France."

Who's Austral?

If Melba was cordial to few singers, she was less cordial to other sopranos, least cordial to other sopranos who also came from Australia. As Melba's career was winding down, the young Florence Austral turned up at Covent Garden with a spectacular heroic-dramatic voice, the temperament of a Valkyrie, and the projection of a star. Melba was not glad. It may have galled her especially that Austral excelled in Wagner, perhaps the only music Melba loved but could not master.

Melba did not cross paths with Austral at first. But one night they shared the stage in a gala, Melba in a scene from *La Bohème* and Austral in one from *Aida*. The next morning, Melba walked into the theatre to run right into Austral and a stage manager.

"You know Madame Austral?" the official asked, preparing to introduce the two.

"Austral?" says Melba, looking right through her colleague. "Who's Austral?"

"You sang with her last night."

"Oh," Melba answers, turning to go. "She was black then."

Melba As Voice Teacher

Finding herself more or less locked in Australia during World War I because of the danger of travel, Melba initiated vocal classes in Melbourne at the Albert Street Conservatorium, where she not only started newcomers off but realigned the voices of singers who had suffered what Melba took to be incompetent training. Arriving one day at Albert Street, she overheard a student having a lesson on the second floor, let out a cry of agony, and rushed up the stairs shouting, "Stop that girl! She's singing off her soft palate!"

An Australian Official's Wife Reviews Melba's Performance As a Dinner Guest

"Delightful! You know, she does allow you to feel so much at home in your own house!"

Melba's Father Reviews a Melba Concert

A forthright and conservative Scotsman who had come to Australia at the age of twenty-three and prospered as a building contractor, Melba's father David Mitchell never quite took to his daughter's stage career. He did hear her sing on her homeland tours, however. At dinner after she had sung in Melbourne, Melba asked him if he had enjoyed her concert.

Her father said, "I dinna like yir hat."

Melba Negotiates for Party Entertainment

Melba happened to enjoy a dance band at a Melbourne nightclub and thought it would lend spin to a party she was planning at her country place, Coombe Cottage.

When the bandleader presented himself at Melba's invitation, he and she hit it off at once, most especially after he described his heritage as "Australian, with a dash of Scotch"—Melba's, too, more or less.

Melba asked him what he would charge to play at her party. He quoted an immense figure.

"You mean," said Melba, "you want more for one performance of your band than I pay my grand opera orchestra to play for a whole week."

"Well, if I were giving a concert in the Melbourne town hall I could get fifty fine sopranos, any one of whom would be glad to sing for a guinea. If I want *you*, it would cost me a thousand guineas."

Melba had met her match. "It's a deal," she said.

Melba Gives an Encore

Melba must have been in terrific voice at one concert in Ballarat, for a huge portion of her audience followed her to her hotel to chant, "We want Melba! We want Melba!" Attracted by the noise and the possibility that the diva might appear upon her balcony to deliver a valedictory speech—or even to sing!—passers-by swelled the crowd and joined in the calls.

Among those present in the hotel were some newspaper reporters who had come to Ballarat to cover a conference of the Australian Natives Association. Having concluded their business that afternoon, they were well advanced in alcoholic revelry, and one of them decided to have a little fun with the crowd. He, too, had access to a balcony overlooking the street. Donning a florid dressing robe and wrapping a towel into a turban to simulate the appearance of a diva relaxing at her night table, he threw open the French windows and manifested himself upon his balcony as the mob cheered for their Nellie.

Then came silence, as the people of Ballarat made ready to hear the silvery voice, Australia's gift to music, opera, and the world. But the silver they heard was rust clear through and the voice startlingly shaky.

And the valedictory that their Nellie delivered was: "I wish all you buggers would go home and let me get some bloody sleep!"

The Passing of Melba

As the diva of the age, Melba gave the most epochal of farewells, on the stage of Covent Garden on the night of June 8, 1926. The program was a gala of Melba specialties: Act Two of *Roméo et Juliette*, the Willow Song and Ave Maria from *Otello*, and Acts Two and Three of *La Bohème*. The other participants were of no particular moment—Charles Hackett sang Romeo, Browning Mummery, Rodolpho, Aurora Rettore, Musetta, and the young John Brownlee, Marcello. This was strictly Melba's Night of Nights, a culmination of the ages in which opera counted the celebrity of its spectators as heavily as that of its singers. After this Night, the opera world took little interest in who was out there in the darkness.

Thus the sense of occasion. Had it been 1910, no one would have sensed that the opera world was undergoing a transition. But everyone in Europe knew that the world had changed after World War I, and Melba's farewell seemed like a very last salute from the golden age to its survivors. How appropriate, then, that Melba present the *envoi*, Melba the most public of opera's figures, most international of persons, most wondrous of singers.

Here is what she said:

I have so many people to thank tonight. It was such a . . . a great and glorious evening. But you can imagine what a sad evening it is for me. To think that I shall never again perhaps sing within these beloved walls. Covent Garden has always been my artistic home—and I love it. I love it more than anyplace in the world perhaps. But all things must end. And now I have to thank the management for their unfailing courtesy and kindness to me. I have to thank my dear, *dear* big public, for their great gratefulness to me. I have to thank the orchestra for their patience at many tasks and rehearsals and who played so beautifully in the evening. I have to thank the dear stagehands, all willing to help in any way they can—and, even tonight, they have presented me with a little souvenir, which will always be so precious. And I also have to thank my dear old friend Austen, who has been at the stage door for forty years and all of those forty years . . . for thirty-six years . . . he has always put me in my carriage and always bids me good night.

Her next words were drowned in applause.

And now, there is only one word to say, and that is farewell. I won't say goodbye because farewell is such a very beautiful word. I am sure you all know that it's part of a prayer, and means "fare *thee* well," which I all . . . I wish you all. And I feel *sure* . . . that you wish me the same!

Her voice broke on the last four words; even a goddess has feelings. She had sung well and spoken well, and the house rose and cheered: the era was over absolutely.

> The break in Melba's voice was quite genuine—one can hear it on a recording of the event. Also genuine were Melba's tears; the backstage staff thought her so upset at one point that they held the curtains closed, despite the public's continuing cries, out of consideration for the diva's feelings. But Melba whirled on them, shouting, "Pull back those bloody curtains!" Or so legend tells. In another version, she was utterly overcome, and an attendant held the curtain till he felt she was ready to go on with the call.
>
> However overcome Melba was, she recovered fast enough in her dressing room. When one of the house staff suggested that, in her speech, she forgot to thank the box office, she thundered, "The box office should have thanked *me!*"
>
> Like many of opera's farewell appearances, it was not the last. Illness kept her from another farewell at the Monnaie, where she had made her opera debut, but she sang again in London at a benefit at the Old Vic, and made a farewell tour of Australia.
>
> One footnote to all this: Beverley Nichols, the author of *Evensong*, the novel that outraged Melba's following, also wrote her farewell speech—a portrait of a very different Melba from the one he pictured in his book. And one last question: what was the "little souvenir" that the stagehands gave her at Covent Garden? Nobody seems to know.

OLIVE FREMSTAD

Fremstad was of that unusual class of soprano who dominates the scene in her prime but quickly loses reputation after leaving the stage and exists from then on as an aficionado's buzz term. Where her contemporaries Geraldine Farrar and Ernestine Schumann-Heink are still with us in spirit, Fremstad is gone. Farrar and Schumann-Heink left an extensive repertory on disc while Fremstad, who hated the feckless reproduction of her apparently magnificent instrument, released only fourteen. Perhaps, too, as a Wagnerian Fremstad is rivaled by too many other important reputations from that Wagnerian heyday; and she did specialize too direly, singing—after her first years as a mezzo—little more than Brünnhilde, Venus, Elsa, Kundry, and—her greatest role—Isolde. Part of the reclame of the Met's famous 1910 revival of Gluck's

Armide—a sterling effort with Caruso, Amato, Gilly, de Segurola, Louise Homer, and Alma Gluck, conducted by Toscanini—lay in the unusual choice of Fremstad as the elegant sorceress. Toscanini himself thought her outstanding in the part.

She was outstanding in general, a diva of the old school. Backstage, she would go into a trance as she donned costume and makeup, virtually dissolving into her character. Yet she was alert enough when some smart tenor attempted to rally a claque for a high note in her presence. There were contradictions in her social background as well, for while she was raised in the American Midwest, the daughter of a Swedish doctor who became something of a circuit pastor in Minnesota, she remodeled herself along the lines of Lilli Lehmann, with whom Fremstad studied in Berlin, becoming the compleat Wagnerian, with Bayreuth experience and German oaths. ("Um Gotteswillen!" was her favorite.) She was cosmopolitan, then, born in Stockholm but middle American, a mezzo but a soprano (some critics always claimed that she was abusing her voice in high parts), and a homeless traveler who, moving into the next furnished apartment or hotel suite, would immediately unpack the "homelike trunk" of personal and nostalgic articles so as to create her little nest.

She was not easy to get along with, not a trouper. Like Melba, she knew she was great and expected to be treated with deference. At rehearsal she would denounce a stray note in the orchestra as "Ein Skandal!" She constantly rebelled against the Met tradition of holding the dress rehearsal the day before the premiere. She made her longtime secretary Mary Watkins run the Fremstad marathon along Riverside Drive, the game being to see how many lamposts each could pass without taking a breath—who could match Isolde for breath control? She was forever concerned about her "cachet" (her fee) when asked to do something not specified in her contract. She was superstitious, capricious, and testy. But she was one of the great ones, so distinctive a diva—yet so representative—that Willa Cather modeled Thea Kronberg, the heroine of *The Song of the Lark*, on Fremstad.

She was utterly of the theatre, poised and intent, obsessed with the meaning of the words, and a handsome, statuesque woman to boot. The notorious single performance of *Salome* that the Met put on before bluenose paranoia cancelled it might have been considerably less shocking if the Met hadn't cast Fremstad as Salome, for she was not a one for ambiguous portrayals. She actually visited the city morgue to find out what a human head feels like after death, discovered it to be quite heavy, and used this information on stage: when the head of the Baptist was handed to her, she staggered under its weight, provoking gasps of very real horror in the house. (As we shall see, this was not the end of Fremstad's fascination for severed heads.)

Fremstad's theatricality, however, could hurt as well as help her. Working with Toscanini on *Tristan* before full cast and orchestra, she became so involved in the music, so relentlessly stirred by what Toscanini had made her hear and believe, that she suddenly lurched forward and begged him to dismiss her for the day: "Maestro, non posso più!'": I cannot go on! Her dramatic gift hurt her worst of all when she was cut off from the stage, for she was too stimulated a being to accept unemployment. She was a singing actress; the concert life held nothing for her. Once out of the theatre she dwindled in the slow death of aimless retirement at Nawandyn, the vacation palace she built in Bridgton, Maine. She gave her last concert in 1920, but lived till 1951, just as the great age of Wagner singers was coming to a close.

Fire the Cook!

The help could never get used to Madame. When she was in one of her Moods, nobody could please her. If it was right, it was wrong; if it was wrong, it was an outrage.

Imagine the cook's bewilderment. Trying to delight Madame, she would dare something ambitiously novel and earn high praise. "Delicious!" Fremstad would exclaim. "You must serve it again soon! Don't forget!"

After ten or twelve days, the cook would triumphantly revive the honored dish, whereupon Madame would snarl, "Must we eat the same thing each day? Does she call this food?"

Madame went through rather a lot of cooks—and the cooks weren't fired: the cooks quit.

Please Don't Scare the Servants

Did Madame *have* to sweep through the apartment with such furor on Kundry days? Naturally, Madame would want to get into the part; and, true, Kundry is savage. But if Fremstad sang many more *Parsifal*s, the supply of available domestics just might give out. Finally, secretary Watkins attempted to reason Madame into making less commotion in the household, despite a nagging notion that it was probably more important that a great Kundry let off a little steam than that the servants enjoy sound democratic relations with the boss.

In any case, Madame was angered at the suggestion that she compromise her habits in any way, especially on *Parsifal* days, as the Met at that time gave it only as a matinee, thus constricting Madame's pre-performance tension into a few morning hours.

"Um Gotteswillen!" was how Madame put it.

Immediately Watkins backtracked, attempting to remind Madame of the glory of her Kundry, of her rare sense of entitlement in the part.

"Don't you try to soothe me!" Madame cried.

Baffled, Watkins just looked at her.

"And *stop shouting!*" Madame screamed.

End of debate.

Fremstad Buys Furniture

Considering herself a wandering minstrel, Fremstad gave little thought to the personality of the various households she occupied. Finally, Watkins decided it was time Madame made herself a home. Renting, for once, an empty flat, the secretary went to Wanamaker's (the Bloomingdale's of the time) and charged, to her own name, over two thousand dollars' worth of furniture.

Nowadays, delivery would take a month and everything would be the wrong size, the wrong color, or broken. In Fremstad's era, the pieces would turn up in three or four days. After a week, in a panic, the secretary telephoned Wanamaker's.

There was a reason for the delay: Watkins was a secretary. Therefore, how could she charge such a fortune in credit?

Madame had been listening on the extension, and now she burst into flame. She would take her business elsewhere! She had never been so insulted! Miss Watkins is her secretary and made these purchases for her!

"And who," asked Wanamaker's, "may I ask, are you?"

"*I'm Madame Olive Fremstad of the Metropolitan Opera Company!*" Her high B in "Dich, Teure Halle" never rang with greater thrill.

Gurglings, excuses, and assorted mercantile truckling ensued on the Wanamaker's end of the phone. An official came on to assure Madame of the store's good will and the speedy delivery of the furniture.

"And *prix d'artiste!*" Madame thundered.

The discount of fame.

Tristan, Isolde, King Mark, and Unidentified Friend

At the Met, Watkins's duties included racing out after the last note had sounded to revive Madame and adjust her toilette. The public, of course, never saw these ministrations, for the Met dropped a shield curtain to cover the stage while the house drapery was parted for the principals' bows.

Unfortunately, while the Met was on tour in St. Louis, Watkins forgot to consider the possibility that procedures elsewhere might vary from those at the Met: such as by not having a shield curtain. Scarcely had *Tristan und Isolde* ended and the curtain shuddered close on the dying peace of the Liebestod than Watkins dashed out with the mirror, the brushes, the throat spray, the lozenges, and such when the curtain rose again, leaving Watkins in street clothes of the late-middle ragtime era, lined up with the figures of medieval romance.

The public was convulsed and Fremstad outraged. "Raus!" she hissed. "Raus, um Gotteswillen!"

Watkins was too embarrassed to try to cross the stage. Instead, she ducked behind Tristan's deathbed.

The stagehands thought she was the best thing in the show.

Kundry on Wagner

The daughter of a stern Methodist, Fremstad often looked at the world— and art—from the vantage of fundamentalist "witness." Once she said, "I consider the whole opera *Parsifal* to be just an elaborate revival meeting."

Olive the Conqueror

Madame was considerably unnerved about singing her first Isolde in Munich after a decade of Wagnerian eminence at the Met. True, Munich wasn't Bayreuth. But if Munich wasn't the Wagnerian cultural capital, it had a Wagnerian tradition of even longer standing: Munich saw, for instance, the premiere of *Tristan und Isolde*, in which Fremstad was now to appear.

The visit began badly. First, Madame gave herself stomach trouble on a lunch of Bratwürste. Then, walking on stage at the first rehearsal, she tripped and fell flat on her face. "It's an ill omen!" she cried. "I will fail here as Isolde!"

"Nonsense, Fremstad," said the Brangäne, Sarah Walker, known as Madame Charles Cahier (also, briefly, as Mrs. Morris Black; but that's another story). "Have you never heard of William the Conqueror? When he invaded England, he tripped and fell on the shore as he disembarked. But he was a fast thinker. He grabbed two handfuls of English soil and said, 'Thus do I grasp this land!' And now," Cahier went on, "let me see your palms!"

Fremstad displayed them: black with stage dirt.

"There!" Cahier concluded. "So what are you worried about?"

Despondent since her fall, Fremstad suddenly grew radiant. "Cahier," she observed, "you are wonderful!"

The Passing of Fremstad

Where Nellie Melba left her theatre only when a failing instrument left
her no choice, Olive Fremstad was forced out of her theatre in her prime.
Why did Gatti decide to drop Fremstad, retaining Johanna Gadski and
importing Melanie Kurt for Fremstad's roles? Were there artistic or
practical or personal problems?

It began when Fremstad heard rumors that she was to lose her Met
contract. (The news even found its way into *Musical America*.) When
Fremstad confronted Gatti in his office toward the end of the 1913–14
season, he told her that her narrow repertory made her too expensive.
She cost the house as much as any star, yet sang fewer roles than any—
and there was all that trouble she made about not rehearsing within a
day of a performance. She was not game; she was not a team player.

"When have I ever refused to learn new roles?" Fremstad challenged
him, "even that disgusting Giulietta?" All-star evenings of *Les Contes
d'Hoffmann* were all very well, but if Fremstad had to play a courtesan, let it be the Wagnerian kind you find in the Venusberg, not a co-
cotte floating through a Venetian sewer.

But Fremstad had refused to learn one part. "Mona," said Gatti, so
simply, so eloquently: *Mona*, Horatio Parker's opera, new two years
before, which Fremstad had refused. A sort of Wagnerian *Norma*, it
marked another stop along Gatti's fruitless search for an American
masterpiece; and, who knows, it might have gone over if Fremstad had
lent her magic to it. (Louise Homer assumed the role.) In any case, it
was a fiasco, as Fremstad now pointed out. "I was right to turn it down!'
she cried.

Gatti was unmoved. "The facts are that we find ourselves dissatisfied
with the limitations of your repertoire. You have repeatedly told us that
you are unhappy here under conditions which we cannot ameliorate.
We wish no longer to distress you and are therefore taking you at your
word. We view your departure from the company with regret, of course,
but will make no further effort to detain you." Artistic problems? Practical problems? Personal problems? Gatti capped his speech with a blow
of his fist on his desk; and that was the end of Fremstad's Met career.

Hiding her dismay, Fremstad pretended that this would fit in nicely
with her concert schedule, which she was planning to expand. She asked
one last favor, to make her Met farewell as Isolde, her most potent role.
Was there perhaps a *Tristan* coming up?

There was one left, on the last Saturday night of the season.

Fremstad asked for it.

"We shall see," said Gatti.

The news of Fremstad's severance from the Met made headlines in the musical press, especially as the Met declared that Fremstad had asked for an *expanded* contract while management had wanted to give her a curtailed one. Fremstad took the lofty option and, like Isolde embarking for Cornwall, hid her humiliation and said nothing publicly.

Then she learned that the last *Tristan* of the season had been assigned not to Olive Fremstad but to Johanna Gadski. Fremstad was granted a last Elsa, not one of her best parts. Worst of all, Gatti scheduled Fremstad's Met farewell for the closing Sunday night concert, one of the weakest evenings in the Met season because the company traditionally departed for the spring tour that day, leaving the concert to a miscellany of second-line talents.

When Isolde was at last stung into action, she delivered her Narration to Brangäne; Fremstad merely cancelled the Sunday concert without a word of explanation. Gatti's people urged the press to report this as another instance of Fremstad's lack of company spirit. But a climate of public support at Fremstad's last performances, and the resulting descriptions in the newspapers, suggested that New York thought more of Fremstad than Gatti did. Her last Kundry inspired an astonishing ovation after Act Two—this at the Met's annual Good Friday *Parsifal*, at which applause was forbidden after the binding acts and only tolerated after the Magic Garden Scene. "Goodbye!" Fremstad whispered, moved to tears as the public called her out again and again. "Goodbye!" Her last Venus—provocatively in tandem with Gadski's Elisabeth—was sold out.

Then came the *Lohengrin*, Fremstad's last night in the house, April 23, 1914. So many boxes of flowers arrived at Fremstad's apartment, each with a mournful note, that Fremstad's secretary felt as if someone had just died. Someone was about to—for opera, especially Metropolitan opera in the Wagner wing, was Fremstad's very life. True, she feared the improvisation of theatre, the unlooked-for happening. As she was about to take a nap to rest the voice for the ordeal of having to outdo her Isoldes in a less than heroic part, her secretary mentioned that Fremstad might have to give a speech. Fremstad became so frightened that she couldn't sleep.

Melba, observant of the official niceties, commissioned her farewell speech from a writer; Fremstad left hers to chance. It came at the end of Act Two. Her first appearance in the opera received a grand salute, and Act One ended in cheers—but not till the Church Scene—of Elsa's aria, "Euch Lüften, die mein Klagen," her scene with Ortrud, and the great massed finale of the wedding—did Fremstad get the chance to do what she did best. Some say she poured Isolde into Elsa, expanding the

Traum into a kind of Narration and translating "Euch Lüften" into a mini-Liebesnacht. This seems unlikely; and would surely have produced a *Lohengrin* out of sync with its own imperatives. In any event, Fremstad never sounded better, and the crowd went wild as the second-act curtain fell, demanding call after call. Responding to the occasion, the other singers left the stage to Fremstad, and the stage manager allowed Fremstad's dressing-room flowers to be presented to her on stage, despite Gatti's brand-new ban on floral tributes (imposed, it was said, specifically to detract from Fremstad's glory). Then came the calls for a speech.

Fremstad panicked. But Louise Homer, the Ortrud, pushed her forward, and, grasping a tassel of the great gold curtain, Fremstad spoke to her Met public for the only time in her life:

Before I leave I must thank you from the bottom of my heart for your unfailing kindness, your encouragement, and your sympathy. I have always tried to give you of my best—my *very* best.

Buoyed by the warmth of her reception, Fremstad extended her arms to her fans, letting go—not symbolically, but the point is taken—of the Met drapery. Her last night. One love duet to go and then. . .

Goodbye, dear friends. May God bless you and may we meet again someday where all is peace and harmony.

There came in answer a silence, a crescendo of gasps, sobs, and cheers, and a smashing great thunder of love and sorrow. Again and again they called her back, as the gossips compared readings of her last words. Was the line about "peace and harmony" a slap at Gatti? The third act threatened to start the whole business all over—they even demanded another speech!

"Another speech," Fremstad told them, "would spoil my first one."

In all, Fremstad got fifty calls that night, some of them *after* the fire curtain came down: the crowd refused to budge, and back up went the asbestos—four times. At last, the conductor, Alfred Hertz, came on. This was a rare gesture, for a difficulty in walking forbade him the stage on most evenings. He joined Fremstad, kissed her hands, and escorted her to her dressing room. There, the excitement continued, and a superb supper followed, of the kind that only golden-age opera singers knew how to eat. The event had been so fulfilling and so exhausting that the moment Fremstad got home she fell into bed.

It's stupid and vicious to say so, but Fremstad should have died that night, like Isolde at the end of the Liebestod. To part from the theatre was to give up her nourishment and stimulation. She sang in other theatres for four more years and was to return to the Met when, ironically, her rivals Gadski and Kurt were sent home when the United States entered World War I. But a ban on German opera cancelled the deal, and a disheartened Fremstad gave up singing altogether in 1920. There was nothing left for her then, and she forced the time to pass, worrying over Met casting, sampling the latest Wagner records, listening to the Met Saturday broadcasts, following the rise of Flagstad, Lawrence, Traubel, and wondering what kind of farewell she might have given if Gatti had allowed her one last Isolde after all. Sadly, it took her thirty-one years to die. Rest in peace.

One Last Fremstad Story

Any tale is anticlimactic after The Farewell, but we ought to look in on Fremstad as voice teacher, the occupation she took up, like many of her colleagues, upon retirement. Fremstad was not a gentle coach. Only those with a spirit of iron could survive her course, for training included viewing the inside of a mysterious box that sat on the piano under a red silk scarf.

One day, Fremstad was about to unveil the secret for her secretary to see when a student showed up for a lesson.

"Don't!" the student screamed in terror. "I won't look at it again! I'd rather leave forever!"

"Leave then, poor child," said Fremstad. "Better now than disappointment and heartbreak later." Turning to her secretary as the student fled, Fremstad added, "She has no guts, that one. Opera is not for her." Then she showed the contents of the box to her secretary.

It was a human head, pickled and sliced in half from cranium to neck.

ENRICO CARUSO

"Why was Caruso so great?" is possibly the most common question that outsiders ask of opera buffs. No anecdote can tell us: for if opera is, as Rossini said, "voice, voice, and more voice," Caruso had it, and a story cannot tell us of sound. Anyway, others had voice. Why is Caruso especially famous for his?

It was partly a matter of time, and partly of place, but mainly of voice. It was second of all a great one, but first of all a musical one, not technically apt as the Rossini tenorino's must have been, but meltingly suave in lyricism and fierce in declamation. This was always the wonder of Caruso: so tender, yet so aggressive, a beau ideal in tenors. There was Jean de Reszke before him, Alessandro Bonci during, Beniamino Gigli and Giovanni Martinelli after, Luciano Pavarotti and Nicolai Gedda today. Each is unique. But all cede to Caruso as a setter of standards. In the soprano line, many voices offer a standard of measurement—think of Tetrazzini, Muzio, Ponselle, Rethberg, Flagstad, Callas, Tebaldi. But there is, in the word "Caruso," an awesome renown of entitlement never challenged. His time was the beginning of the century, when recordings carried singers' fame into the home, acculturating opera as a middle-class institution, a marker of status, a collectible; and his place was the Met at its peak of glory. Why was Caruso so great? Because he was the first to exploit a spectacular voice on a spectacular level.

Not that Caruso did any exploiting per se. He was very nearly a victim, for the primitive recording technology, like the movie camera, was unpredictable as to whom it would favor and whom humiliate. Caruso it loved. Fred Gaisberg entered opera legend for his tale of The Day They Recorded Caruso when Gaisberg was advance scout for the Gramophone Company. Gaisberg heard Caruso at La Scala in Alberto Franchetti's *Germania* in 1902 and negotiated a deal: Caruso would record ten arias to piano accompaniment for £ 100 (about $500) in one afternoon, all the time the singer could spare. The head office in London wired Gaisberg: FEE EXORBITANT FORBID YOU TO RECORD. But Gaisberg jumped at it—with that voice, who could deny history?

The discs of course made a fortune—not because Caruso was famous and therefore sellable; he wasn't famous yet—but because the voice turned out to be the most phonogenic of the time. The horn shied away from the valor of the dramatic soprano, curdled a lyric's top notes and lost her low ones, couldn't fathom a bass's bottom range. But Caruso fit into the machine like a natural. When he reached the Met in 1903, Caruso mated voice and place; and the sensational popularity of the Victrola and its concomitant, the Victor Red Seal twelve-inch celebrity single, made him the master of time as well. Any American household that called itself respectable had to invest in a Victrola and a set of Carusos. As America rode through World War I into the age of technology, it carried Caruso along. This, by the way, is why those "Carusos in the attic" are not only not rarities, but have no resale value whatsoever. Everyone in the land bought them. And they still sell, on LP, in increasingly ingenious transcription. But no science can make them sound as vibrant as they did on those old wind-up monsters. They weren't just souvenirs of Caruso; they were what Caruso would have sounded like if he sang in your parlor.

Never had there been so famous an opera singer who was also well liked. Before Caruso, opera people were largely regarded as greedy, mischievous fools. Have we not seen the like in Ravelli's torn *gilet* and Patti's shoe? Caruso was seen as a fine fellow, friendly, helpful, and honorable. And so he was. The public's good will buoyed him during a ghastly episode in which he was arrested for having made overtures to a woman in the monkey house of the Central Park Zoo. Often, vilification of a public figure—especially one from the ridiculously colorful world of opera—is a cause for general amusement. But this time the public sided with Caruso. The policeman who arrested him seemed an opportunist, the woman Caruso supposedly molested simply disappeared, and there was no evidence to support the charge. Caruso was found guilty and fined ten dollars, and the press tried to sell it as a scandal, but readers wouldn't buy it. On the contrary, the Met audience had greeted Caruso warmly the next time he sang, heartened no doubt by the fact that Marcella Sembrich was singing with him. Sembrich was a notably moral soprano whose very presence was a good housekeeper's seal of approval. If Sembrich didn't think Caruso a masher, nobody could; and no one did. Caruso just didn't seem like that sort of person.

Perhaps he didn't seem like an opera singer, either—certainly he lacked the figure for Rodolpho, Cavaradossi, the Duke of Mantua, Don José, Dick Johnson, and his other great roles. Nor was he much of an actor, though critic Henry Finck rhapsodized over the way Caruso drained the bottle in *L'Elisir d'Amore:* "He tried to reach its depths with his tongue, he squeezed it as if it had been a lemon, he shook it and peered into it with an anxious eye, rejoicing that it still held some of the precious stuff." At least Caruso was Italian—that's authentic opera. Would he have have had half the impact on records if he had been American? There's a certain rightness in fame that has nothing to do with entitlement—and note that when this son of Naples made his hometown debut, he suffered a tepid reception and poor reviews. Yet this was the same voice that astonished the world through the acoustic horn, and the Naples role was one of Caruso's surest, this same Elvino in *L'Elisir d'Amore.*

It would be interesting to know what Caruso's reception might have been like had he returned to Naples after he had become the world's greatest tenor; but though he often visited his family, he never sang there again. Elsewhere, his fame never betrayed its expectations. Appearing through the entire Met season year after year, usually twice a week or so, Caruso implanted himself as a symbol of likable and nearly unerring greatness. Then, too, as his somewhat baritonal voice deepened in color, he adapted to it, *used* it, so that each new season revealed a yet more interesting singer. His fame won him more fame, and he died at his height—died fighting, at that—so his passing could only be felt as a grievous and untimely loss to music. His fame has not given out yet; the legend persists. Why was he so great?

He just was.

Caruso Auditions for Puccini

La Bohème was not a flash success. Its Turin premiere, in 1896, though conducted by Arturo Toscanini, failed to thrill the public and earned terrible notices. It was crucial, then, that its second, third, and fourth productions be cast for certain success; otherwise the piece would vanish forever, perhaps to be replaced by Leoncavallo's version, shortly to appear.

It was just about this time that the young Enrico Caruso was on the rise, counting off the provincial dates till he could manifest himself at the San Carlo, the Costanzi, the Scala. Caruso was to play Rodolpho in Livorno, only a few miles from Lucca, Puccini's native city. So this *Bohème* naturally took on a certain importance. Puccini's publisher Giulio Ricordi was satisfied with the other principals—but the Rodolpho must prove to be the man of the hour, and it seemed unlikely that an inexperienced tenor of no reputation whatsoever would be that man.

There was only one way out: let this Enrico Caruso sing for the composer. So Caruso did: "Che gelida manina."

And Puccini said, "Who sent you to me—God?"

A Secular Pope

Vincenzo Lombardi, Caruso's coach and first major enthusiast, told conductor Leopoldo Mugnone that it was just a matter of time—not much time, besides—before the tenor was famous. "Soon," said Lombardi, "he will be earning the top fee."

"When I become Pope," said the scornful Mugnone.

Not long after, Caruso made his Rome debut in Mascagni's *Iris*, as Osaka. It was a prime Caruso part, lyrical and passionate, with an expansive love duet right in the middle of the evening and lots of bright, high lines to show off the ring of the voice. Not too high—Caruso was never comfortable above B flat. Just lots of As and Gs, sweeping down and up again in those pulsing ⁶/₈ metres Mascagni loved.

Caruso enjoyed a great success as Osaka, for a handsome salary, and lo, Mugnone himself conducted. After the performance, Lombardi came backstage and fell on his knees before the maestro.

"What are you doing?" Mugnone asked.

"My duty. You have become Pope."

Heard But Not Seen

When young Grace Moore first arrived in New York, she sang in musical comedy but fed her operatic ambitions by patronizing chiropodist Lilian Blynn to mix with Blynn's impressive clientele of Met stars. One time, Blynn put off Moore's appointment because Caruso was coming in. Moore begged to be allowed to stay, hidden behind a screen, so she could get a peek at the greatest tenor in the world.

Blynn was worried about the ethics of the stunt, but Moore insisted. Behind her screen, she waited, too shy to look. She heard a rustling, a sigh. Would Caruso sing, perhaps? A snatch of "La donna è mobile"? "Che gelida manina"? The Flower Song?

Caruso did sing, but no aria. What he sang was, "Lil-yan, Lil-yan, feex my leetle toes."

Caruso and the Earthquake

Unlike many companies, the Met prides itself on never cancelling a performance. But on April 18, 1906, on tour in San Francisco, it had little choice, for at dawn that morning the San Andreas Fault shuddered and the city broke apart.

As San Franciscans have been assuring the rest of the country ever since, it wasn't the earthquake that was so terrible: it was the fire. The upheaval ignited a thousand blazes to consume the wooden town, but Caruso was not concerned with the precise cause of his discomfort. The press reports that tell us of Caruso's day vary greatly: he was seen here running in panic, or there ensconced on his suitcase, weeping; he was in pajamas—no, a fur coat over his pajamas; beg pardon, fully dressed but with a towel draped around his throat.

The truth of the matter is stranger than the fictions. Caruso fled the Palace Hotel carrying but one item, the inscribed photograph of Theodore Roosevelt he had received earlier in the tour in Washington, D. C. —and not in the White House, but backstage, true homage from the President. Maybe Caruso simply snatched the first notable object he saw; maybe he was planning ahead, for the photograph served the tenor as identification and safe-conduct whenever he encountered a police barricade. The inscription affirmed that Caruso was indeed Caruso, and what more formidable reference than T. R. to vouch for one's character?

Caruso slept outside that night, fearful that any refuge he might take would collapse on top of him. "Give me Vesuvius," said the Neapolitan: at least when a volcano erupts you can run away. " 'ell of a place," he concluded. "I never come back here."

He never did.

Colleagues

John McCormack greets Caruso: "How's the world's greatest tenor?"
Caruso replies: "Since when have you become a baritone?"

Caruso Sings Bass

In this, one of opera's most popular tales, Caruso is singing Rodolpho with the Met on one of their Philadelphia Tuesdays in 1913. When bass Andreas de Segurola, the Colline, found himself almost entirely out of voice, Caruso suggested he try to bark his way through the role. After all, it really doesn't call for singing till the last act, when Colline gets his solo moment in the Coat Song, "Vecchia zimmara." Surely de Segurola could croak out one tiny aria.

The hoarse Colline made a go of it—till "Vecchia zimmara" approached and de Segurola realized he did not even have enough tone to talk through it. Caruso, reading terror in his friend's eyes, pulled him close as if Rodolpho were clutching Colline for sympathy, and, their faces turned upstage so the audience couldn't pierce the ruse, the tenor sang the aria for the bass.

Except for the conductor, nobody noticed.

> It sounds like a marvelous stunt, but the aria is quite short and lies spang in the middle of the male voice. Celebrating the fun, Caruso recorded it, and as a vocal experiment it does not stand out from his other discs as much as one might imagine. If you want Caruso in an unfamiliar role, try his version of "Over There."

Woman Bites Tenor

Teaming Caruso with Geraldine Farrar was one of Gatti's most inspired acts of chemistry, for between his voice and her personality, their operas really sang.

They got on well together, too. As the Highball Story in the Farrar section will reveal, their jousting was amiable. Except once, in a *Carmen* in 1916 that followed soon upon Farrar's first Hollywood summer, when she filmed a silent *Carmen* with Wallace Reid under Cecil B. de Mille, who encouraged Farrar to realize the tempestuous nature of Bizet's gypsy with vigor. Naturally, Farrar returned to New York ready to give somewhat more to Carmen than New York was used to. Her fight in Act One with the cigarette girl was a holy terror (not least for the cigarette girl) and her dance in Act Two was pungent. Then, in Act Three, she threw herself at Caruso with such abandon that she not only socked but bit him. Whereupon Caruso tried a little realism himself and threw Farrar to the stage with such force that she bounced.

During the succeeding intermission, the two battled it out while house officials prayed to the muses that the Met's two biggest box-office attractions wouldn't do or say anything permanent. Nor did they, and Act Four went off more or less as Bizet wrote it. The press played up the excitement, however, and no doubt spectators at the next Caruso-Farrar *Carmen* took their seats in hope of seeing the fireworks ignited anew. But this pair was too big for that, and their embrace after the

Flower Song seemed more fond and sweet than usual. Caruso and Farrar had made up their quarrel—if, indeed, they had ever had one.

> Farrar says they didn't. "Fantastic stories were spread abroad that I assaulted chorus girls," she later wrote. "That I chewed the ears of timid supers and and slapped King Enrico such a resounding smack that the audience gasped, as it caused him to falter in his song and sputter maledictions. All pretty reading, perhaps, but none of these charming inventions occurred." If not, then one of opera's most insistent stories is a hoax—a little like saying that Filippo Marchetti, not Verdi, wrote *Rigoletto*.

The Passing of Caruso

Though Caruso had been a Met mainstay since 1903, totaling over 600 performances of some forty roles, the public could scarcely get enough of Caruso, and was profoundly shocked to see him in trouble during *L'Elisir d'Amore* at the Brooklyn Academy of Music on December 11, 1920. The tenor was spitting blood with every phrase, staining his costume and making trips to the wings to towel off his mouth.

Caruso had been ailing for some time, though he had tried to keep it from his colleagues. His wife he could not fool; when she saw him coughing blood into the sink in his dressing room, she sent for Caruso's doctor, Philip Horowitz. Shortly after Act One had begun, Horowitz was in the wings, beckoning to Caruso to leave the stage. Caruso, with every eye in the chorus and orchestra inquiringly upon him, ignored Horowitz's signals. The opera must continue.

Meanwhile, Gatti's assistant Giuseppe Bamboschek was frantically phoning Manhattan to tell Gatti what was happening. Gatti ordered the performance suspended. By this time even Caruso was willing to call it a night, and the audience, who had been sitting in helpless worry, watching their hero battle some terrible ailment, was glad to go along with the decision.

An odd piece fits into the story here: Horowitz examined the tenor and found no major problems. Surely this should have been cause for worry—there clearly was a problem, and possibly a major one. But Caruso was delighted to tell Gatti that he would be fine for the next performance, and the press relayed the happy story to the world. The tenor fired off his own reports in cables to his friends and allies in High Middle Carusoese. Otto Kahn's read "Thanks God it was nothing to be alarmed."

But it was. Caruso's body ached horribly throughout a *Forza del*

Destino, sung with the old Caruso ring a mere two days after his Brooklyn trial. "Caruso," the *New York Times* disclosed, "was as frolicsome as a schoolboy and beaming all over his broad countenance with happiness over his complete recovery and joy at the depth of welcome sent to him across the footlights." But a few days after that he was forced to cancel a performance, and sang *La Juive* on Christmas Eve in such pain that Toscanini, in the audience, came backstage to worry over Caruso's health with Gatti. Caruso sounded fine, yes: because he was determined to sing at his best. But the effort showed in his face.

The next day, during a family Christmas party, the pain attacked again, so viciously that Caruso could no longer put off dealing with it. He had pleurisy; with complications this might lead to pneumonia. No less than six doctors attended him, and a barrage of announcements kept the world informed of Caruso's progress. The tenor underwent surgery on the verge of his forty-eighth birthday, and came through well enough. But his changed appearance spooked his colleagues. He had lost fifty pounds, his glow had died to a wan glimmer, and he couldn't stand up straight. This was survival, not health.

Caruso traveled to Naples for the summer of 1921 to recuperate. There Gatti visited him in early July. HIS CONVALESCENCE IS MORE THAN NORMAL, he telegraphed to the Met. HAVE NO PREOCCUPATIONS FOR HIS FUTURE CONDITION. HE WILL SURELY SING COMING SEASON. Gatti followed up his visit with a letter, asking Caruso what roles he looked forward to trying come fall. "I cannot say anything," Caruso wrote back. "I am not yet in good health. Dear friend, as I write, I see my wife sitting in a corner and weeping."

Three days later, Caruso was dead.

FRANCES ALDA

Alda was another of the many Marchesi pupils who kept alive the ideals of lyric weight and coloratura training in in age increasingly impressed by the power of Wagner and verismo, with the resulting neglect of coloratura. In the end, Alda did sing a great deal of contemporary opera—and sang it well. But unlike Melba and Farrar, Alda put her stamp on nothing in particular and today is mainly remembered as having been the lover and then wife of Giulio Gatti-Casazza.

It took Gatti years to talk Alda into marriage, but, long before, their liaison had been an open secret in New York. This may have led critics to underrate her—the talented earn their roles and the untalented sleep with the boss. But Gatti gave Alda nothing that she didn't deserve. It seems amazing that there are so few stories of Alda's promoting a vehicle, though she was certainly free with advice on casting.

She was as feisty a diva as ever lived, with a cutting sense of humor—she appears in her colleagues' memoirs invariably as a comic villain. But she was a first-rate artist. Perhaps what held her back from true stardom was her repertory. Weak in the technique needed for the Marchesi roles like Gilda and Ophélie and weak in the force needed for the big verismo roles like Zandonai's Francesca da Rimini, Alda never established an identifying specialty. When she was well cast, it was in operas that few cared to hear, like Wolf-Ferrari's *Il Segreto di Susanna* or Rabaud's *Mârouf*. Even Lalo's *Le Roi d'Ys,* a tuneful piece closing with a doomsday flood and produced with Rosa Ponselle and Beniamino Gigli as well as Alda, registered faintly with Met audiences.

Then, too, Alda was shadowed by the richness of the contemporary talent. Born in New Zealand, raised in Australia, schooled in Paris, and seasoned on European stages, Alda at last came to the right place at the right time, the Met under Gatti, possibly the greatest regime in opera history. And Alda knew the right people, obviously. But when you share the public's attention with Ponselle and Gigli, not to mention Farrar and Caruso, to live in legend you need more than Alda had. Maybe it was the right place at the *wrong* time, after all. Yet notice, in the story immediately following, with what promise the career began . . .

Alda Auditions for Marchesi

Past eighty, a maestra of many a star and hostess to the greatest musicans in Paris, Marchesi desposited herself in a chair with rigid grandeur and motioned young Alda to the piano.

"I will hear you sing, mademoiselle," she announced. "Then I will say what I think of your voice and whether or not I will accept you as a pupil."

Rebelliously, Alda sang not the expected "Caro nome" or "Vedrai carino" but a parlor ballad in English.

Marchesi was grim, but she bore it.

Alda ignored her and concentrated on the music, playing her own accompaniment and rendering Francis Allison's "Song of Thanksgiving" as if it were "Caro mio ben."

Alda finished.

Marchesi rose and, without giving Alda so much as a glance, went to the double doors giving on the hall, threw them open, and called to her husband—as, we recall, she did earlier in one of these audition anecdotes.

"Salvatore, viens! J'ai trouvé la nouvelle Melba!": I have found the new Melba!

The Old Melba Outranks The New One

In Europe, scouting talent for the first season of Oscar Hammerstein's Manhattan Opera, Cleofonte Campanini heard Alda under ideal circumstances, while conducting a Covent Garden *Rigoletto* in which Alda sang Gilda. Campanini immediately offered her a contract. It was a main chance for the as yet unestablished Alda, and she leaped at it. Not long after she had signed, however, Campanini showed her a telegram he had received from Hammerstein's ace card, Nellie Melba: EITHER ALDA OR MYSELF.

Alda shrugged; in the city of opera, you can't fight city hall. She let Campanini tear up her contract, and moved on . . . to La Scala and an important place in the heart of Giulio Gatti-Casazza. Less than a year later, she had another contract to sing in New York.

At the Met.

Here, Mimi

At the Met, Olive Fremstad was singing Giulietta in an all-star *Les Contes d'Hoffmann*. As always, her secretary and factotum Mary Watkins stood in the wings; but this time, for a change, she carried Fremstad's little dog Mimi. Alda came up, petted dear little Mimi, and said, "Do let me hold it."

Watkins was in no position to say no to Mrs. Gatti, and handed the dog over. Suddenly, Alda set Mimi down, aimed her at the stage, gave her a push, and cried, "Go!"

Mimi went: straight for her mistress, Giulietta. Mimi's irruption into the canalworks of Venice broke up the performance; Fremstad was so startled that her voice dried up. She was angry, too; and when she confronted her secretary, Alda was nowhere to be found.

Actually, this occurred not at a performance but at a dress rehearsal, if a public one, so no harm was done. But Alda's prank may have been somewhat less than improvised: for in due course Giulietta was taken from Fremstad and reassigned to . . . yes, Frances Alda.

Alda Quits

One night shortly after she finally married Gatti, Alda happened to be watching a dress rehearsal when she heard voices discussing her in the next box. She knew them: one belonged to the Boston impresario Henry Russell and the other to Met Board power Otto Kahn. It was Kahn

Alda had overheard saying, "Now that Alda is the director's wife, it would be much better if she did not sing here next season."

Leaning over the railing, Alda pushed back the separating drapery, her eyes flashing. Kahn looked as if he were facing the ghost of Sophie Arnould.

"I suppose it would be all right if I were his mistress instead of his wife!" Alda raged. In fact, it had been, for years. "I resign *right now!*" And she meant it.

Alda spent that contested season touring the land in concert; she found it hectic but invigorating. During the winter, Otto Kahn reached her by telegram: COME BACK—YOUR PLACE AT THE METROPOLITAN IS WAITING FOR YOU. Was this gallantry or genuine need? Kahn was gallant, certainly, and his faux pas must have been nagging at him. But Alda was a great singer, the kind every company needs, if only to supplement the Farrar and Ponselle nights. In any case, Alda came home.

Eclectic Music

As Gatti's sweetheart, Alda was not exempt from participation in his constant productions of new American operas, which generally meant signing on for an absolute guaranteed fiasco. Alda's least gratifying role in this series was Roxane in Walter Damrosch's *Cyrano de Bergerac*, a work so derivative that a runthrough sounded like a history of nineteenth-century music.

One day at rehearsal, Alda was unsure about whether or not there was a cut on the next page, and asked, "Where do we go from here?"

The conductor replied, "From Gounod to Meyerbeer."

Ponselle Pays a Visit

In New York buying antiques for her Baltimore retirement palace, Villa Pace, Ponselle caught sight of Alda. Ponselle hurried to escape, fearing a scene, but Alda saw her before she could leave, and it was "Rosa, dear!," "Frances, darling!," and kisses, kisses. Alda, too, had a new retirement palace, on Madison Avenue in the sixties. She insisted Ponselle come up for a tour of the place.

No sooner had they walked in than Alda rang for her five servants. When they assembled, she snapped out, "This is Rosa Ponselle, the greatest soprano who ever lived—so have a look and get back to work!"

An Old Friend

In Versailles at Lady Mendl's Villa Trianon, Alda spent lunch next to a pleasant young man who claimed to have shared the stage with her once.

"In Chicago," he recalled, "Back in 1910. You came from New York to sing in *Rigoletto*. There was a big blizzard and the train was late, and everybody at the rehearsal waited and waited for you to get there. Finally, when you did come, you looked at them all and said, 'Listen, this is how I sing Gilda. First I do this, then I do that. I come on here. I go off there. Now everybody can go home.' You waved your hand and left."

Alda laughed. She couldn't place the man, but no wonder: he had been one of the little pages in red velvet who held the curtain back during the bows.

"And now you are?"

"Mainbocher."

LEO SLEZAK

Slezak was one of those rare men born to sing Wagner's tenor leads. A strapping, princely looking fellow, he sported a great ringing sound, as pliant in tender moments as heroic in the big numbers. It seems surprising to learn that he had a sense of humor as well; not only did he tell good stories on himself, he seems to have invented a few, too.

One Lohengrin story, at least, is true: on his London debut at Covent Garden, the entire audience got up and left the theatre *during Act One!* As this was near the start of Slezak's career, his first important engagement (and in the role he expected to make one of his great ones), it was not only startling but highly discouraging.

Actually, the audience was making not an artistic statement but a patriotic one: news of the relief of Mafeking* hit London on the night of Slezak's debut and was announced from the stage just before the duel between Lohengrin and Telramund. Obviously, another three hours of Wagner was not on any Briton's agenda that night.

In any case, Slezak moved on to the Vienna State Opera under Gustav Mahler, and made his history. He even gave a son to the theatre, Walter, who came to America to play Continental characters in Broadway operettas, starring in the first productions of Kern's *Music in the Air*, Romberg's *May Wine*, Rodgers and Hart's *I Married an*

---

* Mafeking was the small town occupied at a turning point of the South African War by Col. Robert Baden-Powell and surrounded by the Boers. Though the Dutch never pressed their advantage and the fighting amounted to little more than skirmishes and the hurling of dud shells, the 217-day siege aroused near-hysteria in England, and there were riots when Baden-Powell's forces were reinforced.

Angel, and Harold Rome's virtually operatic *Fanny* (opposite Ezio Pinza, a credit Leo might have relished). In his twenties Walter looked exactly like his father, and opera buffs delight in the famous photograph of the two in matching Lohengrin outfits, taken when Walter was about four years old. He even sports a tiny beard to match Papa's.

Slezak Auditions for Wagner's Widow

The Wagner family, maintaining the Bayreuth Festival after the composer's death, was always looking for fresh talent, especially for the youthful roles like Eva, Walther von Stolzing, Elsa, and Tristan, which too often went to veterans with the part's voice but not its looks. In 1896, hearing promising reports of a dynamic young Lohengrin in Brno, the Wagners invited him—Slezak, of course—to Bayreuth to audition.

It was Slezak's first year as a soloist, so this was a great opportunity—and a daunting one. He was to sing on the historic stage for Frau Wagner herself, Cosima Liszt von Bülow Wagner, related by blood or marriage to three of the century's greatest musicians and herself autocrat of Bayreuth.

Slezak was led out to sing during a break in rehearsals for *Das Rheingold;* everyone perked up to attend to this new Wunderkind as Frau Wagner asked him what he was going to sing.

" 'Vesti la giubba,' " said Slezak.

Everyone froze. No, not everyone—the pianist gasped and the Thor nearly fainted. Frau Wagner coldly suggested Slezak might better sing something by The Master; that is, if he knew anything besides *Pagliacci*. Slezak obliged with a bit of *Das Rheingold*, received the Bayreuth equivalent of "Thank you very much!" and was rushed out of the Festspielhaus in the hope that he would leave the vicinity as soon as possible. He did not get the job.

But he did get a little fame out of it. For a number of years afterward, Leo Slezak was known from Gelsenkirchen to Klagenfurt as "the fellow who tried to sing *Pagliacci* in Bayreuth."

Slezak's Service to the Citizens of Breslau

Slezak met his wife when they were both working in Breslau, he in opera and she as an actress. Apparently, she was not an inspired tragedienne, and did not object when Slezak suggested she retire to play the role of Frau Slezak for life. She made her farewell as Joan of Arc in Schiller's *The Maid of Orleans,* and, at the end of the evening, as she reached the line, "Joan goes, never to return," the audience cried out, "Hoch Slezak!": Hooray for Slezak! The tenor insisted he had nothing to do with it; still she never forgave him.

A Dog Knows His Master

Slezak suffered a weight problem. His ever-bulging stomach threatened to humiliate his Lohengrin and Raoul in *Les Huguenots,* so he had constantly to go on diets, supervised by his wife and ceaselessly sabotaged by the hungry singer.

A trusting soul, Frau Slezak failed to realize that something was up when suddenly her Leo began to accept his tiny dinners docilely. One day, Frau Slezak found the dog Schnauzi holding point in Slezak's study, the animal's rigid snout aimed at a desk drawer. Opened, it disclosed a two-foot Hungarian salami.

"Now you've spoiled my surprise!" cried Slezak. "I got that salami for you and the children!" Frau Slezak believed him, and there the matter ended.

But, from then on, Slezak called Schnauzi Judas Iscariot.

Junior Buys a Car

Back in the days when most people didn't ride in cars, much less own them, young Walter bought one: he was just beginning a career in silent films and was feeling notable. It was a tiny convertible, fire-engine red, named Nora after his sweetheart of the moment, and Walter called his father to share his joy.

"Who recommended your chauffeur?" asked Leo, accustomed to huge, opulent machines fit for a personage, his family, and entourage.

"What chauffeur?" said Walter. "*I* am the chauffeur. I took driving lessons, and—"

Leo let out a moan of agony like Mario in Scarpia's torture chamber. "Elsa!" he called to his wife. "Come quickly, the boy is driving a car. He will kill himself!" Through the receiver, Walter heard his mother's sobs, as his father lectured him endlessly on the perils of the road. Finally, Walter reminded Leo that the call had been placed collect.

"Oh, my God!" Leo wept. "*That too?*" He immediately hung up.

The Classic Leo Slezak Story

Backstage at *Lohengrin* before his first entrance, Slezak was bemused to see the swan-boat take off just before he got into it: a stagehand had jumped the cue. As the boat glided into the opera without its silver knight, Slezak turned to someone and asked, "Wann geht der nächste Schwann?": What time's the next swan?

The line has such ring that it seems surprising that Slezak never used it as a title for any of his three books of memoirs. No matter: son Walter used it for his.

The Other Classic Leo Slezak Story

Enrico Caruso sang the knightly Renaud with misgivings when the Met mounted Toscanini's spectacular reading of *Armide*. It was Olive Fremstad's show, and Caruso knew it. Moreover, he felt ridiculous in the costume. But Slezak claimed to have enjoyed taking over the role. He loved to tell how he enlivened the show by dragging out for a curtain call an impressively white-bearded gentleman who just happened to be standing around backstage. Presenting the man to the public, Slezak genuflected before him, and reporters rushed backstage to get the story.

"That was Gluck, the composer of *Armide*," Slezak explained. "He told me that never in his life has he heard his opera sung as magnificently as I have sung it tonight."

The next day several newspapers reported the incident, unaware that Gluck had died in 1787, and a furious Gatti fined Slezak one hundred dollars. Donning a mourning veil, the tenor put in an appearance at the offices of Met *éminence grise* Otto Kahn and the fine was cancelled.

The story, however famous, is apocryphal: Slezak never sang *Armide* with the Met. In an earlier version, recounted in one of Slezak's books of recollection, the tale occurs in an unspecified place, during a rehearsal rather than a performance, and the victim is not the press but a credulous fellow tenor. Furious at the deception, he thought Slezak was at it again when a portly Italian came backstage to congratulate this singer on his Canio in *Pagliacci*. "Who are you?" asked the singer. "Sono maestro Leoncavallo," the stranger replied—*Pagliacci*'s composer, no less. "Don't you try that game on me!" cried Slezak's former dupe, stamping off. "You probably died a hundred years ago!" Unfortunately, it *was* Leoncavallo.

The less colorful version of Slezak's *Armide* story is doubtless the authentic one, but I included the Met version because it is better known. In any case, the picture of the New York press failing to place Gluck is persuasive: at *Armide*'s Met premiere, one paper, announcing the cast, noted that Alma Gluck was "no relation to the composer." Louise Homer sang in that *Armide,* too—no relation to the Greek poet.

JOHN McCORMACK

A devoted family man with no sense of theatricality does not suggest
an opera tenor, especially not in the Italian wing. Yet John Mc-
Cormack was one of Caruso's few coevals who was arguably his equal.
It was a small voice, one better suited to the recital hall than to Covent Garden, the Met, Hammerstein's Manhattan Opera, and the other
places wherein McCormack made his name. "Tell your damn orchestra to play softer!" was the reply of McCormack's early sponsor Sir
John Murray Scott, when an official of Covent Garden worried over
McCormack's potential in volume.

Yet the very smallness proved advantageous in the end, for it led
McCormack to the discovery that he was more personable in the intimacy of the recital—or, better, in the recital's honesty: for Mc-
Cormack gave recitals to thousands at a sitting. Opera was too grand
for him; its attitudes were beyond his belief, and the costumes made
him feel silly. Only as Rodolpho, he said, did he feel truly at his ease,
hanging around with his hands in his pockets and shrugging his
shoulders as if playing himself. (He looks odd, though, in the goatee,
traditional in the role at the time.) It seems right, then, that when
Hollywood switched over to sound film and hired opera singers to lend
their prestige to the venture, Lawrence Tibbett, Grace Moore, Lily Pons,
and Gladys Swarthout all played operatic sorts of parts with plenty of
Extremely Prestigious Grand Opera Selections—while McCormack
played an everyday sort of guy and sang Irish ballads.

His film, *Song O' My Heart,* was in fact one of the few really successful films built around an opera singer, precisely because its lack of
pretension coincided exactly with McCormack's. "There stands
McCormack right before your eyes," *Photoplay* exulted, "singing with
all the tenderness and beauty for which his voice is famed." Not acting or striking poses, but presenting, in his own persona, the music
that most moves him and that he hopes will move you. That about
sums up the film's action, and its achievement—it reminds us that some
of the greatest opera singers were not really meant to sing opera. Mozart, Verdi, Puccini, Wolf-Ferrari, and all the others have their own
psychology and physiology. A fellow might be very musical yet not
suit their particular musicality. If McCormack's recording of "Il mio
tesoro" is the best ever made—some say so—still McCormack could
not do more than most tenors in making Don Ottavio come off as
anything but the weak link in *Don Giovanni*'s chain of characters.
Truth to tell, McCormack's Ottavio was less forceful than most. But
on the platform, holding his famous little black book of lyrics (for assurance rather than for practical need, as he never so much as glanced
at it), he could fascinate a population—at concerts in the New York
Hippodrome, he sang to seven thousand people, including one thousand seated on the stage behind him. Max de Schauensee likened him
to Paderewski and Kreisler in their ability to "reach the heart most
directly" and to Caruso in the "forthright charm that, free of any
complications, made its effect with a minimum of time and effort . . .

Even when he was singing in a huge auditorium, he always gave the sensation of person-to-person intimacy."

He was a natural, an affable chap who was one of the most famous Irishmen alive. In odd truth, McCormack was of Scottish parentage (though born in Athlone, on the River Shannon) and became an American citizen. These are the trivia that one forgets, or never hears; what stays with us is the image of a man without the flamboyance of most of the people in this book—but with voice and technique to challenge and in many cases better anything they could do.

It's Every Tenor's Nightmare

Making his operatic debut in January of 1906 at Savona, Italy, in the title role of Mascagni's *L'Amico Fritz* and billed as Giovanni Foli, McCormack reached the middle of his big aria in Act Three when he realized that he was not going to make the high B flat that climaxes the number. It's an exposed note; the aria may be said to lead up to it as a prayer leads up to "Amen," and it could not possibly be ducked.

McCormack hit upon a daring solution, based on the, to him, loud orchestra. Comes the B flat, he will open his mouth as wide as possible, throw out his arms in a pose suggestive of Tenor Doing High Note, and let the orchestra sing the note for him.

He does it.

And the audience is so thrilled it demands an encore.

Promising Ethnicity

When Oscar Hammerstein signed McCormack for the Manhattan Opera House, he is supposed to have said, "An Irishman singing Italian opera in New York? He'll sell the place out!"

Beautiful Curtain

Nellie Melba had a way of dying in the last scene of *Roméo et Juliette* that touched many a heart. She would arrange to drape herself over the dead Romeo, effecting a picture of beautiful doom that might have adorned an art nouveau poster. Like it or not, McCormack had to tolerate being draped upon when he sing Romeo on one of Melba's Australian tours—but, one night, while going into her drape, she accidentally pinned McCormack's ankle to the steps they were lying on. In great pain, McCormack tried to squirm into a more comfortable position, and Melba whispered, "Don't stir, John. Tableau! *Tableau!*"

"Tableau be damned," he replied. "Get off my ankle!"

Babies, Take a Bow

This isn't a great story, perhaps; but anyone who has raised children should enjoy it. John and Lily McCormack had two, Cyril and Gwen, and when the kids were still quite young they were taken to Carnegie Hall for their first taste of a McCormack concert. They sat with their mother in a box, and were to be taken home after the first half, though in the event they were having a fine time.

A friend led them backstage to say hello to their father as they left, and, as the audience was still applauding, McCormack suddenly reappeared from the wings with Cyril on one hand and Gwen on the other, the two children smiling up at their father. All three bowed to the pleasantly startled public—none more startled, and more pleasantly, than Mrs. Lily McCormack.

Smart Kid

Someone asked Cyril at about this time if he, too, entertained musical ambitions.

"Oh no," said the boy. "I'm going to *work*."

The Greatest Cast Never Assembled

One great regret in McCormack's generally quite satisfying career was the Don Ottavio he didn't get to sing in Salzburg in 1914. An almost ferociously imposing cast had been hired: Lilli Lehmann as Donna Anna, Johanna Gadski as Elvira, Geraldine Farrar as Zerlina, Antonio Scotti as Giovanni, and Feodor Chalyapin as Leporello, all under Karl Muck leading the Vienna Philharmonic, possibly the world's greatest opera orchestra. Lehmann was at the end of her career and Chalyapin no one's idea of a Mozart stylist. Still, the production promised to be one of the great events of the day. A greater event cancelled it: the outbreak of World War I.

McCormack Whistles for Paderewski

In Hollywood while making *Song O'My Heart,* McCormack attended a party honoring the pianist Ignace Paderewski. At dinner, McCormack told the company about a bird he heard singing one phrase over and over.

"Whistle it, John," said Paderewski.

McCormack whistled.

"Again, John."

McCormack whistled again.

"Once more, John."

"What's the big idea, Maestro?" McCormack asked.

"Oh John," said Paderewski, smiling. "I like to hear you whistle."

MARY GARDEN

Because her personality mesmerized the public, commentators who never heard her have established the legend that she had no voice. It seems unlikely that a soprano without a voice could have made her debut as Louise—at that, on the stage of the Opéra-Comique while the *Louise* rage was at its height and all Paris flocking to hear it, and at a time when the Opéra-Comique boasted a number of first-rate sopranos. True, Garden was a substitute, stepping in for Marthe Rioton at the start of Act Three. It happens, however, that this act begins with "Depuis le jour," the opera's most popular highlight, five minutes of soaring rhapsody. Are we to believe that a soprano without a voice got through two acts of *Louise* to enchant Paris, Monte Carlo, New York, and Chicago entirely on personality?

There's no question that Garden cut a fascinating figure, offstage as well as on. Where other sopranos sang the standard roles of their vocal category, along the Gilda-Amina-Marguerite or Sieglinde-Desdemona-Agathe axes, Garden preferred new roles that no one else sang, premieres wherever possible—and roles, especially, that gave Garden a chance to exploit her riveting plastique. No Marguerite for her, but rather Thaïs, Tosca, Sapho, Monna Vanna, Natoma, Katiusha (in Alfano's *Resurezzione*): sensual, giving women. Paradoxically, Garden was just as notable in trouser roles like Massenet's Chérubin; and even invented one, for *Le Jongleur de Notre-Dame*. Massenet wrote the part (that of a strolling player whose act brings a statue of the Madonna to life) for a tenor. Garden coopted it, with such success that, while Massenet was unhappy, he let it pass.

Mélisande was Garden's greatest role, according to Garden, the one with which she most identified. Perhaps she preferred it because, of the roles Garden created, Mélisande lived on: where are Natoma and Monna Vanna today? And in some ways Maeterlinck's doll princess relates closely to Garden, in her ascetic approach to life and in the sense of characterological mystery she created wherever she went. When Garden entered a room, people who knew very well who she was found themselves murmuring, "Who is she?" Yet she could be roguishly feminine on a whim or for a purpose. When tycoon Harold McCormick proposed Garden to take over the Chicago Opera and his fellow board members demurred, Garden appeared before them to argue her case. "If I could just talk to each of you gentleman alone," she most provocatively said, "I am sure I could convince you." Thus Mary Garden took over the Chicago Opera.

She had one greater role even than Mélisande, and she knew it: as manipulator of the press. Now, half a century after she retired, she is recalled as her colleagues are, for a stunt here and a great role there, for her Scotch burr, which she retained from her Aberdeen birthright through her American childhood and the otherwise flawless French of her maturity. She may be even less well recalled than, say, Marcella Sembrich or Lucrezia Bori, because they recorded well and plentifully while Garden never quite cottoned to the acoustic horn. But back when Garden was in her prime, she was one of the most famous singers in the world—precisely because of this talent for getting into the newspapers.

Garden must have been the first diva to realize that once you lure reporters into letting you become news, you will remain news thereafter. All you have to do is stay active and remain available for interviews. This Garden did, with a merry manner and an expertise in aiming conversations toward her objective, letting the newsmen wangle the next headline out of her so they could feel like the coauthors of her reputation. They liked that. For a woman who recommended abstaining—as Garden did often—she sure knew how to help a man to like himself.

No amount of news tales will support a reputation in opera without a talent behind those tales, and everyone who heard her agrees that Garden had that talent. She must have been something, for in real life she was tiny and thin, the kind of person who could get lost in a closet. Yet, on the stages of the biggest houses, she enthralled thousands at a go. Perhaps the saddest aspect of the recent arrival of home opera video is that they didn't start making it till the Malibrans, Lablaches, Chalyapins, Callases—and Mary Gardens—were all used up.

Two Mélisandes

Claude Debussy assured Albert Carré, chief of the Opéra-Comique, that Garden was the ideal choice for Mélisande. The Comique's leading soprano, Marguerite Guirard, had her eye on the part as well—and, as Guirard was Carré's lover, he found himself in a dire position. He had no choice but to respect the composer's wishes, but his *petite amie* Guirard would not give up the role without a fight. On the day of the dress rehearsal, she bore down furiously on Garden.

"What are you doing here?" Guirard demands.

Garden, already dreaming herself into Mélisande's trancelike grace, remains calm. "I came to rehearse Mélisande."

Guirard then explodes in a hail of abuse and threats. But Garden thinks that this virago is the loved one of the chief of the house, and laughs to herself at the exquisite vanity of a foolish world.

"I'll show you who's mistress here!" Guirard vows.

"You win," says Garden.

A Feud à la Garden

At Hammerstein's Manhattan Opera, Garden enjoyed a sensation as Thaïs with Maurice Renaud in 1907. It was New York's first taste of the piece, and French opera was in vogue, especially Massenet, especially Massenet with Mary Garden. Naturally, Garden was angered when Lina Cavalieri was unexpectedly announced to take over the part. No impresario would willingly pour off sell-out chemistry like Garden-as-Thaïs for a substitution; there had to be an intrigue somewhere (an intrigue named Cavalieri, Garden was sure), and Garden determined to root it out or take the next boat back to France.

"Explain!" she demanded, confronting Hammerstein.

"*I'm* running this opera house!" he replied.

So she pulled out her magic press-magnetizing kit, made the mystic passes, and, *presto!* the papers carried the news that Mary Garden was sailing for France.

Hammerstein immediately capitulated, and Garden blithely resumed her sensation. But Cavalieri was furious. As The Most Beautiful Singer in the World, she had been planning to have her own sensation in the part, one that begins in a courtesan's diaphanous veils and ends in piety and prayer (not to mention death). Actually, someone might have warned Cavalieri that the sensation had more to do with Garden (and with Sibyl Sanderson, the original Thaïs) than with the role itself. No matter; Cavalieri's scheme to steal Thaïs from Garden had failed, and she responded with angry denunciations of her rival to the newspapers.

Of course the reporters went to Garden for her side of it, so in the end Cavalieri's plot had backfired: Garden not only retained Thaïs, but took in a load of publicity as well. Still, no matter how much the boys prodded, Garden would tell them nothing of the Thaïs caper. She spoke of new roles, new operas, new clothes, new vacation spots. She gave them enough to fill their Garden files for four or five stories—but, on the present matter, nothing. Indeed, our Mary could scarcely concentrate on the interview at all, it seemed, for most of her attention was taken up by an incredibly spoiled and demanding Pekingese lap dog, who would whine if it wasn't being petted every moment.

At last the reporters called it quits. If they couldn't get the story, at least they had passed another arresting hour with the spectacular Mary Garden. Graciously, she saw them down the hall to the elevator, carrying the still insistently abominable little Pekingese.

As the men got into the elevator, one of them asked, "What's the dog's name, Miss Garden?"

"I call her Cavalieri," said Mary with a smile. "So long, gentlemen."

So they got their story after all.

Give a Girl a Break

Garden was delighted when John McCormack invited her to share a concert with him, as his public was known to be warm and appreciative, whereas hers was often merely curious, attracted by her publicity. When she thanked McCormack for the opportunity, he joked, "Well, Mary, you seldom get your name in the papers, so I thought I'd give you a boost."

Zoological Opera

An outdoor performance of *Carmen,* as outdoor performances will, spiced the pageant with live animals, including two donkeys who began to bray while Garden was singing the Habañera.

Later, backstage, a reporter asked for Garden's reaction to the incident.

"What's so unusual about it?" she said. "There have always been asses in grand opera!"

Mankiller Garden

Garden had a penchant for napping before a performance, and at such times not even the press could penetrate her seclusion. In Amarillo, Texas, Garden turned down an interview with the local critic so she could rest, and he responded in print, quite unkindly. Garden took him to task in her turn, and soon an all-out feud developed—though, admittedly, it is somewhat difficult for a world-famous singer to war in worthy proportion with the music critic of a small town in Texas.

Eventually, Garden sang in Amarillo again, and this time the two called a truce. The man was so attentive that his wife joked that she might lose him to Garden.

"Don't worry," the diva told her. "When I start wrecking homes I won't begin in Amarillo."

Everybody's Favorite Mary Garden Story

Chauncey Depew stares at Garden's decolleté and says, "Tell me, Miss Garden, what's holding that dress up?"

Garden looks him spang in the eye and answers, "Your age and my discretion."

Garden's Theatre Party

Disappointed that she couldn't try the adventure of living through an occupied Paris, Garden spent World War II in her native Aberdeen with her mother and sisters, all of them constantly in search of ways to cheer up Allied soldiers. One Christmas, Garden asked a general if there was something in the Garden manner that she could do for his troops—not the usual fruit basket party, something unique: the R & R equivalent of what Garden was like on the stage.

The general asked his men, and, as they said they wanted to go to the theatre, Garden bought them tickets to a Noël Coward show. Coward later said they made a terrific audience, neat, alert, and appreciative—not least of Coward's lovely ingenue, Judie Campbell. After the play, when the soldiers got into the trucks for the ride back to camp, an officer cried out, "Is everybody in?"

And the men shouted back, "Everybody but Judie!"

Garden at a Naval Hospital

On another mission of mercy, Garden and her sister took a load of eyeglasses to King's Seat Hospital, having heard that many men had lost theirs in battle and had nothing to read with. By luck, the miscellanous assortment of spectacles suited the needy. But this story is not a happy one. Introduced to the distinguished visitor, one of the wounded sailors—"a very young boy," Garden recalled, "with great big eyes"—looked up in surprise. "Not the real Mary Garden?"

"Yes," she proclaimed. "The *real* Mary Garden. She's come to see if there's anything she can do for you. Is there anything you'd like?"

"Yes."

"What is it?"

"I want to go home."

Garden Speaks

"Claude Debussy?" Garden said to the writer Vincent Sheean. "I'd as soon have a love affair with the Pope!"

Yet there were hints of a Debussy-Garden romance in the Garden legend, and this composer and role were essential components of the Garden aura, remember. It wouldn't have done much for Garden's mythology for her to leak the revelation that Henry Fevrier had conceived an obsession for her. All her other composers had lost their luster, even Massenet, whom Garden had never cared for, anyway. No, it was Debussy with whom she must connect.

One day in 1946, Garden gave a lecture in New York's Town Hall. Unknown to her, the audience included the other Scottish Mélisande, Maggie Teyte, who had never forgiven Garden for attempting to keep the role for herself. Why, Teyte was only now, at the age of sixty, getting to present her Mélisande to New Yorkers, at that not in their major house, but at the neglected City Opera in its shabby barn on Fifty-fifth Street. This was Garden's doing—when both women were prime, Garden had sung Mélisande all over the map, edging Teyte out everywhere that mattered.

Teyte, accompanied by friends, sat regarding Garden with a beady eye as her old rival elaborated upon her legend, acting out the many scenes of her fabulous past, a past filled to repletion, it seemed, with fawning men and enraptured audiences. Massenet adored her, of course. Messager doted. Carré went wild. And Debussy . . .

Teyte stiffened.

. . . Debussy had loved her beyond limit. How he had implored her, how different his life would be, he told her, if she would love the man as she loved his music; how truly he had come to know his own opera through the miraculous art of Garden. His music and his love were one. As Garden had obliged him by creating his Mélisande, so must she now complete the act by becoming his wife.

The public was transfixed; Teyte was not. Visibly irritated, she heard Mary Garden reach the climax of her eulogy of Mary Garden. "Of course," she said, "you know," and they did; they listened and knew, hanging on every word: "I really *am* Mélisande."

"Oh, for God's sake!" roared Maggie Teyte.

GERALDINE FARRAR

Caruso coined her motto, "Farrar farà": Farrar will do it. Will find a way, will pull it off, will triumph. Caruso was right. Farrar was one of opera's most resourceful singers, like Schröder-Devrient, Malibran, and Callas, a unique artist. She had many gifts, including a lovely timbre, flawless musicality, and a superb sense of theatre. Perhaps her greatest quality was her identification with each role, the sensibility Farrar so individually projected as Elisabeth, Zazà, Butterfly, Carmen, Suor Angelica. Examine photographs of Farrar's colleagues from role to role and one sees the same person in a series of costumes. But Farrar looks like a different being from one character to another, so much so that it becomes hard to get a fix on her beauty till she turns up, after retirement, as the Met's grande dame, white-haired yet firm-busted, and caught *in situ* with Milton Cross while delivering musical analyses of the Saturday broadcast operas at the pianoforte.

She was a born actress, though nothing in her middle-class Massachusetts background indicated a stage career. Her father ran a store and played baseball in season; her mother raised one child, this one. (Their name, by the way, is accented on the first syllable: FAR-rar.) Young Farrar was always on, always playing some role. At the age of ten, she was courted by a slightly older boy whom she rebuffed when he revealed a lack of interest in music. Not long after, he drowned in an ice-skating accident, and immediately Geraldine became the Widow Farrar, moping into a black-bordered handkerchief and avoiding her pals' playtimes. As she later recalled it, she had no feeling for the dead boy: his tragedy simply gave her a dramatic outlet.

Farrar's parents fostered her artistic bent, and when her pleasant adolescent voice showed signs of developing into a genuine instrument they changed their lives to see her through to fulfillment. On money borrowed from a neighbor (a fortune, and the soprano paid it back at the first opportunity), they took her to Europe for training and experience. Already, she was so distinctive an attraction, a beauty in an age of clumsies, that the intendant of the Berlin Hofoper, Count von Hochberg, engaged Farrar on a three-year contract before she had any stage experience whatever. Moreover, he allowed her to sing Marguerite, Violetta, and Nedda in Italian while the rest of the cast sang in German. On a technicality, she could not actually join the company; the poster announcing her debut in *Faust* listed her, *als Gast* (as a visitor), as "Miss Geraldine Farrar aus New York."

This is a significant billing, for Farrar was always the young American, a do-it-yourself talent who goes out there a youngster and comes back a star. For so her European visit made her. After her debut, on the basis of her success, she applied to Lilli Lehmann for polishing, and Lehmann put her through The Course. Still, Farrar was self-invented; the personal projection that made each of her great roles special unto her was something she devised for herself. There were no great stage directors in those days. What one learned of interpretation came from coaches and conductors like Mahler and Toscanini. And, yes, Farrar worked closely with the latter at the Met. One can hear the difference in her recordings. Those from her German years offer the fresher voice but largely unrealized characterizations; the later American Victors present an incisive vitality of being. Still, Farrar always had it, from the skating accident on—a sense of who she might have been in different times and places that inspired her in the theatre as no one else was. Her colleagues were regulation; Farrar was an odd fit.

Back in America, she came into a kind of inheritance, as if there had never been any question that Geraldine Farrar of Melrose, Massachusetts, would be the ultimate Met star. Fremstad had the bigger voice, Ponselle the better; but of all American sopranos Farrar seemed most American and most unlike anyone else. What could be more American than to become a movie star, to have screaming fans (the "Gerryflappers") to whom you are role model and idol? Yet what other American sopranos made such movies, had such fans? Who else had a sensational liaison with Germany's Crown Prince, another with the film actor Lou Tellegen, whom Farrar married, unwisely? What non-Italian could hold the stage with Caruso and Scotti in Puccini and still be thought the key element? Caruso was a miracle of nature and Scotti an astonishing performer. Yet when other sopranos sang with them, the house takings fell off. Farrar must have been a miracle of a performer.

Her reign, from the Berlin debut in 1901 to the Met farewell in 1922, marked the emergence of the theatre personality in opera, overthrowing the rule of the Garcia-era singer who entertained through force of musicianship alone. Farrar's voice was her vulnerable point, a very lyric instrument forced to accommodate the passion of Butterfly. And twenty-one years, even of absolutely front-line work, is not a long career. Yet her art reproached that of the stand-and-deliver singer who might be able to distinguish Puccini from Massenet but not Mimì from Manon. Farrar shot a wry smile at Toscanini from the stage the night she substituted at the last minute for Emmy Destinn in a drastically undersold *Butterfly*—undersold because the great singer who was also a great performer was going to make it harder for the great singer who was not a great performer. Thus Farrar made her history, and thus Farrar was essentially an American artist. It is an American notion that music theatre is as much theatre as music; they've known this on Broadway since Victor Herbert's day, the day as well of Geraldine Farrar. After she passed, they knew it at the Met, too.

Her retirement was bad news to Gatti, especially as he had just lost Caruso. Rumor had it that Farrar was leaving in fury at the success of Maria Jeritza, another performer-singer who challenged Farrar in her parts. But it had always been Farrar's style to leave at the top. She abandoned film when still a big draw, and rejected all offers when sound came in. What a *Carmen* they might have made with her! No, it cannot have been Jeritza. Farrar called time arbitrarily. And when she called time, time it was.

She was strong willed, very New England. When the United States entered World War I and everything German was *verboten,* Farrar refused to lend her name to jingoistic ploys. She helped sell Liberty Bonds, but recalled the kindness of many who supported her in her Berlin days too well to indulge in the hysterical rhetoric of the time. Long after the war, a friend, noting the signed photograph of Wilhelm II on Farrar's piano, said, "I see you have restored the Kaiser."

"Restored?" Farrar replied. "He stood there all through World War I!"

Farrar Auditions for the Met

The mysterious explosion of the U.S. Battleship *Maine* in Havana harbor in 1898 contributed not only to American war hysteria but to the rise of Geraldine Farrar. The Met decided to give a benefit of something special, the proceeds to go to families of the *Maine* victims, and

choice had landed on *Mignon,* with Nellie Melba in her first local Philine, when sixteen-year-old Farrar arrived in New York. Through a throat
doctor who treated opera singers, Farrar met the wife of Met manager
Maurice Grau; it was Mrs. Grau's happy thought that Farrar would
make a splendid Mignon, her looks and voice perfect for the gamine so
often cast with veterans old enough to be Mignon's grandmother.

Farrar was aware that she was not ready to sing opera, especially at
the Met. Some years of vocal study and professional experience stood
before her—yet the possibility of singing on the stage of Melba and the
de Reszkes tempted her. At least she ought to audition; if only for form's
sake. Others, walking out on that stage, would be deflated by the very
size of the place; Farrar was stimulated. Of course she exercised her
typical theatricality by dismissing the pianist and singing at the keyboard to her own accompaniment: Farrar was always Farrar. But she
was not always a great singer; Grau, at least, thought her well ahead
of greatness just then. Farrar would not sing Mignon.

Grau was too nice a man not to offer this remarkable young woman
something for her trouble. Would she like to sing in one of the Met's
Sunday night concerts? It wasn't "real" opera, perhaps, but it *was* the
Met.

Farrar did things all the way or not at all. She said no.

"But it might be valuable to you," Grau pointed out, "to have your
name on the billboards of the Metropolitan Opera House."

"You will see it there some day," she replied. The rise of Geraldine
Farrar had begun.

Farrar told this tale on herself in her first small volume of memoirs,
The Story of an American Singer, published in 1916, when she was at
her height and felt the need to structure her legend. Years after she
retired, she produced the much larger, quite elegantly styled, and presumably definitive *Such Sweet Compulsion,* and there she revises the
story somewhat ambiguously—so ambiguously that it is less her implication than the reader's inference that Grau offered her Mignon.
Moreover, Farrar clearly states that Melba herself "urged the debut."
According to Farrar, her mother turned down the Met Mignon on the
grounds that she was too much the tyro to deserve it. This may well
be. But when Farrar did make her debut, in Berlin not long after the
Met episode, she had undergone less than decisive training under one
Maestro Graziani—and are we really to believe that the congenitally
jealous Melba encouraged Grau to challenge her Philine with the
beauteous teenager, at that in the opera's title role, a role that dominates the action in almost every scene? In either version, though, the
story does suggest a first taste of professionalism that must have convinced young Farrar that she had chosen the right course for her life.

Sixteen years old and already auditioning for the Metropolitan! Farrar farà.

Farrar Pays the Penalty for Subversive Personality

Germany is such an orderly country that its opera companies, reinless everywhere else, must observe niceties of reason and cleanliness. So Farrar discovered on a guest jaunt in Magdeburg with her frequent Berlin partner Karl Jörn. As Magdeburg followed a provincial line of opera production, officials there naturally allowed Farrar and Jörn, with the sophistication of their Berlin swank, to devise their own staging for *La Traviata*.

One of Farrar's innovations involved a little teasing byplay in the "Libiamo": she wanted to express Violetta's capricious amusement at Alfredo's ardor by snatching his wineglass and smashing it onto the floor. They loved it in Berlin.

But in Magdeburg, to Farrar's amazement, a stagehand in court theatre uniform suddenly materialized in the midst of Violetta's party guests bearing with great dignity a whisk broom and pan. Ignoring singers and audience, he stoically swept up the shattered glass and marched off.

The next day, the theatre bookkeeper billed Farrar twenty-five pfennigs for glass breakage.

Farrar As Salome

In 1905, Richard Strauss invited Farrar to Dresden to the premiere of *Salome*. Composer and soprano were already colleagues from performances in Berlin and Munich, and, even this early, Strauss was scheming to inveigle pretty, youthful, svelte sopranos into trying a part that was otherwise certain to belong to aging Junos by the very nature of the vocal writing and huge orchestration.

Would Farrar agree to sing Salome in Berlin if the composer altered the composition to suit a lyric voice?

Farrar would not. No alteration would get her through that score.

"Farrar," said Strauss, "you have such dramatic possibilities. You can act. You can dance half-naked. No one will care if you sing or not."

The mighty scoring intact, Emmy Destinn sang Salome in Berlin—"and looked," Farrar reported, "like a misplaced *Walküre*."

Battle of the Titans

One of opera's favorite stories finds Farrar confronting Arturo Toscanini at a rehearsal for the first Met *Butterfly*. Toscanini had just arrived at the house to expound the purity of starless art; Farrar, by two years his senior at the Met, argues for the clarity of performer charisma. He wants to set tempo; she wants to set tempo. It's a shoving match between two immovable objects.

The maestro must give way, Farrar insists. Why? "I am a star," Farrar explains.

Toscanini's reply varies by version. Met historian Martin Mayer quotes the *New York American*'s transcription: "The stars are all in the heavens, mademoiselle. You are but a plain artist, and you must obey my direction."

George Marek's biography of Toscanini gives a colorful alternate: "Geraldine, the stars are in heaven. Here we are all artists, good artists and bad artists. You are a bad artist."

There is even a German version, complete with a pun that doesn't translate back into English and that could not possibly have come out of Toscanini: "Ein Star is für mich ein Vogel": "A star(ling) is to me a bird."

And did Farrar truly reply, as Francis Robinson recalls, "The public pays to see my face, not your back"?

Certainly, there was some contretemps between the two, and Toscanini did speak of "the stars in the heavens" or something like, because Farrar referred to the incident in her second book. In any case, the two settled their differences and made music.

In fact, they became lovers.

Reunion

Toscanini's involvement with Farrar threatened to imperil his marriage, and he decided to take his family back to Italy. The lovers' parting was rough but their memory stayed fond, and some time after Toscanini visited Farrar for dinner. It was a lavish one: for hors d'oeuvre, Farrar served caviar.

"I slept with that woman for seven years," Toscanini said to a friend. "Wouldn't you think that she'd remember that I hate fish?"

He's Had a Highball

Cio-Cio-San was Farrar's most successful role at the Met, her most constant part in a most popular opera. Others might sing Carmen or

Marguerite, two Farrar specialties. But one attempted a Met *Butterfly* at one's peril.

Naturally, Victor wanted to record highlights of the Met production, and duly trucked Farrar, Louise Homer, Enrico Caruso, and Antonio Scotti to Camden, New Jersey, to preserve their portrayals. But, according to opera legend, Caruso turned up for the recording of the love duet somewhat inebriated, and an offended or amused Farrar improvised commentative English lyrics, and Caruso responded in kind.

Impossible. The Met's two greatest stars sparring into the acoustic horn? The lines Farrar and Caruso supposedly revised are Butterfly's "Sì, per la vita!" and Pinkerton's "Vieni, vieni!," just before the reprise of the big tune that closes the first act. As legend tells us, at this point Farrar sang, "He's had a highball!" and Caruso responded, "I had two!," losing a syllable of the original line.

The disc Victor issued, DM 110, finds the two singing these lines as Puccini set them. Yet the legend persists. It is thought that the interpolations were made, but in an early, rejected take. Victor never issued it—but some aficionado apparently did. It has been heard. Farrar does seem to sing "He's had a highball,"—sort of—but Caruso responds with the assigned "Vieni, vieni!" Perhaps the highball dulled his sense of humor.

Farrar and the Geese

The role of the Goosegirl in Engelbert Humperdinck's *Königskinder* joined Butterfly and the *Tannhäuser* Elisabeth on Farrar's list of the great Farrar parts. She thought Humperdinck's music achingly beautiful. For the Met public, who supported the work for a little era, the music was secondary to the fun of watching Farrar handle her corps of trained geese. Humperdinck, who had come over for the Met premiere, was taken aback; he had anticipated nothing more enchanting than stuffed animals. Using live ones was Farrar's idea, and at her persuasive request a team of them was drilled to respond to the soprano as if she were the dear little queen of their secret club.

The geese have little to do over the course of the evening; their key scene came just after the curtain rose on the sight of the goosegirl, Farrar, humming to herself as the animals patter about and gather close, entranced by her song. A bit later, she would clap her hands to call them to her, and they came, waddling about her as she asked, "Gefall' ich euch?": Do you like me? Did they? Did Fafner like treasure? It was a picture Met patrons loved: their Geraldine captivating the animal kingdom as she had captured New York.

Obviously, the picture could only be painted with carefully mustered geese. As the story runs, the Met gave a *Königskinder* outside the official precincts, in Brooklyn in one version, Chicago or Philadelphia in others. For some reason, no one thought to bring along the trained geese, and unprepared amateurs were rented, as one hires local supers to carry spears in *Aida*.

The geese behaved well enough when they were deposited on stage, and waited patiently behind the curtain during the orchestral prelude. But when the curtain rose and Farrar went into her humming tune, the birds began to honk and flap their wings, then rushed all over the stage in an effort to get away from the noise. Ever the artiste, Farrar decided to play it, petting and trying to soothe them; but the geese sought only to escape. A few of them found their way into the wings, one fell into the orchestra pit, and one attacked the Witch (who enters after the humming song). Worse yet, they continued to gabble behind the scenes, evading stagehands who tried to round them up. Now and then throughout the first act, a goose would come rampaging onto the stage, utter sounds perilous to the appreciation of Humperdinck, and career off again, while Farrar and her colleagues tried to keep *Königskinder*'s fairytale sweetness deft and fleet.

It wasn't easy. A Prince wanders through the forest to the Witch's dwelling and engages the goosegirl in love duet. Yet he had only to present Farrar with a caressing phrase and a goose would come quacking and grouching behind him, on its way from one would-be captor stage right to another stage left. Let Farrar initiate a *tendresse,* and half the flock would come rushing in, race around her, and go out whence they came. Not till the act ended and the curtain had fallen could the backstage personnel take the geese out of the opera.

The story belongs to opera's oral tradition, passed from generation to generation by opera's people. Did it really happen? Well, if you cast geese in your opera, it's bound to.

Why Farrar Tried Carmen

It was critic Henry Finck's idea. Think how aptly Farrar's sensual realism suited Bizet's gypsy! And with the usual soprano's higher options in the line, it would suit her vocally as well.

But by this time Farrar had learned a secret of maintaining opera stardom: sing only those roles you can make uniquely yours. Gone, now, were her Violetta and Marguerite and Manon, those championship parts in which each newcomer challenges the reigning power as sharpshooters call out the local gunslinger. Now Farrar was Butterfly, Zazà, the

Goose Girl, Madame Sans-Gêne: "Gerry roles" in which none could top her. As for Carmen, Farrar told Finck that Calvé could not be equaled, and that was that.

Finck insisted.

Farrar held firm.

"Very well," says Finck. "I am going to suggest in the *Post* that the fascinating Lucrezia Bori, who resembles you so strikingly in many ways, should do it."

Not long after, Farrar changed her tune: to the Habañera.

Farrar Entertains at a Party

All performers are irritated by partygivers who expect them to perform on request. Some give in and make the best of it; some politely resist. Farrar met the nuisance head on. Once a hostess said, "Dear little songbird, do please sing that heavenly *Butterfly* entrance, I so seldom hear it." Whereupon the fearless Geraldine rose to leave, telling the woman, "I am so sorry, but if you would arrive in your box before the middle of the second act, and stop chattering, you *would* hear it—in the opera house, where it belongs!"

Why Farrar Did Not Take Up the Theatre When She Left Opera, in Her Own Words

"I might be tempted by [David] Belasco's offers," she told Henry Finck. "But one doesn't become Sarah [Bernhardt] of the Celestial Voice overnight because one gets weary of the Metropolitan and its cacophony. Twenty-odd years of slavish prostration to the lyric art is by no means a recommendation to evolve a dramatic genius. One would be more apt to evoke the caustic comment from singers: 'she's better in the movies,' and from actresses: 'she's better in the opera.' Personally, I think I *am* better away from it all."

AMELITA GALLI-CURCI

Galli-Curci found herself in South America in 1916, cut off from Europe by fear of U-boats and without an engagement. She decided to chance a trip north to the Met: and here her legend begins. It has become rather factored over the years, with contradictory versions. In one, she sang for Gatti-Casazza; and sang, as she frequently did, flat. In another, she did *not* sing; but inquiries were made, on both sides. Galli-Curci asks if the Met would be interested. Gatti asks what is she like? But he asks Caruso, who has just sung with her in Buenos Aires, and says she was a flop. Was she indeed? Or was Caruso getting his own back because at one rehearsal the pianist failed to arrive and Galli-Curci sat in for him, playing a faultless accompaniment while heeding the singers and conductor *and* singing the heroine? Naturally, this got the soprano a lot of company attention. Naturally, this annoyed Caruso. But would he, so comradely, have minded that Galli-Curci helped out at the keyboard? After all, she originally was trained as a pianist. What part of which version are we to believe?

At least it is certain that the Met was well stocked with coloraturas when Galli-Curci arrived in New York, that she moved on to Chicago, and that there, at what was supposed to be a humdrum matinee of *Rigoletto,* Galli-Curci had little more than to slip onstage, look dear, and open her mouth to enjoy one of the biggest sensations in opera history. The audience was so enthusiastic that the company director came backstage at the next intermission to renegotiate Galli-Curci's contract—at double her set salary.

The soprano's success was virtually designed—coerced, even—by her manager Charles Wagner. Playing her Chicago press against New York curiosity, working with Victor in the marketing of Galli-Curci's records, and teasing the Met with concerts hither and yon in the northeast, beyond the reach of critics but close enough to set gossip going among the vagabond cognoscenti, Wagner built Galli-Curci's fame into such proportion that, provided her voice held up, she must take the Met as she took Chicago.

She did, at first, and remained at least enjoyable, though the New York critics quickly tired of her wayward intonation and lack of characterological gusto. She was a relic in her own time, the last of the Patti coloraturas, plying old repertory in the tactful old manner that Farrar and Garden had made obsolete. Entirely self-taught, with a sweet girlish timbre, a dullish middle register, and an amusing top, Galli-Curci had nothing special to offer her era; her Met predecessors Frieda Hempel and Maria Barrientos sang a wider repertory with greater éclat.

But Galli-Curci was a great recording artist. Her discs were effective souvenirs of Galli-Curci live, for, being neither a fascinating performer nor the bearer of a truly sensual tone, she came through nicely at home. Soon enough, the process of acquiring records to recall the theatre experience reversed itself: many people bought Galli-Curci's records first, loved them at first hearing, and began to attend her performances to see what the voice looked like, hear the eyes, so to say.

If only she could have controlled that famous flatness of tone, which worsened over the years; or expanded her repertory. But she lacked both the voice and the temperament for the contemporary roles that Farrar and Garden made so much of, and after battling the flatness for years she at last gave it up as insuperable, something genetic, perhaps, a part of her. Sadly, this proved true. The flatness had been a symptom of a goiter condition, and eventually Galli-Curci had to undergo an operation. She came out fine: she, not the voice. After an unsuccessful comeback as Mimì in her beloved and loving Chicago, twenty years after that amazing *Rigoletto*, Galli-Curci retired, to sit at the piano day after day, working toward a resuscitation of her voice and a second career.

The voice never came back.

Galli-Curci's First Rave Review

Though young Amelita was studying piano with dedication, the keyboard's percussive quality annoyed her. It had no true legato, as a singer would, so the girl took to singing along with her Mozart sonatas and Chopin preludes, filling in the sustained line that stood beyond the piano's reach.

On the day that she came home from the conservatory with a gold medal, she favored a family friend with her unique duet. "Lita," said the man, "as a pianist you will have an excellent career, but as a singer you will have a great one!"

The friend was Pietro Mascagni.

A Boycott

As a native of Milan, Galli-Curci naturally had her eye on La Scala from the start of her singing career. Very early on, she decided to put herself forward for the title role in *La Sonnambula,* ready and waiting on the *cartellone* for the coming season.

Or no, not waiting: Rosina Storchio had been cast. Perhaps Mingardi, La Scala's chief, was simply trying to maintain relations when he offered Galli-Curci the very secondary role of Lisa. Mistake. "Caro Mingardi," said Galli-Curci. "Don't forget this: I shall never put my feet in this theatre again."

Easier said than done: but Galli-Curci did it. To embroider the revenge, she made a point of singing in other Milanese houses; this merely needled Mingardi. Not till her spectacular American success was Galli-Curci able to sew it all up. La Scala, now under new management, sent the soprano a sealed contract with the roles and fee left to her to fill in as she chose. She duly sent the contract back to them.

Unopened.

A Soprano's Credo

A tenor with a vociferous claque had been sharing his calls with Galli-Curci, when suddenly he urged her to go out alone. How generous— but Galli-Curci knew he would in turn take a solo bow so his hirelings could shake the theatre with their cheers. "No, thank you," she said. "I make my reputation while the curtain is up, not while it is down."

McCormack Gets Tough

Thrilled that her New York appearances repeated her Chicago success, Galli-Curci decided to settle in America and put her haphazard European career behind her, along with her unsympathetic husband, Luigi Curci, Marchese di Simeri. To legalize this act of cultural transformation, the soprano took out citizenship papers.

Meanwhile, John McCormack was planning to give a concert in the gigantic Hippodrome, make a fortune, and hand it over to veterans' charities. He invited Galli-Curci, but she claimed that she was too tired.

"I am sorry to hear that you are tired," McCormack fired back. "I am tired, too. But so are the soldiers and sailors in whose honor I asked you to sing. So I am sending your telegram of refusal to Washington, D.C. Maybe they will think you are too tired to become an American citizen."

If this seems harsh, it should be remembered that the years during and just after World War I were marked with a tense patriotism—and that McCormack also was in the process of being naturalized, and thus may have felt more strongly than birthright Americans on such matters as servicemen's benefit concerts. In any case, Galli-Curci's second husband, her accompanist Homer Samuels, was American, so she became a citizen after all.

Persuasive High Notes

High in the Catskills was Galli-Curci's retreat Sul Monte (On the Mountain), where she would rest, dream, and practice, letting the backstage of the opera world carry on its intrigues and scandals without her. One morning some laborers were working on the road outside her house while she was going over some music, and at length the foreman knocked on her door.

"You the lady who's been singing all morning?" he asked.

"Yes. Have you enjoyed it?"

"Look ma'am, it's not that, exactly. I just wanted to ask if you'd mind not hanging onto that top note so long next time. My men have knocked off for lunch three times already."

KIRSTEN FLAGSTAD

Flagstad was the no-nonsense diva, the kind who, asked if there was a secret to singing Wagnerian heroines, would give a direct, concise answer. If she lacked the fervor of her contemporary Frida Leider or her successor Birgit Nilsson—the involvement in those heroines that brings a ferocious sense of dishonor to Isolde's Narration or abandon to Brünnhilde's Oath on the Spear—still the very majesty of Flagstad's voice lent her portrayals majesty. From the afternoon of her Met debut, on February 2, 1935, as Sieglinde, Flagstad was set apart as an artist uniquely endowed to sing Wagner, to establish a standard of power and beauty in these parts that no other soprano, perhaps, would be able to match.

No doubt it was Flagstad's long service in lyric roles that allowed her vocal production to develop. After twenty years of Nedda, Micaëla, Mimì, and Marguerite, she had developed her tone to Wagnerian roundness, a great column of sound that faltered only on the highest notes, and that not really until the last ten years of her life. Such are the demands of the Wagnerian repertory that, after the days of Jacques Urlus and Jean de Reszke, of Olive Fremstad and Johanna Gadski, critical and popular admiration tended to center on single specialists in the great roles—such as Friedrich Schorr's Hans Sachs and Wotan, or Lauritz Melchior's Tristan and Siegfried. The vocal and dramatic demands in this repertory are too great for more than one expert to emerge in a generation.

In Flagstad's time, there was a small corps of essential sopranos— yet did any of the others challenge Flagstad's vocal mastery? Even Leider, famous in Flagstad's parts over a decade before Flagstad sang any of them, eventually ran into trouble encompassing Wagner's range at full power. At a Met *Walküre* in 1933, Leider suffered such difficulty staying with Brünnhilde's music that one of the third-act Valkyrie team, Dorothy Manski, stood by in the wings after her exit to assist if there was an emergency. Sure enough, Leider literally ran out of voice just as she began "War es so schmälich," her great scene with Wotan that leads to the Farewell and Magic Fire Music. Manski spelled Leider from the wings, so adroitly that only those in the first rows were aware of Leider's dilemma. After a few bars, Leider took up her part again, and by sheer will summoned the dead voice back to life. She did not croak her way through the act: she *sang* it, with desperate grandeur, as if anything less than total intensity would allow her sound to dry up again. The effort must have told horribly on her instrument.

Flagstad never ran into such troubles, though after she retired from stage work she cut down on the most daunting passages. When Decca-London Records wanted to capture Flagstad's Brünnhilde in a complete *Walküre* in stereo, she balked. She was willing to record Act Three separately and the Todesverkündigung in Act Two, and would also revive her Met debut role of Sieglinde in a complete Act One. But she would not attempt the "Ho-yo-to-ho," with its perilous high notes. Flagstad was not only adamant but sensitive on this point. She broke off relations with EMI when news leaked out that, on Flagstad's recording of *Tristan und Isolde* under Wilhelm Furtwängler, Elisabeth Schwarzkopf had supplied the two Bs in the Narration and the two Cs in the love duet.

As many have pointed out, when one deals with a voice like Flagstad's, proficiency in high notes is a small matter, especially as high-note trouble is a failing common to veteran Wagnerian sopranos. Throwing out so much weight so constantly in the middle register tends to weaken the top. This, of course, is what preserves the lyric soprano's high notes over a long career. Singing roles like Lily Pons'— Lakmé, Lucia, Gilda, and so on—will not abuse a well-trained instrument. Isolde and Brünnhilde will.

On the other hand, the sensual glory of those giant voices rolling out to fill a theatre is part of Wagner's attraction, and here Flagstad was indispensable. Not only did she revitalize the Wagnerian repertory in America; she kept the Met solvent in its dark days of the late Depression, on one hand by singing two performances a week to a box-office sellout, on the other hand by keeping her salary demands modest. Like Farrar and Caruso a generation before, Flagstad and her constant partner Lauritz Melchior instituted a fixed Met chemistry, an act that had only to appear to make a performance classic. The sound of those two in full cry is still the first memory in every aficionado heart that was there when they were. Covent Garden, too, treasures the recollection—Flagstad and Melchior in *Tristan* under Fritz Reiner and Thomas Beecham in the late 1930s is said to have been the *Tristan* of the century.

It is interesting that neither of these two made their reputations at Bayreuth, then as now the home of the dedicated Wagnerian and the place where a great Isolde and Tristan affirm their greatness. Both sang there, but early on, Flagstad in small parts and as Sieglinde and Gutrune, Melchior somewhat before his days of brilliance. By the late 1930s, she was based in New York and he was too outraged by Hitler to consider singing in Germany. Then came the war, and when Wagner's grandsons reopened the Festival, a new generation had grown up to replace the old-timers and try out Wieland Wagner's experiments in acting Wagner as well as singing him. Though Flagstad's voice held up in all its color and light long enough for her to launch Decca-London's complete *Ring* project, learning Fricka especially for *Das Rheingold;* and though she virtually died working, as founding chief of the Norwegian National Opera, Flagstad was by the 1950s somewhat outdated, a little venerable.

Yet many say she was literally irreplaceable: has not even been challenged. Again, it is the voice, that effortlessly penetrating sound that struck one as a crashing wave of recklessly pure beauty. The clarity of Flagstad! *That* was irreplaceable. She came to the Met unheralded, at that mere second choice to Nanny Larsen-Todsen, famous for the Bayreuth Isolde she sang under Toscanini. Larsen was hired, but Larsen cancelled, and the Met accepted Flagstad, who—it is scarcely believable, though we have heard this a hundred times—was on the verge of retirement. She first raised her voice in the house at the dress rehearsal of *Die Walküre*, and before the second act had begun, news swept through the building that something astonishing was happening on stage. Flagstad's first night was a great triumph (though Gatti had to send someone around to the press room to drag the critics out of their nightly bull session to attend the new *Wunderstimme*). As the season continued, she began to immerse herself, role by role, in the character gallery she would come to own—Isolde, Kundry, Brünnhilde, Senta.

She sang little else: Beethoven's Leonore, Gluck's Alceste, and Purcell's Dido; and she as well specialized in what might be called Nordic song, trying to popularize Grieg and Dørumsgaard between sections of Schubert and Schumann. Other Wagnerians roamed more widely. Leider sang the Marschallin and Donna Anna, Marjorie Lawrence a stupendous Salome, Germaine Lubin a rota of classic French parts, Nilsson a whole swatch of the heroic-dramatic Italian material—and Lilli Lehmann sang everything. Flagstad was the essential Wagnerian: taking her Dido as impulsive curiosity, her entire repertory, once she discovered her forte, was either Wagner parts or parts that led up to Wagner; Gluck and Beethoven being resonant inspirations in the conception of the Wagnerian heroine.

Flagstad's supremacy as an artist has been contested by those who resented her lack of theatrical bite. They thought her regal placidity, her efficient aplomb, insufficient in bringing Wagner's tortured women to life. Her Kundry was nothing like the wild sinner Wagner imagined. She learned the words and music—in a few weeks, on urgent demand—and marched out and sang; did she stop to consider what Kundry has done, what is in her mind, who are her friends and enemies?

The official line on Flagstad's character—her supremacy, let us say, as a person—has not been contested. All agree that she was professional, pleasant if cold, loyal, easily (and usually permanently) offended, and very stubborn: all in all, rather Norwegian. She was a great patriot, despite her long years away from home, bristling whenever anyone Wagnerized her name in pronunciation as "Flagshtat." "I am very attached to my country," she told Lanfranco Rasponi, "passionately so, really, and I love the winters there where no light transpires and the summers when darkness does not exist." She spoke with haunted gravity of the North Sea, that most Wagnerian of waters, of its beauty and terror. "I am afraid of man," she said, "never of nature."

And men gave her trouble, vilifying her for a supposed Nazi sympathy of hearsay and invention. She had returned to Norway in 1941, and had no contact with the Nazis, but her husband, it appears, was close to Vidkun Quisling, and died in prison shortly after peacetime cleaned fascism out of Norway. With her home life thus shattered—her one child, a daughter, lived in America—Flagstad decided to take up the stage again, and some of her American appearances were harried by pickets and a nasty press. Here, as we shall see, her Norwegian stubbornness supported her: she had done nothing wrong, so she held her ground and sang, no matter what anyone did to silence her. This, too, was part of the Flagstad phenomenon, a secret lying dormant in the placidity and aplomb: determination.

Flagstad's secret to singing Wagnerian heroines, by the way, is "Always wear comfortable shoes."

Enter Isolde

Late for a rehearsal of the third act of *Tristan* at Covent Garden, Flagstad pulled up in her taxicab just as the company had reached the moment for her first line, sung offstage, as Isolde rushes up from her ship to the dying Tristan. As it happened, the huge doors at the back of the house were open, and when Flagstad heard her cue, she paid her driver, turned to face the opera house, and let loose with the response, "Tristan! Geliebter!" In the flower market from which the opera house takes its name, all business was suspended in amazement as the glorious voice rang out, but onstage not a beat was missed. The Tristan, Set Svanholm, sang his reply as Flagstad calmly walked into the house through the back doors and gained the stage precisely on cue.

How Flagstad Performs *Die Walküre* in Gothenburg

Peter Brook, Covent Garden's Director of Productions and *enfant terrible*-in-residence, made it his mission to sweep away the old, anti-theatrical customs. But it was with a certain bemusement the Brook encountered the most outdated custom of all, that wherein the star sends some minion to the theatre to inform the staff as to Madame's placement in each scene of the piece at hand. In one of the last such events in opera history, Kirsten Flagstad's manager took the incredulous Brook through Flagstad's Brünnhilde.

"At this point," he said, somewhere along the way, "Madame Flagstad comes to the front of the stage and turns left." A droll recollection struck him. "Except for one time in Gothenburg—when, for *some* reason, she turned *right!*"

"I see," Brook replied. "The Gothenburg Variation!"

Brook's pun, of course, refers to Bach's *Goldberg Variations*.

Flagstad Sees It Through

When Flagstad made her first concert tour in America after World War II, in 1947, authorities feared harassment not only from pickets outside

theatres but by hecklers in the auditoriums. Her first recital, in Carnegie Hall, was not assaulted, but there were reports that someone in
Philadelphia was prepared to spend a fortune to drive her out of the
city.

When the time came, the Academy of Music was swamped with
demonstrators outside and littered with a group of college-age kids,
distributed throughout the house in seats that had been bought in one
huge clump. A suspicious ticket-seller had registered the seat numbers,
but the police could do nothing till trouble actually started. Just before
they were to go out, Flagstad's accompanist Edwin McArthur told her
to leave the stage if anything happened.

Flagstad refused. "I'm not a bit afraid," she said. "I'm not going to
let them win, whoever they are."

The booing caught her by surprise. In Europe they whistle to dis-
courage you, so the odd noise was more puzzling than offensive. The
stinkbomb, too, was bewildering. Flagstad hadn't seen it thrown—didn't
even know there was such a thing. She did notice a very odd smell, but
put it down to concert nerves.

The shout of "Na-zi!," broken into two distinct syllables, was unmistakeable, as was someone's response of "I dare you to repeat that!"
and the immediate repetition. (Was this the confrontation of a rat and
a Flagstad loyalist, or the setup of two confederates?) The consistency
of the booing, too, was hard to miss, as it ran from the last note of
each number right up to the first note of the next. The more they tried
to dishearten her the more she dug in her heels. "You know how stubborn a Norwegian can get," she said later.

She sang the concert thinking that in one sense the harassment was
for the best: "Now it's come out in the open, where I can face it." But
Flagstad had never been legally charged, so how could she be cleared?
She would simply have to fight her way through it, through such con-
frontations as these, her accusers anonymous, dimly glimpsed; and the
accusations a headline of rumor, like that shouted "Na-zi!"

As Flagstad gained the wings after her first set, a policeman backstage told her, "You sure got guts, lady."

Critic's Choice

Ernest Newman had a special interest in Wagner, and heard most of
the great Wagner singers from the very early 1900s on. This is quite a
panorama: Elsas melting and tense, Sentas desperate and convinced, Isoldes intimate and epic, Brünnhildes vital and tragic, Kundrys sensual

and robust—Lehmann, Nordica, Gadski, Fremstad, Kurt, Leider . . .
And whom, first of all, did Newman prefer?

"Thank God," he said, "I have lived long enough to hear Flagstad."

Conductor's Pleasure

A slightly different reading of the Flagstad phenomenon was taken by
Hans Knappertsbusch when he conducted her recording of the first act
of *Die Walküre*. Learning that three hours of taping time remained in
which to get down a mere sixteen minutes, "Kna" asked his producer
John Culshaw what they were to do with the rest of the session.

Culshaw reckoned they might go on with new material if Flagstad
didn't get tired.

"Tired?" said Knappertsbusch. "She won't get tired. She's built like
a battleship!"

GERMAINE LUBIN

If primitive peoples punished scapegoats in times of danger, to pro-
piate evil forces, civilized peoples punish theirs after the danger is over,
unleashing evil forces of their own. Post-World War II France is a case
in point: in the eagerness to arrest and denounce, many innocent people were branded as collaborators. This held true particularly in the
performing arts, where nearly anyone who had appeared on a stage
in occupied France and had a personal enemy could count on being
charged, even punished.

Germaine Lubin was one of the prime victims, because she sang not
only at the Opéra during the War, but in Berlin and Bayreuth in the
late 1930s. A handsome woman with a gorgeous instrument, Lubin
was an outstanding Wagnerian, with a personal warmth, an epic vulnerability, that none of her rivals had. Naturally the Wagner family
and Nazi leaders wanted her for key productions of *Tristan* and *Parsifal*. Not only was she possibly the best Isolde and Kundry, but too
many gifted foreigners had refused to perform in Germany. Toscanini's boycott of Bayreuth, and later Salzburg, embarrassed the Nazis;
thus Lubin became a political as well as an artistic pawn.

The only crime Lubin committed was exercising a strong will. She
alienated many of her colleagues with her prideful sense of self and
her certainty that she was the greatest French singer of her time. Thus
many people were gunning for her after the war ended. For every musician who came forward to attest that Lubin had used her prestige
with the Nazis to save his life, there were five anonymous denunciations. She was arrested and freed several times over on ludicrous
charges. Because she was so famous, Lubin was singled out to pay for

all collaborators, to redeem France. At length, she was sentenced to
five years of National Disgrace, during which she was not permitted
to sing. Unfortunately, these would have been her last five good years
in opera, so there was no point in attempting a comeback later on.
Lubin turned to teaching, and to reminiscing in bitter despair. She was
never silent, and has not forgiven.

She was never cleared, either. Popular memory and even some his-
tories still name her as a traitor. But some Parisians recall, with a sorrowful thrill, the graffito that appeared one day on the wall of the
Opéra—"Rendez-nous Germaine Lubin": Bring back Germaine Lubin.

Silence!

In Paul Dukas's *Ariane et Barbe-Bleue,* Bluebeard's fifth wife finds her
predecessors imprisoned in the basement of his castle, and offers them
freedom by smashing open a window to reveal a beautiful sunlit meadow
lulled by soughing wind and pounding ocean waves. During a performance at the Opéra, Lubin was distracted at this moment by stagehands chattering loudly behind the scenes, and, when she had broken
open the miraculous window, leaned out as to listen to the wind and
the waves. Actually, she was telling the stagehands, "Messieurs, if you
don't shut up immediately I shall stop singing, approach the public, and
tell them why."

They shut up.

A Dinner with Friends

"In all my life," Hitler told her, "I have never seen and heard such an
Isolde."

This was Bayreuth, summer of 1939. Lubin had sung her first Isolde,
and the Führer had come backstage to offer his personal congratulations and express his regret that she was not attending the usual reception at Wahnfried.

Lubin chose instead to meet German friends in a restaurant near the
theatre. When she entered, the entire place sprang to its feet and gave
her an ovation. Her table partners did better yet: they repeated to her
Hitler's proposals for Operation Lubin. She would stay in Germany,
have whatever she wanted, and sing everything forever. "I would do
anything for her," Hitler had vowed. "After all, I have already given
her my photograph!"

Lubin broke into laughter at this nonsense. "Tell the Führer," she
said, "that I want nothing from him—except to be left in peace."

Silence at the table. Utter silence.

An Old Friend

In 1973, a distinguished-looking man approached Lubin during an intermission at the Opéra.

"You remember me, Monsieur?" she asked.

"Madame, there are faces one does not forget."

Thinking of her five years of "degradation nationale," Lubin replied, "It was not so long ago that you seemed not to know me at all."

He fled.

MARIE POWERS

An unusual-looking mezzo of dynamic presence, Powers was the sort of singer who would have had difficulty surviving in the mid-1800s, but who might have made a niche for herself in the early 1900s in character cameos, and who, in the mid-1900s, was able to secure a little fame in character leads. The reason lies in the difference between twentieth-century opera and the opera of Patti's era, when lovely tone and dextrous technique mattered more than presence, and when repertory didn't offer enough character parts to build a career on. After 1900, opera expanded its vocal and characterological range. Ancient operas with character parts—Monteverdi and Lully, for example—began to be heard again, and new operas often gave a great opportunity to sopranos who didn't sound like sweethearts or princesses. Then, too, opera was more theatrical in these later days; by 1950, it actually *needed* the presence of a Marie Powers.

She found a berth in Gian Carlo Menotti's operas especially, singing the title role in *The Medium* and mother parts in *The Consul* and *Maria Golovin*. She even recorded the first two—would a Marie Powers have been invited into the recording studio in 1900? Unlikely. It was not as successful a career as it might have been; the following stories suggest why. But in her prime Powers made her contribution to the vitalizing of American opera production, and to the growing belief that America's best instincts in music theatre are developed on Broadway—where, in fact, Powers introduced her Madame Flora and Mother Sorel—and not in opera houses.

The Artiste Greets Her Fans

In the 1940s, Powers signed on with the impresario Fortune Gallo, who toured the American hinterland with the old warhorses. Avoiding the big cities, Gallo concentrated on small towns starved for opera, where the audiences could be extremely enthusiastic.

Powers enjoyed the warm receptions. She was getting on in age, and the goal of important stardom was beginning to fade into the hope that she could just continue earning a living in music. There were nights, then, when she felt like something less than a great prima donna.

On one of these nights, after an endless day, weary and dispirited, Powers came out of the stage door to find a horde of opera lovers with programs for her to sign and hands to shake. All she wanted was to make it to her boarding house and creep into bed. But the diva in her told her she must do *something*.

So she drew herself up, put on her grandest manner, announced, "I'll choose *three!*," grabbed the hands, pens, and programs of the nearest three people, shook, signed, and swept through the alley to her bus stop.

Back at the stage door, a dazzled crowd stood transfixed. "Now, *that*," said one of them, "is an opera singer!"

The Artiste Considers

Two idealistic young actors, Chandler Cowles and Efrem Zimbalist, Jr. (son of the violinist, later of television and Hollywood), decided to bring Menotti's double bill of horror and comedy, *The Medium* and *The Telephone*, to Broadway in 1947. Claramae Turner, the contralto who created the squalid heroine of *The Medium*, decided not to come along, and Menotti searched desperately for a replacement. The part is the very center of the evening—a weak Madame Flora promised certain failure.

It was the writer Lanfranco Rasponi who sent Marie Powers to Menotti—but the singer who appeared at the appointed audition was not Marie Powers, but one Madame Crescentini, a diva of formidable *grandezza*. She is interested, yes; she will think about it. She has sung in many important theatres; she must consider her career. Opera on Broadway; this is strange, this is dangerous. She is gala. She cannot be rushed.

Suddenly Madame Crescentini plopped onto a sofa and said, "Oh, for God's sake, let's cut this out. I've got exactly forty cents in my pocket and I may as well say yes. Of course I'll do it."

She made her reputation in it.

The Artiste Proposes a Sacrifice

Powers eventually proved a quite difficult proposition. She was a genuine madcap—during *The Medium*'s Broadway run she commuted to the Ethel Barrymore Theatre on roller skates—but a turbulent pro as well, obsessed with her billing, her fame, her Contribution to the roles she played. Madame Flora and Menotti to an extent created Marie Powers; but by the time Powers played the Mother in Menotti's *The*

Consul, she had begun to act as if she had created *The Medium* and Menotti.

Like *The Medium, The Consul* was produced on Broadway, in 1950, and Powers openly resented playing a secondary role—Patricia Neway, as Magda Sorel, was the work's protagonist. Powers did have a special moment all to herself, a lullaby scene sung to her dying grandchild. But Neway not only had the work's biggest part (she is scarcely off the stage at all), but the most promising solo, "To this we've come," a moving indictment of the world bureaucracy, especially pertinent at the time, as Eastern Europe fell to the Soviets and many displaced or otherwise vulnerable people attempted to emigrate to the West.

In despair at seeing this musical and dramatic plum fall to another, Powers devised, during the rehearsal period, an eccentric revision of Menotti's score, by which Powers could sing "To this we've come" instead of Neway. Menotti resisted, and Powers and he went into a screaming fight, in Italian, to paint traditional Broadway *geschrei* with an operatic *colorito.* Finally Powers said, "It means so much to me, *caro,* that I have taken sacred vows that if you will give this aria to me, I will never again drink, I will never again smoke, and I will never again have sex."

To which Menotti went into a laughing fit that rendered him nearly helpless. At last he found his voice. "It's not worth it, Marie," he said.

MARIA CALLAS

Because she worked best in an atmosphere of challenge and backstage intrigue, a born daredevil; because she was hot copy in society dish columns; because she suffered as many disasters as triumphs, sometimes both at once; because her glamor was contentious and her talent arrogant . . . in all: because she lived skating the blade, left the stage after a mere ten years of glory, failed in "retirement careers" as movie actress and stage director, made a pathetically atrocious comeback, and died too soon, Callas's importance as a historical figure is not clearly understood. Musicians know it. The aficionados know it. But the one who knew it best, and who best articulated the principles of Callas's historical status, is dead: Maria Callas.

In essence, Callas's mission was to turn opera back from singing as lovely noise to singing as expression, of text, character, mood. When it was new, in 1600, opera was an intensely musical declamation of poetry. The libretto was all-important, the music virtually secondary, and there were no star singers. By the 1700s, as Angelica Catalani's husband pointed out for us in these pages, all one needed was a star "and four or five puppets." Opera was singers. Callas proposed a compromise. The stars would remain, but instead of raising their lovely noise they would express, personify, sing *on the libretto*. In short, Callas redirected opera forward to the past: to the golden age of Malibran.

Coaxing an instrument out of an imperfect vocal endowment, she made her entree in heroic parts—Gioconda, Turandot, Kundry, Isolde. But she was determined to edge into authentic bel canto, into the great roles of Malibran's time and into some others that led up to or followed them—Médée and Giulia; Lucia, Amina, and Elvira; Violetta and Hélène; and, *sanctum sanctorum*, Norma. Callas would neither peck and chirp her way through them nor hurl them forth in a messy lump, as had been the practice of late. Callas would sing these parts with a full battery of technique and line, accent and color.

She retrieved the lost ideal of the compleat singer, as adept in plangent lyricism as in vehement utterance, with a classical plastique of fierce elegance. "It is soprano, basta!" she insisted in her Juilliard master classes. One voice, many roles. She taught a dedication to refocus opera; by her example, she made her colleagues acknowledge that, in this most complex of arts, only the best is acceptable. She was exceptional, yet she acted as if she were the norm. And, in her view, she was. She remains the line of comparison every soprano must meet.

Callas's dedication was the wonder of her peers. Her Manhattan childhood was not one enriched by the love and lore of arts and letters, and during World War II she was isolated in Athens, whither her mother had moved with Maria and her older sister Jackie. All Callas had to draw on when she launched her career at the Verona Arena in 1947 was some parlous stage experience in a cultural backwater and lessons from Elvira de Hidalgo, a coloratura of the old school who had retired to Athens. Not much, in all, in the way of musical nurturing: an apprenticeship, no more.

Yet once Callas got to Italy she soaked up musicianship from her maestros and theatricality from her directors. And somehow, instinctively, she had conjured up much of her private golden age all by herself. For suddenly she was teaching style, now in Rossini, now in Bellini, now in Verdi, now in Puccini. Where had she learned it? Her vocal quality—not only the natural sound, but the way in which she used it—was so unusual that she practically had to barge into opera. "That woman will never sing at La Scala," Antonio Ghiringhelli told Gian Carlo Menotti. "Never! *Never!*" Yet Ghiringhelli had to give way in time, and Callas took La Scala. For, once one accustomed one's ear to her Gilda or Mimì, a legion of great coloraturas and lyrics paled in the memory, lost their glitter. And glitter, Callas showed us, was all they had had.

She was a tireless rehearser, always singing full out, always begging the maestro for another runthrough. Fearing that Callas was exhausting herself in preparation for the Scala *Alceste*, director Margherita Wallmann told the soprano to take it easy in the morning; Wallmann would work with the chorus at ten, so Callas wouldn't be needed till noon. But at ten the next day, there was Maria. "You know, Margherita," she said, "it's really better for me to attend your chorus rehearsal. That way, I'll be better prepared when it's my turn. It will give me an idea of your approach."

She was determined to be *assoluta*, the best; this ignited her dedication. Wallmann also directed Callas' Scala *Médée*, and conceived an astonishing *coup de théâtre* for the finale: Callas, lying prone on a stairway, head downward, as she lifts her eyes to heaven and sings a powerful invocation to the gods.

"Margherita!" Callas cried. "It's impossible! I'll never be able to do it!" She actually wept.

Wallmann was willing to revise the blocking, but Luigi Oldani, Ghiringhelli's right arm, told Wallmann not to change a thing. "It's terrific," he said. "and la Callas is an ambitious woman. You'll see, she'll do it."

Of course she did.

That determination to be the best not only led Callas on to the impossible, but delivered her as well into a series of feuds and scandals that less driven singers would have been able to avoid. As we shall see in the stories that follow, Callas had never been peaceful when disdained by impresarios or unappreciated by audiences. But in her early years she was not famous enough for the hearsay of this rugged encounter or that bitter retort to travel. Callas was unsung. However, from January 1949, when, at La Fenice in Venice, Callas followed a series of *Walküre* Brünnhildes with the *Puritani* Elvira—from grandest Wagner to most nuanced Bellini—her fame began to spread. After important appearances at the Florence May Festival in 1951, at the opening of La Scala at the end of that year, and at Covent Garden in 1952, Callas became opera's most talked-of figure, as those who had heard her—and those who hadn't—tried to understand why the obviously flawed voice could do such spectacular things.

Fame, alas, puts one's mistakes into bold relief, and Callas seemed to collect a veritable series of scandals just when she had achieved greatest prominence. "Another Callas walkout" was the press cliché of the era, as Callas abandoned a last Scala *Sonnambula* at the 1957 Edinburgh Festival to attend Elsa Maxwell's Venetian ball without explaining that the company had announced Callas for the last performance without her agreement . . . as Callas insulted all Italy in early 1958 by leaving a Rome *Norma* after Act One with no less than the President of Italy, Giovanni Gronchi, in the offended house, having foolishly tried to sing literally without voice . . . as Callas stirred up the volatile Scala public during *Anna Bolena* the following April by hurling Anne Boleyn's most defiant lines into the auditorium—but they loved it, and cheered her, *absolved* her . . . till she managed to insult the Scala's Ghiringhelli and the Met's Bing, the two managers most essential to her career.

Then, too, there was Callas's extremely varied assortment of guides and confidants. To be the best, one must know the best; Callas had ideal teachers in Tullio Serafin, Carlo Maria Giulini, Luchino Visconti, and Franco Zeffirelli. Serafin, a kind of keeper of the flame of Italian opera as conductor and coach, helped Callas make her transition out of the dramatic repertory of Wagner, La Gioconda, and Turandot into bel canto—it was Serafin who pushed Callas into the Venice *Puritani* when she herself had doubts. Giulini stepped into Serafin's role as musical mentor when Callas gained La Scala, and supervised some of her greatest events there—it was Giulini who flouted the house's historic ban on solo curtain calls by sending Callas out alone after their *Traviata,* thereby affirming the gathering feeling that Callas was "la regina della Scala" (Queen of La Scala), incidentally offending the Alfredo, Giuseppe di Stefano, who walked out of the production and briefly joined the chorus of the Callas detractors. Visconti, who with Margherita Wallmann staged Callas's Scala productions, helped refine her *ottocento* plastique, the better to set off her historicism; and Zeffirelli, Visconti's protégé, succeeded Visconti as Giulini did Serafin when the diva made another of her periodic shifts in symbiotic loyalty.

All these were worthy cohorts, complementary to a soprano who was raising opera's standards. But where did Giovanni Battista Meneghini fit in? Where Elsa Maxwell or Aristotle Onassis? Meneghini, Callas's first husband, shielded her in her difficult first years in Italy, when she was overweight, insecure, and unknown. She actually took his name onto her posters, sandwiched between her two, and let him negotiate her contracts, yet he was not the sort of man a Giulini or Visconti willingly socialized with. What must they have been thinking of this alliance? Maxwell, a gossip columnist, was fit to companion show-biz luminaries, not a guardian of opera's first principles. Remember, Callas was one American opera singer who saw herself as a singer of nothing but opera. Grace Moore made "Ciribiribin" her theme song, Helen Traubel sang Romberg in Hollywood and Rodgers and Hammerstein on Broadway, Eileen Farrell sounded the blues, Beverly Sills recorded Herbert and Friml. Callas, though American born and bred, would have none of it; her idea of popular music was Puccini, at least compared with Bellini. And if Callas was Norma, Elsa Maxwell was Little Lulu. How could Callas bear Maxwell and what she represented? Yet she befriended her, took up the international scandal-rag society Maxwell fawned upon. And all this led to Onassis.

When Callas threw Meneghini over for the Greek shipping tycoon, she tossed away her last connection with the stage, with Giulini and Visconti and all that La Scala means to those who keep the flame of Italian opera. For all Meneghini's bluster and backstage paranoia—which directly fed Callas's own—he at least saw Callas as a musician. Onassis saw Callas as a collectible, something, like Winston Churchill, to be displayed on his yacht. Onassis collected Callas on the condition that she give up opera. Tragically, she agreed. After a scant decade of greatness—at that a greatness compromised by the scandals and feuds—Callas accomplished the ultimate walk-out, giving up her entire career.

Callas is a rich source for chronicle, clearly—but a poor one for anecdote. Too much of the boiling diva comes through and too little of the unique talent who, through the baleful beauty of her singing, revivified an entire shelf of classics that had fallen into abuse through misunderstanding. In Berlin, when Callas, Giuseppe di Stefano, and Herbert von Karajan led the Scala company in *Lucia* the audience was so entranced at how this former canary's cage of an opera had been remade into music theatre that it demanded—and got—an encore of the Sextet.

Not only did the era of Callas reinvestigate the familiar; it also rediscovered the forgotten. Much of postwar opera has reclaimed its heritage—*Les Troyens,* for instance, or *Les Vêpres Siciliennes,* or *L'Incoronazione di Poppea.* A major reason was the failure of contemporary composers to fill the theatres with new works. But another reason was Callas. The so-called bel canto *riesumazione* (exhumation) focused attention on the past as a treasure house of art in need of reauthentication. Callas's series of revivals with Wallmann, Visconti, Giulini, Bernstein, and Votto at La Scala in the mid-1950s urged responsibility upon opera in general, and tempted Callas's coevals and successors to test their gifts against hers.

But who remembers Callas for this? She was the wild Greek who dropped a hundred pounds and a dull old husband to become Onassis's chic Parisienne. She was the walk-out queen, fighting with half the opera world, cruelly goading that nice Renata Tebaldi, insulting Italy's President Gronchi by departing *Norma* after the first act, and warring with the impresarios most crucial to her future. Did she not take the most unflattering photograph in opera history backstage in Chicago, after her last Butterfly, when a process server sneaked up with a summons she had been dodging for years and slipped it into her kimono? (At least one witness heard her scream, "I am an angel! You can't do this to me!" She didn't look like an angel—she looked like the picture of Dorian Gray.) Did she not slap the Scala public in the face with Anna Bolena's "Giudici? Ad Anna?" as if to say, *"You* dare to judge *me?"*

What a grasp the woman had, yet what exactions she made on herself. It was as if she realized that glamor mattered so much she must divest herself of her industrial-strength physique if it killed her; as if through feuds she would make herself extraordinary; as if only by not adapting to her ruined instrument could she seem irreplaceable; as if Wallmann or Visconti might advise but Onassis shall command. Why did Callas insist on singing the most difficult roles after she had lost her grip upon them? One does not make one's farewell in *Norma.* Why did Callas let Onassis deny her the stage, so that when she began to consider returning, she was scarcely able to get through anything? How her friends begged her to take the Carmen she had recorded into the theatre. But no: "I'm not going to give some stupid critic," she answered, "the chance to say I've lost my voice." She went out on her old material, onstage in *Tosca* and *Norma* and, too late to be anything but a demoralized wraith pleading for love, in the horrendous worldwide concert tour with di Stefano, artistic meltdown.

Her death, soon after, was a shock; it shouldn't have been. The challenge she had lived on, the dedication, saps one at work and leisure alike. Callas had burned herself out.

Serafin's Recipe for Risotto alla Pilota

In her early years in Italy, Callas followed up her Verona debut with performances in Rome, Naples, Florence, Genoa—in every major city but Milan. Even after her attention-getting tour de force, singing Brünnhilde and Elvira (in *I Puritani*) back to back in Venice in 1949, La Scala's Antonio Ghiringhelli remained hostile to Callas.

It is possible that Ghiringhelli disliked her because she was conductor Tullio Serafin's protégée; Serafin and Ghiringhelli could not abide one another. Still, diplomacy required Ghiringhelli to salute Serafin one night in late 1949 when the two turned up on the same night at Biffi Scala, the celebrated restaurant near the opera house. At the table with Serafin were Callas and her husband Battista Meneghini; Ghiringhelli ignored them, though he knew well who they were.

Oridinarily, Serafin would have traded coolly concise greetings with Ghiringhelli. But this night he tried to be friendly, for, with Callas right there, perhaps conversation might lead very naturally to possibilities for the soprano at La Scala. And so Serafin spoke of *Norma*.

Ghiringhelli had experienced at first hand the world shortage of Normas only the year before. He had staged a disaster around a valiant but miscast Maria Caniglia and, one after the other, three mediocre tenors, and he was not pleased to hear Serafin refer to it, however obliquely.

"To do *Norma* is not as difficult as you think," Ghiringhelli told Serafin as Callas sat by, quietly miserable. "As a matter of fact, I intend to present one that will make history."

"Ah yes? And how do you propose to do that?"

Ghiringhelli had no *Norma* in the works, and all four of them knew it. He blustered and repeated himself—but before he could retreat Serafin said, "I am from Rottanova di Cavarzere, from the environs of Venice. We have a famous rice dish in our area—risotto alla pilota. Do you know what you need to make risotto alla pilota?"

"What do you need?"

"The rice."

Serafin went on to indicate Callas as the rice in the risotto, the singer without whom Ghiringhelli could not give a decent Norma. Ghiringhelli resisted—he let Callas tread the sacred Scala stage the next year, subbing for Renata Tebaldi in *Aida*, but only as a "guest artist"—in other words, an outsider. He did not so much as greet her before the performance or salute her after. But two years later, when Ghiringhelli finally presented Bellini's masterpiece, he used the old recipe favored in Rottanova di Cavarzere: Callas as Norma. Her colleagues were Ebe Stignani, Gino Penno, and Nicola Rossi-Lemeni, but Serafin did not conduct. Though he made recordings with the company, he never raised his baton in performance at La Scala while Ghiringhelli was in charge.

A Slight Disturbance

In Brazil in 1951, Callas was astonished to find her name expunged from the posters advertising her scheduled Toscas. Stalking into the impresario's office, the soprano demanded to know why he had replaced her.

"Because you were lousy the other night."

Grabbing a large bronze paperweight, Callas dared him to repeat that, at the risk of having his skull remodeled.

Luckily, others were present. The impresario deftly waited till Callas was disarmed, then threatened to call the police.

At that, Callas threw herself on her nemesis, smashing him with a knee to the stomach—and this was the early Callas who weighed a tenth of a ton. The impresario moaned, closed his eyes, and collapsed. Probably the right move under the circumstances. Meneghini immediately took Callas's arm and led her out of the office, fearing that the impresario might actually be dead.

Back at the hotel, he asked her, "Don't you think you overdid it?"

Not only did the impresario survive: he sent Callas her performance fees—including those for her cancelled Toscas—and plane tickets for the next trip home. The *next* one.

Callas the Heavyweight

Callas's first complete recording for EMI was *Lucia di Lammermoor*, taped in Florence with Giuseppe di Stefano and Tito Gobbi under Serafin. One day at lunch, Serafin warned Callas that her heavy figure was becoming a problem.

Callas noted that good eating made for good singing. Anyway, she wasn't *that* big.

Gobbi recalled that there was a weighing machine just outside the restaurant, and the company repaired to it to test Callas's resistance to earth's gravity. Shocked at the reading, Callas took off her coat and shoes. Still the result dismayed.

About a year later, Gobbi was leaving the theatre when a voice called to him. He turned to see a slim, beautiful young woman smiling at him. Granted, a celebrated baritone is occasionally hailed by admiring fans, but this woman seemed to know him. "What do you think of me now?" she asked.

It was Callas. The transformation into diva assoluta had begun.

Callas Pays a Compliment

Listening to a broadcast of one of Renata Tebaldi's recordings with Dorle Soria, Callas remarked, "What a lovely voice! But who the hell cares?"

Another Callas Compliment

Having recorded *La Traviata* early in her career, before her collaboration with Carlo Maria Giulini at La Scala rendered her the Violetta of the age, Callas wanted the chance to redo the part, in stereo, with a more impressive cast. Plácido Domingo, just coming into prominence, was suggested as Alfredo, and the two were introduced.

Speaking of opera, Callas tensely remarked that she was losing interest in the stage because there were no satisfactory conductors. Or directors. Or singers.

"Thank you, Maria," said Domingo, laughing.

Callas Goes Shopping

In Milan, Callas was sitting for a photograph to be published in *Harper's Bazaar*. For cachet, the session was held in Verdi's old rooms in the Hotel Milan, and a jeweler promised to lend Callas an antique emerald necklace worth twenty million lire. To the singer's irritation, the jeweler arrived with a detective to watch over the emeralds.

Pacing, watching, even breathing, the detective made Callas nervous; and she asked the jeweler to dismiss him. The jeweler refused. Someone must protect his necklace from theft.

Callas strode over to her checkbook, wrote out a check for twenty million lire, and handed it to the jeweler.

"Now it's mine," she told him. "Both of you get out."

Klemperer 1, Callas 1

Walter Legge, the artistic director of EMI Records, took Callas backstage after a concert led by Otto Klemperer, who told the soprano that he had heard her twice. Her Norma was "very good," her Iphigénie en Tauride "horrible."

"Thank you, maestro," said Callas, smiling.

"But I am sure Herr Legge will agree to invite you to sing at a concert here with me. What would you like to sing?"

"The arias from *Iphigénie,* maestro," Callas sweetly replies.

Callas Knows Nothing About Cooking

Callas is ill, and her friend Marlene Dietrich, a noted cook, arrives with a prime cut of beef which she boils into the most spectacular soup in the history of the stove. If it doesn't cure you, at least you'll die happy.

Callas tastes. "Delicious," she says. "What brand of cubes do you use?"

The Art of Improvisation

Tito Gobbi was one of Callas's most congenial colleagues, partner to some of her most striking portrayals, not least his Scarpia vis-à-vis her Tosca. One night, during Act Two, as Callas clung to Cavaradossi while Scarpia's men dragged him away, she was pushed back so roughly that she lost her footing and fell quite heavily.

Staying in character, Gobbi sent a message with his eyes: "Are you all right?" She was. Excellent—because both had realized the dramatic potential of the chance fall, and began to calculate the next moves. Gobbi crossed to her and extended his hand to help her up with a deft disgust. On her next line—"Salvatelo!": Save him!—Callas seemed to climb up his arm in pathetic desperation. "Io?" runs the response. *"Voi!"*: Not I—*you!* On the last word Gobbi pulled away, letting Callas drop to the floor.

The whole business was spontaneous, but so brilliantly executed that, as Callas sank back, the public, totally caught up in the story, gasped in outrage at Scarpia's tactics.

There were giants in those days.

Brennt Callas?

Callas and Gobbi were singing *Tosca* at Covent Garden in 1964. Not realizing it, the soprano had leaned too far into the flame of a candle and her wig was beginning to smoke. Without losing a note, Gobbi pretended to draw Tosca into an embrace, meanwhile beating out the sparks. Trusting her colleague, Callas played the action and let Gobbi dispose of the emergency. When he had done so, she whispered, "Grazie, Tito."

Says Gobbi in his memoirs, *"That* was Callas."

Callas's Unique Timbre

During rehearsals for this Covent Garden *Tosca,* a titled woman happened by the house and begged the doorman to let her take a look at Callas—just a glimpse, if he'd allow. Oathed to his office, he refused. Would he at least prop open the window so she could hear the celebrated Callas, the once-in-a-century sound? This much the doorman would do.

Unbeknownst to both, Callas was home in bed with a cold. Assistant director John Copley was filling in for her, in an amusingly grotesque treble version of the soprano voice. As the doorman pulled open the window, Copley let out a tremendous scream and "sang" through a few of Tosca's most importunate lines. It sounded like Old Mother Hubbard finding a gila monster in her cupboard.

"Ah!" whispered the eavesdropping noblewoman to the doorman. "The unmistakable voice! Thank you *so* much!" And off she went to tell her friends.

SINGERS OF THE JET AGE

Anecdotes are almost superfluous with the singers of the post-World War II generation, for they have familiarized themselves through media PR—the magazine interview, the talk show, the intermission featurette between the acts of a broadcast, the chatty autobiography, the odd movie, the gossip column, even television commercials. One way or another, today's singers tell their own anecdotes.

Still, the story material does not invariably suggest the amazing transformation that opera has been undergoing in the last few decades. We learn that vanity is as vital now as it was in Catalani's day, that some singers have a sense of humor (and supply deft punch lines) while others have none (and are punched back), that the biggest names garner the biggest salaries. But there are as well rumors of an ancient art being jazzed up, plated with chrome, and wired for modern marketing, as we shall see in Luciano Pavarotti's plane disaster or Plácido Domingo's mixed-media concert. A few years ago, singers didn't travel as frequently—or under deadline pressure—as they do today, and film had no place in the concert hall or opera house. Perhaps the most indicative anecdote in this section is that of Marilyn Horne and her absurd Jocasta costume, a taste of the widespread trend in gimmicky decor.

Another notable impression is the abundance of important voices. We are often told that opera's good days are its old days, that the glory is gone. Actually what is gone is the slow pace of commitment, the variety of style, and the individuality of performance. The material is there; the voices. But a preponderance of time-beating conductors, reckless or gutless directors, and nerd critics is forcing all operas, all performances, into a polished, characterless sound modeled on the age's hot ticket, Herbert von Karajan's Salzburg Festival superproductions. All tenors want to sound like Pavarotti or Domingo, all sopranos like Mirella Freni. Where is the self-starting eccentricity that gave us a Fernando de Lucia, a Mary Garden? The golden throats of the golden age are not gone: but the keen variety is.

One type of voice we are running short on, however, is the heroic. Because today's youngsters push into Wagner at an age at which Kirsten Flagstad was content to sing Lehár, they doom themselves to short careers. Just when their Isolde and Elektra should be expert, they are exhausted. Thus we bid farewell herein to the last of the great Wagnerians, Birgit Nilsson. It was an awkward farewell, for Wagner has never been more popular than now—yet never counted fewer reliable exponents. If these are opera's hardest roles, contemporary opera's racetrack tempo and tactics are making them virtually impossible. One wonders if a roundup of stars of the next generation will see any Nilssons at all.

Zinka Milanov Edits Her Praise

For years, this was a favorite Met story, repeated by house staff and aficionados in ever-widening circles till much of New York had heard it:

Madame Milanov is holding court in the green room after a performance, signing programs and accepting rhapsodies. One of these lacks the ultimate in gush.

"Miss Milanov," says the culprit, "your voice was like silver tonight. Purest silver!"

Milanov knocks him down to size with a look. "It was like *gold!*"

Wow!

Elisabeth Schwarzkopf walks onto the stage at a concert with the Chicago Symphony, radiantly glamorous. A first-timer turns to a friend and whispers in awe, "She *sings,* too?"

The Pro Must Go On

Stage animals, no matter how well prepared, have a shaky sense of occasion, and contemporary opera production avoids them wherever possible. Brünnhilde's horse, Grane, almost never appears anymore, though the Valkyrie addresses lines to him; and while Patrice Chéreau brought Siegfried's bird onstage at Bayreuth, it was caged, to avoid the peril of unscheduled flight.

One opera, however, must have animals, *Der Rosenkavalier,* in the Marschallin's levée. "Hundern so klein!" cries the dogseller. "Hundern so klein und schon zimmerrein!": Little dogs, already housebroken.

Under the hot lights in unfamiliar surroundings, the little dogs sometimes break training. At the Met, one did so—right in Schwarzkopf's lap. Her nightgown absurdly disfigured, how was Schwarzkopf to finish the act?

Never underestimate a diva. Hastily borrowing a needle and thread, Schwarzkopf sewed a pocket into her gown to hide the offending item while the tenor and flautist performed "Di rigori armato," and sang on as suavely as ever.

Buswoman's Holiday

Joan Sutherland was aimlessly warbling in the bathtub; suddenly her husband and music director Richard Bonynge pounded on the door. "If you can't support your voice properly when you sing," he cried, "don't sing at all!"

Well-Lit Set

Taking in the stage picture for the Wedding Scene in the Met's antique *Lucia,* when Sutherland made her house debut, Bonynge noted the overpowering effort of some twenty supers bearing lavish candelabras. "Liberace," he said, "will be livid."

A Golden-Age Encore

In the day of Patti, the prime reason for going to the opera was to hear a star; the more one heard, the better. Encores were a convention. Nowadays, of course, we are too fastidious to accept such indecorous dribbling. The very notion of a soprano's tacking "Home, Sweet Home" into sacred art is too much for some critics to bear.

If there is a contemporary singer whose public reminds one of Patti's, it is Joan Sutherland. When Sutherland visited her native Australia in 1965, the last night of her tour, a *Sonnambula* in Melbourne, erupted into a kind of Patti night. The city must have been denuded of flowers for Sutherland's bouquets, and ladies of fashion were seen to stand on their seats, so intent were they on granting the diva her cheers. As if a century had fallen away, the crowd called for "Home, Sweet Home"— and out came the piano! Bonynge sat in at the keyboard, and Dame Joan, still dressed as Amina and leaning on the edge of the upright, surrounded by local grandees in evening clothes, sang the dreary, droopy, wonderful old tune. At the end, just to remind everyone that this was 1965, not 1865, she put a little topspin trill on the last cadence, sent the phrase home with a roll of her eyes, and shrugged out a smile.

Richard Tucker Gives a Lesson in Verismo Stylistics

Although Tucker was at heart a generous colleague, confident of his talent, he couldn't help resenting the furore attendant upon Franco Corelli's arrival at Tucker's home base, the Met. And, truth to tell, as a species of Italian tenor Corelli enjoyed decisive advantages over Tucker in looks, vocal endowment, and national birthright. Thus it was with mingled surprise and gratitude that Tucker greeted Corelli's request to listen to—indeed study—Tucker's rendition of "O dolci mani" in *Tosca*. Would the great American share his expertise with the younger Italian? Could he perhaps transmit some priceless secret in the sculpting of Puccinian melody? Tucker could and did.

"To sing it right, Franco," said Tucker, "you have to be Jewish."

Corelli Versus Nilsson

Met *Turandot*s of the late Bing era were famed for the Nilsson-Corelli sing-offs that occurred in Act Two, as high note vied with high note. Each has a big one to himself, but they share a C at the end of "In questa reggia," and the two made a point of holding it as long as humanly possible.

One night Nilsson held it longer, and Corelli sulked in his tent. To guarantee his public a third act, Bing paid a visit, advising Corelli to take his revenge during the love duet: instead of kissing her, he should bite her ear.

It is often told that he did; nonsense. What Corelli did was to sing "Nessun dorma" as he'd never sung it before, and to follow this with a line change in the duet. When Turandot sings, "La mia gloria è finita" (My glory is over), Calaf responds with "No! Essa incomincia!" (No ! Your glory begins!). This time, Corelli sang "Sì! Essa finisce!": Yes! Your glory is over!

Poor Franco Alfano. No one sings the love duet the way he wrote it.

Bing on Nilsson

Is Nilsson difficult?

"Not at all," says Bing. "You put enough money in and a glorious sound comes out."

Nilsson on Bing

Nilsson's accountant, preparing her tax form for the IRS, asked her if she had any dependents. "Yes," she said. "Rudolf Bing."

Nilsson's Pearls

If it isn't Bing, it's von Karajan. At a piano rehearsal of *Tristan* in Vienna, Nilsson's string of pearls snapped, hurtling countless tiny baubles onto the floor. As the company rushed around to retrieve them, von Karajan said, "No doubt these are fabulously expensive pearls bought with your Metropolitan fees."

"No," Nilsson replied. "These are cheap imitation pearls bought with your Vienna fees."

The Prima Donna Arrives

Von Karajan's Salzburg *Ring* production came to the Met with an important cast change, Nilsson replacing Helga Dernesch as Brünnhilde. A grateful Bing celebrated this coup by personally welcoming Nilsson to the house in mock grovel. Salzburg had Herbert von Karajan, but the Met had Herbert von Karajan and Birgit Nilsson! The moment comes, the signals are sent out, and Bing salutes his star at the stage door.

"Nu," she utters. "Where's Herbie?"

Encouragement

For some time at the start of his career, Jon Vickers had doubts about whether or not to pursue it. As a budding Heldentenor, he saw a lot of pressure heading his way to become the reigning Otello, Florestan, and Tristan; moreover, he wasn't sure that he would take to the international scene. But others immediately saw him as a major talent on the rise.

"Where have you been hiding?" Regina Resnik asked him when they were rehearsing *Carmen* in Canada.

He shrugged. "I'm just a Canadian tenor, and I don't know if I'll continue or go back to the farm."

"Maybe one day you'll own a farm," Resnik allows. "But you're not going *back* to one!"

The Yolk's on Horne

One problem unique to modern opera staging is bizarre costuming. In the old days singers had costumes made to their specifications, and toured with these blithely heedless of whatever else was in public view. However, in this era of Production Concept, singers are assigned their clothing, and they never know from one staging to the next what they're going to look like.

Marilyn Horne looked like an egg. This was her Scala debut, in March of 1969, as Jocasta in Stravinsky's *Oedipus Rex*. The opera has no action in any real sense: principals and chorus stand immobile and sing in Latin, as, between the numbers, a narrator outlines the plot in the audience's language. The Scala's designer Pier Luigi Pizzi decided that, since Jocasta didn't have to move, she might as well appear as a huge purple egg with only her head showing human features. Horne played the sport, but found it difficult to follow the orchestra.

"Can't you hear what your music is?" conductor Claudio Abbado asked her.

"My music? I can't hear what this *opera* is!"

The Diva As Parent

How does an opera singer balance the raising of children with the running of a career? "For my egotism, I sacrifice my children to travel?" Renata Scotto pleads. *"No!"* When they are older, they might be more independent. But "when they are six, seven, they have to go to school, and they need their parents near.

"I remember my girl say, the night before I left, 'Mama, why you sing? Why?' I don't answer because I don't know what to answer. Finally I say, 'I sing because Mama have to sing.'

" 'But, Mama,' she say, 'if you sing, who will wake me in the morning?' Oh, oh . . . When I speak of my child, I cry."

And thus, speaking of her child, Scotto cried.

Sills's Met Debut (in a Small Role)

Eight years old, Beverly Sills was taken to the Met for her first opera, *Lakmé,* with Lily Pons. One of Pons's attractions in this part was her costume, a two-piece affair with a shimmering midriff of skin.

"Mama, Mama!" Sills shouted. "Her belly button is showing!"

Career Plans

Sills's father has heard enough about this "opera singer" business, all right? Fourteen-year-old girls do not plan to be opera stars. "The child will go to college," says Sills's father, "and be smart."

"No, Morris," says Sills's mother. "The two boys will go to college and be smart. *This* one will be an opera singer."

There's Something Wrong with This Connection

In 1961, Sarah Caldwell called Sills to invite her to play Rosalinda in a Boston *Fledermaus*. They had not worked together before, but Sills had been impressed with a Caldwell *Traviata*. Sills said yes.

"What are you planning to wear?" asked her husband after she had hung up.

"Oh, costumes," said Sills, with a wave of the hand. Anything will do.

Not that season: she was seven months pregnant.

Sills called Caldwell back and apologized. "I can't do your *Fledermaus* because I'm pregnant."

Caldwell considered this for a bit, then asked, "Weren't you pregnant five minutes ago?"

Clothes Make the Tenor

Luciano Pavarotti walks into a clothing store on London's Savile Row, ultimate posh, and says, "Have you anything that would fit me?"

Noting the tenor's golden-age dimensions, the salesman replies, "A handkerchief, perhaps?"

Pavarotti's Plane Crash

Flying from New York to Milan, Pavarotti was unsettled to hear the pilot announce that he was diving into the heavy fog blanketing Milan's Malapensa airport—not to land, but to examine conditions. He shot down sharply and swerved up just as the ground heaved into sight.

Pavarotti was beside himself.

Pavarotti does not like flying.

In fact, at this moment, Pavarotti does not like Malapensa Airport, snap-down trays, cute little pillows, or anything having to do with planes.

The pilot announces that he will circle the airport in the hope that the weather clears. If it doesn't, he could fly to Genoa and land there.

And the golden voice of Pavarotti fills the plane: *"Do it!"*

In the event, the pilot tried to land at Milan, but the fog had so complicated the touchdown that the plane skidded off the runway, lost a wing, and broke in half. Incredibly, there were minor injuries but no casualties. At the aerodrome, the passengers unwound with an impromptu party, and Pavarotti told a companion, "You know, my friend, we were —— lucky."

Janet Baker's Layoff

Baker has an ear for words as well as music: at two and a half she was already picking up all sorts of idioms. Enchanted by the building of a house next to the Bakers, young Janet went over each day with her teddy bear to supervise construction and take care of any special problems. One day a late delivery of essential materials halted work and Mrs. Baker found her daughter playing alone in the garden. Why wasn't Janet over at the site as usual?

Baby Janet gracefully explained, "We're buggered for bricks!"

Beware the Palatch

Elisabeth Söderström did not get a full-scale rehearsal for her guest Marguerites in Leningrad. After all, the Russians know *Faust* and Söderström knows *Faust;* all she needs is a little talk from the stage manager on when she comes on and who will be doing what and so on. Fine with Söderström—only her Russian is not expert and she had a vague idea that she was missing a word here and there. For instance, *"palatch."* At the close of the Prison Scene, she was told, she should drop to her knees facing the audience, and the *palatch* will tap her on the shoulder and lead her off. There wasn't time to get too detailed about all this, so Söderström assumed the *palatch* was a nun and went about her business.

Came the moment, however, Söderström felt not a tap on her shoulder but a demanding tug, and when she turned around she saw not a nun but a gigantic hangman in a black mask.

"So that's what a *palatch* is," she thought to herself, as her head began to swim and her joints turned to rubber: she had been so startled that she fainted.

No to the Movies

A PR agent, noting Plácido Domingo's bent for conducting, suggested filming the tenor leading an orchestra in choice arias, then running the movie in Carnegie Hall while Domingo filled in the melodies. Domingo conducts Domingo!

"But if I make a mess of the concert," Domingo pointed out, "I won't be able to blame the conductor."

"Yes, All Right, You Sing Opera, But What Do You Do for a Living?"

Bass Michael Langdon was on a bus headed for a soccer match when he noticed a man staring at him. "Excuse me," he asked the singer, "don't you live in Sutton Common Road?" They both did—and the stranger and his wife had been wondering what it was that Langdon did.

"You come in at odd times," Langdon's neighbor said. "Sometimes you're in all day, sometimes you disappear for days on end, sometimes you go out early, sometimes you go out late. Now *I* think you're a policeman. My *wife* thinks you're a burglar."

"Actually," says Langdon, "I'm an opera singer."

The stranger absorbed this for a bit, then said, "Ask a bloody silly question and you get a bloody silly answer."

INTERMISSION II
More Operas

RINALDO

Handel Makes ein Quip

Handel's first London opus, *Rinaldo,* was such a success that its publisher made a fortune. Naturally, he urged the composer to come straight to the same house when the next opera was ready. "As it is only right that we should be upon an equal footing," Handel wrote back, *"you* compose the next opera and *I* will sell it."

Choice Seats Still Available

In his later years in London, Handel found the British tiring of Italian opera, with its stolid airs and incredible castratos, and on some nights there were whole pockets of empty places. The royal family, at least, remained loyal. One night, the Earl of Chesterfield was hailed by a friend as he was leaving the theatre in the middle of *Rinaldo.*

"Going so soon?" the friend asked.

"I don't wish to disturb His Majesty's privacy."

LE NOZZE DI FIGARO

Number One in Our Series of Classic Piquant Reviews

Of a *Figaro* at Sadler's Wells in 1936, the *Catholic Times* reported, "Mr. [Warwick] Braithwaite conducted, and the orchestra played Mozart's music."

And there we were, hoping for a little Salieri.

RICHARD COEUR DE LION

Another of Those Stately Georgian Puns

John Philip Kemble, of the great British acting dynasty, was no opera singer. Still, he could get through a tune well enough to play the title role in Grétry's setting of the rescue of Richard the Lion Hearted by his minstrel Blondel, at Drury Lane. Yet however much Kemble might satisfy his public, he could not cheer his conductor.

"Mr. Kemble, that isn't it at all!" the musician cried, when Kemble fell out of tempo in his big scene. "You *murder* time abominably!"

"My dear sir," replied Kemble, "it is surely better to murder it, than to be continually beating it, as you do!"

LA STRANIERA

Collaboration

Between Bellini's first influentially innovative opera, *Il Pirata,* and his two masterpieces, *Norma* and *La Sonnambula,* came this oddly lackluster tale of an unknown woman (the "foreigner" of the title) who turns out to be the Queen of England. *La Straniera* is strangely ordinary after the exciting *Pirata;* yet the finale, an aria for the heroine, was troubling Bellini's habitual librettist, Felice Romani. Bellini rejected the first attempt, the second, the third. At last the poet admitted he didn't know what the composer wanted.

"What I want?" Bellini answered. "I want something that is a prayer, an imprecation, a threat, and a delirium, all at once." This was in effect the recipe for the late bel canto "mad scenes" that were to proliferate thereafter—but of course it is the first essays that challenge, not the later ones. Inspired by his own analysis of what was needed, Bellini ran to the piano and demonstrated, improvising the sort of verses he required to the sort of music he would write for them.

"That's what I want!"

"And here are the words of the aria," said Romani, handing Bellini a sheet of paper wet with ink. He had taken down the verses as Bellini had sung them.

And so was written the heroine's aria, "Or sei pago, o ciel tremendo."

NORMA

Basta, Divo

The tenor Mario Armandi was so terrible that he could get work only as a substitute for other tenors who had been hissed out of town. With his extensive repertory Armandi could cover any standard opera; stepping in for his disgraced colleague, he would brave an already irritated public as a stopgap till some legitimate voice could be found to save the season.

However, Armandi had his pride. One day, agreeing to take over Pollione in Naples, he stipulated that this time he would not serve as a temporary replacement, but must sing the six performances of *Norma* remaining on the *cartellone.* A desperate management assented.

No sooner had he opened his mouth than the public drowned him out with derogatory assessments of his abilities. Inaudible for the entire first act, he came before the curtain at intermission and made a deal. If the public would let him finish the opera in peace, he would then depart Naples; if they continued to harass him he would complete the engagement.

Stunned at the prospect of five more nights of Armandi's Pollione, the house agreed. Once they had heard him for a bit they found him bearable, and, good sports as Neapolitans are, they rather liked his honesty.

In the end, they not only applauded him that night, but cried out that he must stay for the other *Norma*s. I hope he was in good voice.

L'AFRICAINE

Delibes Looks on the Bright Side

It was 1865. Léo Delibes had just been appointed second chorus master at the Opéra when the time came to begin preparations for the posthumous staging of Meyerbeer's last opera. This was possibly the most anticipated premiere of the century, rivaled only by the first nights of Verdi's *Otello* and *Falstaff,* and the entire company, from the Opéra director down to the box attendants, was readying for a stupendous success.

First of all, the director had to hear this masterpiece played through at the piano in the entirety of François Joseph Fétis's realization of Meyerbeer's notebook text. A great moment: historic, sensual, thrilling. It fell to Delibes to give the performance.

Grand opera plumed itself on majesty of proportion, and it took Delibes much of the day to deliver this private world premiere reading. At the end, shaken by the grandeur that lay before him—imagine! the last work of the divine Meyerbeer!—the Opéra intendant turned to Delibes and exclaimed, "What a masterpiece! Don't you agree?"

Delibes was shaken in quite a different way. "Monsieur le Directeur, it's . . . it's awful!"

Delibes was immediately fired. Still, as he told commiserating friends, "At least now I won't have to direct rehearsals of *L'Africaine!*"

FAUST

Opera Wear

After many vicissitudes, the music publisher Antoine de Choudens put his firm on a secure footing by buying the rights to *Faust.* Production of the premiere had been delayed and Gounod was uncertain of its future, so he accepted Choudens's offer of a flat fee of fifteen thousand francs—no royalties. Within a decade of its first night, the score had won enormous popularity and the opera was a gold mine—only for Choudens.

One day, Gounod dropped by the office wearing a notably seedy hat. Choudens asked why the eminent Gounod—composer of the miraculous *Faust,* no less!—should go about Paris dressed so unbecomingly.

"This," said Gounod, "is my *Faust* hat."

As the years went by, Choudens continued to publish Gounod's operas, though some were nearly as unsuccessful as *Faust* was profitable. One of the failures was *Le Tribut de Zamora.* Not long after the *Zamora* score had been published, to vastly few takers, Gounod noticed that Choudens was wearing a spectacularly gruesome something on his head.

"This," Choudens announced, "is my *Zamora* hat."

What's the Opposite of A Cappella?

Tenor Robert Thomas and Bass Michael Langdon were whiling away the off moments backstage at a Welsh National *Faust* when they suddenly noticed, via the house sound system, that the Prison Scene had begun—without them. Dashing onstage, they were in time to deliver the last exchange of the opening recitative, Faust's "Begone!" and the Devil's "I shall wait at the door."

Missing an entrance is unforgivable; still, the two apologized to the conductor, Ivor John. "Don't worry, boys," he said. "I never realized how bloody beautiful that music was until I heard it without the voices."

Monteux Scans the Set

The Met opened its 1953–54 season with a controversial new production of its onetime favorite opera. Rolf Gerard designed for *Faust*'s nineteenth century rather than for Faust's middle ages, and director Peter Brook, as always, sought to give the public something to bite on. The conductor, Pierre Monteux, regarded their work with contempt; this was not *Faust* as he knew it. When he got his first view of Gerard's lavish rendition of Marguerite's house and garden, he said, "Marguerite est donc millionaire!": Marguerite must be a millionaire!

Robert Merrill's Death Agony

In this same production, Mildred Miller as Siebel huddled over Robert Merrill as Valentin, mortally wounded and about to curse his sister before their neighbors. Miller, giving the scene its due, looked beseech-ingly at Merrill, who outdid himself in Method realism. "Oi vey," he whispered. "It hoits."

DER RING DES NIBELUNGEN

The Opera Widow

An oft-told backstage joke finds a tenor's wife complaining to the im-presario:

"Three days before he sings Siegfried, he's too tense; so he won't. Three days after, he's exhausted; so he can't. Your *Ring* cycles are ru-ining our marriage!"

Unusual Commotion at the Valkyries' Rock

Mignon Dunn recalls the night she doubled as Fricka and Waltraute in a Met *Walküre* that was riddled with substitutions. Birgit Nilsson had cancelled because of an auto accident, two or three Valkyries were out, and, at the second intermission, Otto Edelmann, the Wotan, was asked to surrender Act Three to his cover. Edelmann insisted that he felt fine, but management feared he might have been overworked in a heavy sea-son and wanted to save his voice for an imminent Saturday broadcast.

Unfortunately, Edelmann's cover, not expecting to be called upon at such a late hour, had been hoisting one or two with the boys and was in no shape to go on. On he went, however, staggering onstage to the cry of "Wo ish Brünnhild'?"

Valkyrie Heidi Krall leaned over to Dunn. "Herr Vater," she whis-pered, "ist loaded."

He was indeed. Erich Leinsdorf, in the pit, spurred the players on to ever greater waves of sound to effect a *cordon sanitaire* between the helpless Wotan and his audience, the Valkyries created a distraction by violently overacting, the prompter was screaming, the bass's wife pray-ing. Finally, Wotan dropped his spear, leaned over to the prompter and roared, *"What?"*

The curtain came down and the public was promised a resumption of the opera if it would kindly wait while the makeup man prepared a third Wotan.

Otto Edelmann.

Gratitude on a Wagnerian Scale

Launching its gigantic *Ring* recording with a dynamic presentation of *Das Rheingold*—the first ever made—Decca-London arranged for a public playing of the set for the Wagner Society of London. The hall was packed with enthusiasts and Decca's engineers had wired the place to ensure that all the technical effects would make their impression.

After the playing, the recording's producer John Culshaw fielded questions from the floor. None congratulated him, or Decca, or anyone, for pulling off the feat in the face of industry cynicism. The first question was, "When will you make *Die Walküre?*" The second was, "When will you make *Siegfried?*" The third was, "When will you make *Götterdämmerung?*" Then Culshaw himself asked a question: "How many of those assembled here plan to buy this set of *Das Rheingold?*"

Out of some 170 people, twelve raised their hands.

"There's your answer," said Culshaw dryly, "about *Siegfried* and *Götterdämmerung.*"

CAVALLERIA RUSTICANA

The Lesson of the Master

A barrel-organ player just below Mascagni's window was driving him crazy playing *Cavalleria*'s Intermezzo at a tempo appropriate for a gallop. Rushing out of his house, Mascagni grabbed the handle from the organ grinder and turned it to reproduce the music at the proper *Andante sostenuto.*

At first annoyed, the player turned humble when Mascagni explained who he was. Of course the *egregio maestro* had the right to hear his music played to his pleasure. From now on, the Intermezzo would sound as Mascagni instructed.

Indeed, the next day the organ grinder was back at his post, now bearing a placard that read, PUPIL OF THE CELEBRATED MASCAGNI.

HÄNSEL UND GRETEL

Choice Casting

Not long ago, the administration of an opera house passed into the hands of an impresario a bit behind in his opera savvy. Greeting Ingrid Bjoner in his office—Bjoner of the Brünnhildes and Isoldes—the intendant pulled out her file to tell her what the house proposed for the coming season. By mistake, he got the file of a lyric soprano and, leafing through it, suavely offered Bjoner a season of Mimìs, Neddas, and Gretels.

"Gretels?" asked Bjoner.

"Gretels," he replied.

The lady is game. "I'll sing Gretel," she avers, "if Birgit Nilsson sings Hänsel."

PETER GRIMES

More Music!

The scene-setting "sea interludes" that launch each of *Peter Grimes*'s three acts and connect its various scenes are famed for their nature-painting and psychological eloquence. While depicting the turbulent nature of his protagonist, Britten seems to call the very sea and wind into play. Surely there can be no better judged "curtain music" in opera—not a note too many or too few.

It was with some sense of apology, then, that Eric Crozier, who staged the opera's premiere at Sadler's Wells in 1945, asked Britten to lengthen one of the interludes by ninety seconds. This was the storm music (the last of the *Four Sea Interludes,* as they are known in the concert hall), the bridge between the first two scenes in Act One, from the harbor to the crowded pub where Grimes meets his new apprentice. There wasn't time to shift the sets on what Britten had composed, at least not securely. Britten had not written for the vagaries of the cramped backstage of the Wells; he had written what the opera needed at that point, and did not want to change it.

But opera is theatre, and theatre is what is produced, not a platonic ideal of itself. Britten gave in, not agreeably. He told Crozier, "You're like someone who comes along to an architect when he has just finished building a cathedral and gives him a huge block of stone and says, 'You simply must find room for this.' "

Meeting Britten

Thomas Beecham programmed the *Four Sea Interludes* at an Albert Hall concert. Britten was there. Next to him, a young man was following the music from the published score. Proud and gratified, Britten felt that a few words of amity were indicated, and began with, "I see you're interested in Benjamin Britten."

"Of course I am."

That sounded nice. "Why 'of course'?" Britten asked the stranger.

"Because I *am* Benjamin Britten."

This is, if ever there was, a story that prompts a What Happened Then? What do you say in such a case? Nonplussed, Britten came out with

"Oh, are you?" and there the encounter ended. Later he told the tale to a friend, who disturbed him greatly by remarking, "Maybe he *was* Benjamin Britten."

THE RAPE OF LUCRETIA

Eliot at the Opera

T. S. Eliot heard Britten's next opera—on the callous debauching of a saintly woman—at Covent Garden in the company of the librettist, Ronald Duncan. To Duncan's annoyance, a lavatory in the men's room behind their seats in the Dress Circle became stuck in the middle of a rude noise. Duncan, an accomplished household tinkerer, slipped off, silenced the nuisance, and returned.

As they left the opera house, Duncan asked Eliot—his publisher, by the way—if he'd liked the piece.

"Not exactly, Ronnie," said Eliot. "But I was most impressed with your plumbing."

Musicians and Impresarios

Life for a free-lance impresario of the nineteenth century was utterly unlike that of any impresario today. Lacking the supportive exchequer of the great state theatres of the Continent, herding his contentious troupe downriver and cross-country, making the acquaintance of many a rustic sheriff and small-town magistrate, never knowing from one night to the next whether he could count on a sellout or a dead loss, and committed largely to a fixed repertory bounded by *La Traviata* on the east, *Les Huguenots* on the west, *Mignon* on the south, and *I Puritani* on the north, the impresario raised up a precarious art. Singers had no commitment. Audiences were demanding yet not knowledgeable. Production values consisted of genre settings and come-as-you-are costumes out of the nearest trunk. After singing Jason in Cherubini's *Médée* for two years, tenor Giuseppe Fancelli finally quizzed Mapleson as to Jason's precise relationship to the soprano: "Am I her father, her brother, her lover, or what?" Or what, Fancelli: her husband. His ignorance typifies the personnel Mapleson dealt with.

Somehow these preposterous tribulations endear Mapleson to us. His famous memoirs are a combination of thriller (will the show get on?— and which one?), comedy of manners (the man's dry wit under fire is recommended as a study to politicians at press conferences and authors replying to book reviews), and rogue's gallery (of singers). In the end, we wonder why he did it at all. Why did he employ a singer like Sofia Scalchi, who cancelled an *Aida* on the afternoon of the performance, pleading illness, when Mapleson knew that the dinner of lobster and duck he saw being wheeled into her hotel room was not Scalchi's medicine but Scalchi's treat, and that only if Mapleson appeared in the midst of this dinner with a physician in tow could Scalchi be induced to dispatch her obligations at the theatre. Why? Because that's what free-lance opera was like then; if not Scalchi, then Patti, if not Patti, then Gerster; not to mention the tenors. Singers were like children who knew they were so cute they would be forgiven anything. Sheer rogues.

The Colonel, too, was something of a rogue, from his Sunday-regiment title through his rented claques on to his own failed obligations, unpaid costumer's bills the favorite. No doubt one had to be a rogue to stay afloat in such a business. One costumer in New York finally called the law on Mapleson, then visited him in his office in hope that the matter might be settled without the forced closure of Mapleson's operation. The costumer found his man preparing "paper"—free tickets distributed to fill unsold seats—and the Colonel greeted the costumer with such worldly agreeability that the costumer not only called off his lawyers but lent the Colonel a further seventy-five dollars, cash. "I tell you, I know lots of managers," he concluded, "but there's only one Colonel Mapleson in the world."

He was unique, no question. With his buttonhole rose and his disarming manner, he set himself apart from his competitors, and only the accident of his not being offered the management of the Metropolitan Opera prevented his developing a truly fabulous legend. Mapleson was running the rival Academy of Music when the Met opened, so he was not exactly overlooked; but, despite the impresario's natural conservatism, Mapleson was adventurous enough to have made something more of the new house than the various Met managers did. Or was Mapleson simply too much the underdog to participate in anything as secure as a fully outfitted palace? It feels sadly inevitable that the Colonel should have died in poverty, having arranged for the making of so many singers' fortunes.

The opera world Mapleson knew—created as much as inherited—is gone, and no one can lament this. As the following stories reveal, it was a reckless and unartistic world, a concert of star turns. But the Colonel did at least leave his name on one important corner of opera history. His nephew Lionel became the Met's librarian, and it was in this capacity that Lionel climbed high over the stage during performances by Melba, Nordica, the de Reszkes, and others, and took down their voices on a recording machine—the infuriatingly foggy but indispensably revealing "Mapleson cylinders."

The Colonel Creates a Hit

Warned by his music director Luigi Arditi that a new French opera had the makings of a popular success, Mapleson secured the rights and programmed it for his coming season. But as the premiere approached, the box office takings were so poor as to promise a disaster. Thinking fast, the Colonel took all the unsold tickets for the first three performances, mailed them off to various people throughout Greater London, and placed an advertisement offering a pair for sale at a slight premium, owing to a death in the family.

Curiosity was now aroused. The "pair" was of course sold many times over, and the realization that the new work had "sold out" its first three nights gripped the public with a desire to hear this wondrous piece. Nor did the Colonel fail to arrange for an exciting first night. The spontaneous reception was only fair, but a hired claque called the composer to the stage for several ovations, and of course the thrill at having been present at the opening of this much talked-about opera inspired handsome word-of-mouth publicity. By the fourth performance, when London's operagoers were at last allowed to buy their way into this great event, enthusiasm was assured—whether for the music itself or for the cachet the Colonel had given it hardly matters.

The new piece was Gounod's *Faust*.

What the Critics Say

Despite the furore, *Faust*'s first night earned a highly mixed reception from various interested parties. Mapleson's rival impresario Frederick Gye could hear only one melody in the whole thing, the Soldiers' Chorus. Gounod, on the other hand, was quite impressed. Turning to his publisher Choudens during the first act, he cried, "Que Dieu soit beni! Voilà mon *Faust!*": God be praised, *there* is my *Faust!*

Perhaps the most interesting opinion was that of a lord who, when Mapleson asked how he liked it, replied, "This demand is most premature. How am I to answer you until I have talked to my friends and read the criticisms in the morning papers?"

Faust with Rather a Lot of Cast Changes

To get some idea of the rough-and-tumble strategy Mapleson sometimes had to employ to get his shows on, consider the *Faust* he had planned around the popular tenor Sims Reeves. Some confusion over the date of a performance led Reeves to refuse his services, on account of having already ordered his dinner.

That's all right—the Colonel had been to Reeves's house and reordered it for later.

Reeves laughed, and said it was all right with him if it was all right with his wife.

It wasn't. "It's all nonsense," she declared. "Mapleson is an impresario"—she meant the term as describing something between a reptile and a pickpocket—"and wants to ruin you by making you sing."

How could Reeves appear on such short notice? Why, his customary chintz had not been hung in his dressing room! Mrs. Reeves hurried her husband into his carriage and off they went.

It was now 6:30. Mapleson had access to two possible substitutes in Reeves's role, who had sung different scenes from *Faust* on a concert tour. They could double up and save the performance. Unfortunately, one of them happened to be lying on his deathbed.

Being an impresario means never saying die. Rounding up the hearty tenor and enlivening the moribund one with a brew of Château Lafitte, two beaten eggs, and powdered sugar, Mapleson got them dressed, advised each as to which of them was doing what scene, and warned the audience of certain minor alterations in the program. All seemed well, despite a backstage skirmish between the wives of the two Fausts. "Of course you will rejoice!" cried the wife of the dying tenor. "My poor sick husband brought out at the risk of his life, and then simply to undertake an old man's part [in the first scene, before the devil transforms Faust into a young man], with grey hair and beard concealing his beauty, whilst your husband is to come on and make all the love in the garden scene, and get all the applause!"

Just then the Siebel of the evening, Thérèse Tietjens, decided *Faust* was not going on that night—not with her, anyway—and left the theatre. She was promptly followed by the wife of the lively tenor, with her husband in tow.

Now Mapleson had even fewer characters on call than when he had started. In desperation, Mapleson's most constant condition, he retrieved the departed tenor at his home and asked him to return to the theatre—to sing the trouser role, Siebel, no doubt in his own trousers, though he had to shave off his moustache.

"Everything," the Colonel concluded in his memoirs, "went off brilliantly."

This is a preposterous story, though I have it from the Colonel himself. How did the tenor get through Siebel, a part he had never sung, or even learned? The Colonel says he picked it up from hearing his wife, Zelia Trebelli, practicing it. What, recitative and all? Unlikely. Besides, if Trebelli knew Siebel, why didn't Mapleson ask *her* to sing it? And how did the dying tenor—who, by the way, lived for years afterward, stimulated, the Colonel suggests, by the excitement—get through a huge role he had sung bits of in concert? The silliest piece of all in this puzzle is that the male Siebel went on, the Colonel recalls, "in his wife's clothes." But Siebel, though sung by a woman, is dressed as a man. Perhaps the Colonel means "his wife's *stage* clothes"—her costume.

What would Gounod have said if he had been present on the occasion: "Voilà mon *Faust*"?

Mongini Hates His Costume

The oddest thing about the Colonel's tribulations is that they often seem to occur during the performance, yet with one or more principals throwing a tantrum backstage. The audiences of Mapleson's day were not known for patience; what were they doing during these delays?

Take, for example, the night Pietro Mongini, singing the Duke in *Rigoletto*, realized that the house tailor had bungled the alterations on his costume for the last act. The Colonel had already gone home when he was informed that the curtain was being held while Mongini enjoyed an impromptu opera backstage, threatening to skewer the company with his sword.

Hurrying to the theatre, the Colonel met Mongini's wife, who begged him not to approach her husband: he was in such a rage that anything might set him off on a fatal rampage. Mapleson insisted on speaking to Mongini, for the public out front was getting, as the Colonel mildly puts it, "tumultuous." When he gained Mongini's dressing room, he said, "This time, Mongini, I hear you are right," thus gaining the tenor's confidence.

Indeed, Mapleson's tailor had made a mistake, taking two inches out of Mongini's ducal tunic instead of putting two inches in, as requested. The coat itself appeared to be something of a dead issue, as it was lying on the floor in shreds, Mongini's first, and thus far, only victim. But the tailor, Mapleson announced, must be dealt with severely, and his family put out into the streets to starve at the first opportunity.

This cheered Mongini, and when the Colonel ventured to tell him how everyone was raving about his performance, the tenor seemed ready to rejoin his colleagues on stage. But how, without his costume?

The Colonel now saw his opening. Let Mongini go out in his second-act costume, dashingly trimmed with whatever was handy, and let him then deliver "La donna è mobile" and everything would be right. So *Rigoletto* was completed, and the next day the tailor was brought before Mapleson and Mongini and told of the ruin that awaited him and his family for his treachery in the matter of the costume. A bachelor, the tailor had been coached by Mapleson, and suffered the scene tactfully. But Mongini was moved. He begged the Colonel not to let the tailor's family starve. Indeed, if he would overlook the incident and retain the tailor in his employ, Mongini would sing an extra night for nothing. The Colonel agreed.

As to the audience who had waited some two hours for "La donna è mobile," the Colonel does not tell us that they stormed the stage and wrecked the house, so we must assume that they too forgave the tailor, and Mongini as well.

The Colonel Accommodates

Getting two star singers into one hotel in Dublin is not easy—not when they both want the same suite. Soprano Caroline Salla and contralto Anna De Belocca happened into the same apartment at the same time and simultaneously declared, "These rooms will do for me!"

"For you?" Salla cries. "The prima donna has the right of choice!"— meaning herself, of course.

"There are but two prime donne," De Belocca counters. "Moi et Patti!"

There the matter uncomfortably rested, till Mapleson, with the ho-telier's connivance, devised the pretty fiction that another suite, as de-lightful as the disputed one, was reserved for Lady Spencer, wife of the Lord-Lieutenant of Ireland, and could not be rented to anyone else.

Madame De Belocca was intrigued; Lady Spencer sounded like a prima donna of donne. "Could we at least see the rooms?" she asked.

"You could see them," the hotelier said. "But that is all."

The two men proceeded upstairs to the other suite, De Belocca sneaking along behind them. No sooner was the door opened than she dashed inside, locked the door, and announced that Lady Spencer must look elsewhere. Thus Mapleson keeps the peace in the family.

Good thing Patti wasn't there, too.

The Colonel Perseveres

Many of Mapleson's adventures involve the last-minute switching of operas, but this classic snafu during the 1882–83 season at New York's Academy of Music tops everything.

On the afternoon of December 4, the Mathilde for the evening's *Guillaume Tell,* Louise Dotti, came down with diptheria. Dotti's un-derstudy was so nervous at the prospect of going on that Mapleson de-cided to put on *Lucia di Lammermoor* with Laura Zagury. Then it turned out that Zagury, who had listed the role in her repertory, had never sung it.

So Mapleson dropped *Lucia* in favor of *Aida;* but Paolina Rossini, his Aida, was also ill.

Now it looked like *Rigoletto*—no, Zagury wasn't prepared to play Gilda, either. Well, *Les Huguenots,* then, with Emma Fursch-Madi, a native of Bayonne, New Jersey, and a staunch Valentine. Alas, the lady had taken some medicine and was indisposed.

Mapleson was running out of productions. But at least there's al-ways *La Favorita,* with refulgent Minnie Hauk and dauntless Luigi Ravelli. No, sorry, Ravelli had just finished rehearsing *Carmen* and Hauk was looking toward a performance in Brooklyn the next day. Neither would risk it.

Always at his best in a crisis, the Colonel decided it would be *La Favorita* or nothing, and *Favorita* it would be, with Victor Clodio and one Madame Galassi, known to opera fame only because of this story: it seems that two large boils had appeared under her right arm, and she was fainting in agony. By this time—something like an hour before cur-tain—Galassi would have had to be legally dead before the Colonel would write her off. He called in a doctor, saw the boils lanced, and presented Galassi and Clodio in *La Favorita*.

A day in the life of an opera manager.

ARTURO TOSCANINI

The opera conductor as company head, the leader as aristocrat, the musician as visionary, and the celebrity as political symbol, Toscanini owns a textured legend. Much as we may love their work, Wilhelm Furtwängler, Bruno Walter, Otto Klemperer, Victor de Sabata, and others of Toscanini's coevals do not contribute remotely as many adventures, comments, and eccentricities to an anecdote collection as Toscanini does. They had few adventures, made no startling comments. Some even lacked eccentricities, virtually a personal failing in the high-strung world of opera. Even Thomas Beecham, an outstanding wit, had no great encounters, except with fumbling oboists or incompetent singers.

Toscanini, however, figures in heavy mythology—making his conducting debut as a last-minute substitute with no baton experience and before a riotous house; instituting controversial reforms at La Scala that eventually became the basis for our modern code of opera house conduct for artists and audiences; maintaining intense liaisons with some of opera's most spectacular sopranos; defying fascism; screaming atrocious invective at singers and instrumentalists; conducting *La Traviata* "too" quickly and *Parsifal* "too" slowly; beaming, bridling, raging; at length the oldest, the most formidable, and possibly the greatest conductor in all opera.

The essential quality in Toscanini's history is his authority, his reinvention of opera production as an experience centered upon the conductor's artistic absolutism. When Toscanini arrived on the scene toward the end of the nineteenth century, the conductor had no authority. Singers, public, the impresario (somewhat), and the composer (barely) had the muscle. The conductor was there to beat time and signal entrances, for opera—at least Italian opera—had long been a succession of vocal lines accompanied by rhythm and harmony. Singers set standards, the public approved them, the impresarios took care of the background matter, and the composer coached the singers of the premiere. Art was style, style was tradition, and tradition was what you did last week. What, then, had a conductor to do but keep the orchestra together to support the tunes?

Nothing—in Bellini and Donizetti's day. But by the time the young 'cellist Toscanini became a conductor, the opera of Bellini and Donizetti had been expanded by Meyerbeer, Wagner, and Verdi. Composition had become complex, ensemble execution more precarious. To accommodate the music, artistic standards had to rise; but to accommodate the standards, someone had to define and enforce them, and centrally. The composer wasn't available, the impresario wasn't interested, the singers couldn't be trusted, and the public couldn't have cared less.

So it must be the conductor: and, just then, Toscanini appeared.

No one was better suited to do the job of asserting authority. Not only was he a tireless worker, but he had a stupendous memory and could learn a score to the last note of every part. At the Met, he corrected a wrong bass note that the 'cellos had been playing for years; and at Bayreuth he asked for "the cymbal crash" at the end of *Tristan*'s first act. What cymbal crash? There was none in the percussion parts. Out came the manuscript, and lo, Wagner had called for a cymbal crash.* "Hier steht," Toscanini tells them. "Here it stands"—or, roughly, Do As Written. Like Mahler in Vienna, Toscanini discarded the conventional amendments to text patterned by reckless singers and compliant maestros. He was meticulous, yet he never sounded academic. On the contrary, his exactness brought off many passages with a vitality they had not known in living memory. Any other conductor observed the traditional ritardando at the close of the big street scene in *La Bohème;* they still do, in fact. But Puccini wrote none, and Toscanini (who conducted *La Bohème*'s world premiere) played it as written, in tempo, and it had the excitement of a gala Christmas Eve out on the town that Puccini wrote into it.

To his respect for the score, Toscanini added a fiery temperament; that is what made his perfection stimulating. But it also made his rehearsals a bitter trial for anyone not as committed as he was. He could forgive a lack of genius but not a lack of concentration. Naturally, the marshalling of an opera-house or symphony orchestra meant tolerating the chatter, the wayward intonation, the fatigue of sixty men acting as one. Naturally: to any but Toscanini. Give him less than everything you had, at ten in the morning or ten at night, and he would come down like the wolf on the fold. And to singers who showed up for rehearsal half-prepared or otherwise got on his nerves, he could be vicious.

This in itself would have made him most prominent in his profession. But the political troubles of the 1920s and 1930s expanded his reputation beyond music as the most admirable Italian to stand up to the fascists, not by implication or graciously but in outspoken fury. Too, his desertion of Bayreuth after a series of performances that stood among the best in the Festival's history identified Toscanini as a moral as well as artistic perfectionist. By the time he presided over Sunday afternoon broadcasts of the NBC Symphony Orchestra—his orchestra, more loyal and less frequently disappointing to him than other, better, bands—his moral clarity sounded as tensely over the airwaves as did his musical demon.

Some say he was too rigid, too driving. Even Verdi thought Toscanini's perfectionism unyielding, at least too much so for opera. Modestly volunteering to play 'cello in the Scala orchestra at *Otello*'s pre-

---

* Cosima had eliminated it in an early Bayreuth revival, and apparently every German musician had been playing from her parts. Toscanini had studied an early, pre-Cosima Italian edition.

miere, Toscanini obeyed Verdi's markings exactly, even unto a *pppp*, pianissimo moltissimo. Verdi couldn't hear it, and asked him to play louder.

Years later, a more established Toscanini, now acquainted with Verdi as maestro to maestro, reminded the composer of the incident. Why did Verdi object to Toscanini's pianissimo moltissimo? So it was written!

Verdi shrugged. "Who can tell the difference in an opera house?"

Toscanini Makes His Debut

Not long out of school, Toscanini was hired as first 'cellist and assistant chorus master by the impresario Claudio Rossi, who was organizing an opera tour of Brazil. The personnel was Italian, with a few other nationalities represented by the star singers, but the conductor, whom the company did not meet until it arrived in Sao Paulo, was a native Brazilian, Leopoldo Miguez. Rossi's troupe and Miguez got off to a rocky collaboration, they insisting he was incompetent and he calling them uncooperative. Rossi's second maestro, Carlo Superti, was no more efficient or inspired in the pit than Miguez, though he was more likable and, at any rate, Italian. But if Rossi were to fire Miguez and promote Superti, the Brazilian public might turn the performances into a jingoistic riot.

As the tour went on, the singers' resentment of Miguez mounted, till he abruptly resigned, in Rio de Janiero, his hometown, on the day of an *Aida*, June 30, 1886. Toscanini spent that afternoon at his pension with one of the chorus women (either making love or studying the Lieder of Schumann, depending on whether Toscanini was telling the story to a friend or to mixed company), and arrived at work to find the theatre in an uproar, for Miguez had published a letter blaming his resignation on the Italians. With Miguez announced as indisposed (to say the least) and Superti proposed as substitute, the audience broke into such a clamor that the gentle opening of *Aida* could not be heard. Superti gave up midway through the prelude and left the pit to jeers, laughter, stamping, and whistles.

What was Rossi to do? If he cancelled the tour at this point, he would lack the funds to ship his people home. He decided to appear before the crowd and make a personal appeal through an interpreter: but this, too, was shouted down. Already, some of the audience were filing out to get refunds from the box office, and behind the curtain everyone was milling about in despair. It was one of those nights almost common along the Italianate opera circuit, when complications backstage and colorful noises before the curtain produce a deadlock and no music is heard.

At last, some of the company made a suggestion: let the young 'cellist try his luck in the pit. He had spent the leisure of the crossing from Genoa coaching the singers and had impressed them all with his command of the scores. Perhaps his authority would overwhelm the demonstration.

So Arturo Toscanini went out to conduct an opera for the first time. As the legend runs, when he reached the podium he slammed the score closed and sat on it in a bravura gesture that may well have fascinated the house into silence. (Remember, the orchestra played open to general sight on a level with the first floor of spectators.) Whatever the reason, the spectators quieted down, the performance went off in trim to close in cheers, and the company's first 'cellist became the company conductor. As one critic put it of that first Toscanini *Aida*, "Le roi est mort, vive le roi."

He was just nineteen years old.

> The feat of shutting and sitting upon the score has been disputed as embellishment after the act, especially as the picture of a conductor sitting while conducting a performance looks peculiar to modern eyes. However, conductors did sit more often than not in those days. As to the performance itself, Toscanini certainly knew the score by heart, though he always claimed to have made small mistakes in two spots that, ever after, he approached with caution.

Toscanini Quits La Scala

Toscanini's five-year reign as La Scala's music director, from 1898 to 1903, was a stormy one, not only for certain singers and the management, but for the audience, against whom he waged a war of manners. Toscanini hated their chattering, their dilletante love of Italian potboilers and suspicion of foreign curiosities, their greed for voice and disdain of musicianship, their brazen fetish about hearing encores of the most popular arias. The public hated Toscanini's ruthless dedication, his insistent Wagner and his impetuous Verdi, which seemed meant as a reproof of every "tradition" the Scala operagoer had helped institute, every reckless cut and excessive high note. Virtually every production Toscanini conducted occasioned another battle—especially over this business of granting encores.

Toscanini would give them: *sometimes*. In a concert with the Scala orchestra he repeated *Till Eulenspiegel* in its entirety at the public's request, doubtless to congratulate their good taste in taking to the German (meaning "difficult") Richard Strauss. But Toscanini was not in accord with the piling on of encores in a popular number opera; throughout his regime there were skirmishes. The public would request a *bis* (Italian for "twice") and Toscanini would surge on, to cries of outrage that might last for minutes.

The war between Toscanini and the Milanese reached its climax during *Un Ballo in Maschera* on April 14, 1903, the last night of the season. Toscanini was to leave for Buenos Aires the next day, from Genoa, and had asked for permission to depart Milan to make his boat in good time and entrust the baton on this last night to one of his deputies. The management refused, and Toscanini walked into the pit in a black, no-nonsense mood. The first scene went smoothly. But in Ulrica's cave, the public demanded that Giovanni Zenatello repeat the so-called Laughing Song, "È scherzo od è follia," and Toscanini pressed on, whether because Zenatello did not wish to grant the *bis* or because the conductor refused to indulge the appetites of the mob is not clear. Perhaps both. One thing one may say of Toscanini: he would always have his way in the end. For indeed, one of his deputies had to take over the performance, as Toscanini was unable to continue the scene—either too furious, too dispirited, or—according to the announcement made from the stage, bleeding from a wound. He may have thrust his hand through a window in his rage. In any case, he was leaving the theatre.

"What's wrong?" his wife asked, when he arrived home at about the time that the big love duet would be arching to its climax. "Is it finished already?"

Toscanini told her, "For me it is finished."

The next morning he left at daybreak and took the train to Genoa, having informed his employers that he wouldn't set foot in La Scala again.

Toscanini Looks Forward to a Difficult Performance

In 1905 Toscanini conducted an interesting season of opera at Bologna, including *Siegfried,* the world premiere of Vittorio Gnecchi's *Cassandra,* and *Madama Butterfly* with Salomea Krusceniski (supposedly the only soprano whom Toscanini had been mad for who resisted him). Just before the first *Siegfried,* one of the singers, who was nervously making his local debut, asked Toscanini how he thought the opera would go over.

"Eh!," the conductor replied. "I truly cannot say. There are too many

beasts in this piece. There are birds, there's the dragon, there's the bear
. . . and there's *you!*"

Toscanini's son-in-law

Toscanini was not impressed with his daughter Wally's marriage plans.
Bad enough that her intended, Count Emmanuele Castelbarco, was of
noble birth—"Whoever heard of an aristocrat being worth anything?"
Worse yet that the Count was of fair coloring. "Whoever heard," asked
Toscanini, "of marrying a blond man?"

Toscanini, Democrat

At the Met, Toscanini was no more gentle with errant personnel than
he had been at La Scala. One day the orchestra, tired of the slashing
invective, sent a delegation to Gatti-Casazza's office to complain. "Never
have we been called such dreadful names!" they cried.
  Gatti grunted. "You should hear what he calls me."

Tempo, Tempo

Toscanini had become so venerated as a Verdi expert that many younger
musicians came to him for advice on procedure. One maestrino asked
Toscanini how to choose the proper tempo for the Anvil Chorus.
  "Listen to the women when they do their laundry by the river," Toscanini answered. "They get it right every time."

Toscanini Reveals the Secret of Greatness

"It is easy to be a conductor," he once said. "All you have to do is play
the notes."

Toscanini Expresses His Opinion of Fascist Music

In late 1922, shortly after the March on Rome that put Mussolini in
power, Toscanini was conducting *Falstaff* at La Scala, of which he had
resumed leadership the year before. As he entered the pit for the last
act, some members of the audience called for the fascist party anthem,
"Giovinezza." Toscanini, who hated fascists even more than he hated
unprepared singers, simply raised his baton and beat into the Inn Scene.
But the fascists kept calling for "Giovinezza." Infuriated by their rude-

ness—and by everything that lay behind it in their fascist hearts—Toscanini broke his baton and stormed out of the pit.

To ease the tension, an official announced that "Giovinezza" would be played at the end of the opera, and the third act then went off in peace, with an unchastened Toscanini at the podium. At the end of the performance, he rushed onto the stage just as the official was telling the cast—and *Falstaff* closes with the entire cast on stage, from title role to choristers—to stay put to sing "Giovinezza."

"They aren't going to sing a damned thing!" Toscanini shouted. "The Scala artists aren't vaudeville singers! Go to your dressing rooms, all of you!"

Everybody ran out of the theatre. In a pinch, better suffer Mussolini's resentment and Toscanini's approval, than vice versa.

Toscanini's Secret of Good Health

Toscanini again gave up full-time leadership of La Scala in 1929 and went free-lance, traveling the world and concentrating ever less on the theatre scores of Verdi and Wagner and more on the concert works of Beethoven and Schubert. Fellow conductor John Barbirolli ran into him and congratulated him on how well he looked.

"My boy," replied Toscanini—"five years without opera!"

The Toscanini Touch

Admirers of *Die Meistersinger* often overlook the highly textured *colorito* of the opera's second act, which runs from jaunty folkishness into rapt poetry, on to farce exploded into the riot in double-fugue, then the rapt beauty restored, an entire city of families, professionals, and neighbors brought to life in an hour.

Toscanini's *Meistersinger* at Salzburg in 1936 was said to have highlighted Act Two especially. As critic B. H. Haggin noted, "in sound and dynamics, in clarity, in expression—this was the ultimate." Publisher Victor Gollancz thought so, too. He was so taken with Toscanini's second act that, after attending one full performance of the opera, he arrived for the others during the first intermission—and left during the second. "Eccentric, no doubt," he wrote. "But as a result we had a musical experience almost certainly unique."

Even Toscanini was impressed; he wasn't often. In his dressing room after the act ended, he stood like one possessed. "Com'un sogno," he said: Like a dream.

Toscanini on Wagnerian Pacing

At Salzburg, Toscanini was sitting in on Bruno Walter's rehearsal of *Tristan und Isolde* with Margherita Wallmann, who choreographed all Salzburg Festival productions in the pre-Nazi 1930s. During the very long love duet in Act Two, Maestro turned to Wallmann and noted, "If they were Italians, they would already have had seven children. But see, they're Germans: they're still talking it over."

Toscanini Sings

Toscanini got so involved in the music he was conducting that he would sometimes sing along with the orchestra at climactic passages in a sort of tense, wordless, hum. The big tune in "O soave fanciulla," near the end of *La Bohème*'s first act particularly inspired Toscanini: when he led a broadcast performance of the opera with his NBC Symphony in 1946, as Licia Albanese and Jan Peerce rose lyrically to the gala moment, so did Maestro. Rosa Raisa, who had sung under Toscanini at La Scala in the old days, heard the broadcast and wired him: "DEAR MAESTRO IT WAS SO GOOD TO HEAR YOU SING AGAIN."

Wanda Toscanini Reviews a Critic

Toscanini's daughter Wanda, who married the pianist Vladimir Horowitz, generally disliked critics. She especially disliked the *New York Herald Tribune*'s Virgil Thomson, who was somewhat less than enthusiastic about her family's talents. In famous Sunday "thinkpieces" devoted to each man, Thomson called Toscanini "spiritually unenlightening" and Horowitz "a master of musical distortion," and Wanda became self-righteously irate when she spotted Thomson dozing during a concert performance of *Falstaff* conducted by her father.

Spiritually unenlightening, eh? At the end of the work, she confronted Thomson, saying, "I am Wanda Toscanini Horowitz. I saw you sleep from the first note to the last note." Then she smacked him with her program, adding, "I hope you enjoyed the performance!"

Thomson gave it a good notice, though he may have been encouraged by Wanda's making the episode public with a call to a newspaper columnist. Toscanini thought Wanda gave a brilliant reading of her part in her scene with Thomson. "Brava! Brava!" he cried.

Dinner with the Maestro

Violist William Primrose was invited to join Toscanini for dinner at his house in Riverdale. Toscanini's family was away, and he wanted company.

Primrose was stunned at this opportunity. The stories he would hear: Verdi, Puccini, Farrar, Caruso, Gatti, Lehmann! But instead of unfolding his tales, Toscanini silently raced through dinner and packed Primrose into the television room for Toscanini's favorite entertainment: wrestling, with running commentary by Toscanini. "Punch 'im in ze stomach!" the Maestro urges. "Grab 'im to ze leg! Jomp on 'im! Make 'im into mess!"

That was all Primrose heard.

The Last Performance

By the early 1950s, Toscanini was the miracle of his profession. His extraordinarily influential first reign at La Scala had ended five decades earlier, his comparable reign at the Met thirty-five years before. He had known Verdi and Puccini personally, conducted the world premieres of *Pagliacci, La Bohème, La Fanciulla del West,* and *Turandot;* led festival performances of *Fidelio, Die Meistersinger,* and *Falstaff* that were among the greatest ever given; not only stood up to but openly ridiculed Mussolini; and made records so good that some people bought their first phonograph in order to hear them.

He was tiring. On his eighty-seventh birthday, he signed a letter resigning his leadership of the NBC Symphony—according to a rumor that can never be substantiated, at NBC's connivance. A few days later, he led rehearsals for his last broadcast, an all-Wagner concert, and a dismayed orchestra saw an almost ruined man, inconsistent in stick technique and unsure of certain details in the score. The temper was as contentious as ever. "È vergogna!" he shouted. "Vergogna!": Shameful! Finally, his rage mounting, he stopped the musicians and cried "L'ultima prova!": The last rehearsal! And he stormed out, the rehearsal unfinished.

The concert, on April 4, 1954, began with the Prelude to *Lohengrin,* uneventfully. In the following Forest Murmurs, Toscanini forgot to anticipate some changes in rhythm; the orchestra covered for him. Then came Dawn and Siegfried's Rhine Journey, competent. Toward the end of the ensuing Overture and Bacchanale from *Tannhäuser,* however, Toscanini suddenly put down his baton and covered his eyes with his left hand, and the orchestra began to go off. Monitoring the broadcast in the radio control room, Toscanini's protégé Guido Cantelli ordered the concert taken off the air. The station replaced it with Toscanini's recording of Brahms' First Symphony, pleading technical difficulties without further explanation.

Meanwhile, Toscanini had recovered himself, and NBC turned the microphones on again. After the Bacchanale, Toscanini stepped down as if to leave. Gently, the concertmaster stopped him: there was still the Prelude to *Die Meistersinger* to play. Nodding assent, Toscanini returned to the podium. "I conducted as if it had been a dream," he said later. "It almost seemed to me that I wasn't there."

Overwhelmed with emotion but conducting with less feeling than ever before in his life, Toscanini beat time through the last piece—up to the final measures, when the ordeal proved too much for him. Dropping his baton, he left the podium as the orchestra was reaching the closing chords, slowly walked to his dressing room, and locked himself in.

He never conducted again.

JOHN CHRISTIE

Here was the most unlikely of impresarios, a crusty and intolerant English squire where producers of opera tend to be diplomatic and suggestible; an elitist where his colleagues try to be democratic; and his public's host in the most literal sense: the theatre was in his house. Only the Wagners rivaled the Christies in the realm of working family auditoriums, and there is no real rivalry, for while Bayreuth and Glyndebourne are both summer festivals, Bayreuth is hard to get to, uncomfortable to attend, and only stages Wagner, whereas Glyndebourne is convenient to London, a grand place to spend the day, and has built on its signature Mozart and Rossini to take in, most notably, ancient Venetian opera, arcane Richard Strauss, and *The Rake's Progress*.

Eton and Cambridge helped form Christie; he emerged a very bulldog of a gentleman, blunt if willing to accommodate these artistic chaps, and very much his own man, unpredictably resourceful. Having an opera singer for a wife—Audrey Mildmay—helped temper his distaste for backstage shenanigans, and no doubt the success of his venture helped pull him over the rough spots, for from the first Glyndebourne made an important contribution to British cultural life. The small scale of the theatre provided a wonderful sense of contact between stage and spectators, and the rustic Sussex setting (every photograph of operalovers strolling over the Glyndebourne grounds shows at least two or three cows) allowed for a contemplative environment that left the public with a highly fulfilled experience of music theatre composed, achieved, and comprehended.

Perhaps this is because Glyndebourne emphasized the serene prestige of Mozart, most melodic of composers, and most intimately so. From the first performance, of *Le Nozze di Figaro* on May 28, 1934, Mozart was the house composer—and house staff, by hap, depended far more on foreigners than on Britishers. Fritz Busch and Carl Ebert, Christie's guests at Hitler's accidental instigation, instituted the Glyndebourne style, respectively in the pit and on stage. Rudolf Bing signed on after the war, and Vittorio Gui inherited the pit at Busch's death. Casting too was cosmopolitan. Mildmay of course took part, but the famous early Mozart ensembles also took in such as Luise Helletsgruber, Aulikki Rautawaara, Kolomon von Pataky, and Willi Domgraf-Fassbaender.

Glyndebourne, then, was a haven: for displaced artists, for Mozarteans, and for thoughtful opera buffs. Its history is rich in "good old days" nostalgia, though after the first two decades the slashing modern style began to intrude (as we'll soon see, when Christie meets the librettist of *An Elegy for Young Lovers*). But in the main Christie and Glyndebourne symbolize a uniquely tolerant corner of opera history, wherein family money and good intentions set up a very special place for opera—and a production style of realism tempered by elegance—that has flourished for five decades.

An Announcement from the Stage

The spring and summer of 1939 saw a march of events that, most reasonable people knew, must lead to the next world war. On March 31, Neville Chamberlain told the House of Commons that England and France would intervene for Polish independence. On April 7, Mussolini attacked Albania. On April 28, Hitler addressed the Reichstag in what was virtually a position paper on aggression. On May 22, Hitler and Mussolini signed the Pact of Steel. And on July 15, John Christie strode on stage at Glyndebourne after *Così Fan Tutte,* the last performance of the season, to share what he announced as "serious news." The audience braced itself.

And Christie announced that Harrow had just beaten Eton at cricket for the first time since 1908.

A Lift

Designer Osbert Lancaster was driving along Pall Mall during the afternoon rush hour when he caught sight of Christie standing in the middle of the road. Of course Lancaster stopped, and Christie got in, saying, "I knew I'd see somebody I knew who was going to Victoria Station."

Lancaster wasn't; but he did.

Christie Meets a Poet

Christie's idea of a night at the opera was something tuneful above all—thus the early insistence on Mozart and Rossini. When it came to unearthing forgotten antiques, Christie similarly liked the ones that turned out to have plenty of tunes. His taste was remarkably consistent.

Contemporary works pained him; they lacked tunes. He tolerated them in his house, but he wasn't going to try to like them, least of all, perhaps, Hans Werner Henze's *Elegy for Young Lovers*. The libretto, about a heartless poet who more or less murders a young couple so that mourning may inspire his muse, was the collaboration of W. H. Auden and Chester Kallmann. One day at a rehearsal Auden approached Christie, who to that point had strangely not said a word to him.

"Mr. Christie," the poet quoth, "I'm Auden."

"Who?"

"Auden. I wrote this opera."

And Christie snapped back, "You shouldn't have."

THOMAS BEECHAM

Beecham hailed from that old school of maestros who played what they liked and to hell with the rest. Today's conductors plume themselves on being stylishly adept at everything, with emphasis on the acknowledged classics. But Beecham's generation, through its eccentric favoritism, could popularize specialties, as Beecham did Delius, Sibelius, and French opera. "I would give the whole of Bach's Brandenburg Concertos for Massenet's *Manon* and would think I had vastly profited by the exchange," Beecham said.

It's hard to imagine the solemnly dedicated star maestros of today delivering such a provocative statement. But then today's conductors don't figure in lively anecdote the way those of Beecham's day did; nor do they often admit to liking, much less popularize, neglected corners of music. Leonard Bernstein's championship of Gustav Mahler, seldom played when Bernstein began and now regarded as stock repertory, is perhaps the last major act of proselytization on the international music scene. No, today's conductors are pious revealers of text in, they hope, the Toscanini manner: *hier steht*. But if they lack Toscanini's reckless disregard of his colleagues' feelings, they also lack his grim wit.

Beecham had wit. Few other conductors claim as many short takes, such as Beecham's comment to an orchestra after the tuning-up oboe sounded a rather wobbly A: "Gentlemen, take your pick!" Less well known was his zest for inventing nicknames. Glyndebourne, with which

Beecham carried on a cordial feud, was "Christie's Minstrels." * Malcolm Sargent was affectionately dubbed "Flash"—and of course Sargent's successful series of concerts in Tokyo was "A Flash in Japan."

A baronet and heir to a fortune derived from the patent medicine Beecham's Pills, Beecham was as much impresario and conductor, forming orchestras and virtually capitalizing out of pocket his earliest operatic ventures. Starting small, with a group fit to put on a decent *Bartered Bride,* he built outward from the center till he was putting on excellent Wagner and Verdi. Beecham was bold. He mounted contemporary English operas (in which no one but he was interested). He hired unknowns along with notable veterans. He had thespian Nigel Playfair stage Mozart. When Diaghilev's troupe left England at the outbreak of World War I, leaving their scenery behind, Beecham got hold of it and put on a series of Russian operas. If his stories emphasize the man's caustic, risqué wit, it should nevertheless be remembered that he was one of the most influential men in the history of English music.

Fire the Trainer!

Beecham is in the pit at Covent Garden, conducting one of those operas that calls for a horse. At the height of the action, the beast chucks his composure and drops a treasure onto the stage.

"Egad!" remarks Sir Thomas. "A critic!"

Wagnerian Tempo

A well-wisher urged Sir Thomas not to attempt *Götterdämmerung* without conducting from the score. Otherwise, how would he handle all those complex rhythmical changes?

"There are no rhythmical changes in *Götterdämmerung,*" said Beecham. "It goes straight on from half past five till midnight like a damned old cart horse!"

Sir Thomas on *Wozzeck*

"It is an ingenious score, but entirely uncivilized and uncharming. I am not interested in music, or in any work of art, that fails to stimulate enjoyment in life, and, what is more, pride in life."

---

* Beecham's pun refers to the Christy Minstrels, blackface troupes popular in Victorian London and the Continent.

Sir Thomas on Toscanini

Beecham conducted the New York Philharmonic Orchestra in 1928 on a guest shot while Toscanini, the Philharmonic's regular conductor, was on vacation. After Beecham's first rehearsal, the orchestra's managerial committee took him to lunch and asked him what he thought of the band. "They are quite incredibly good," said Beecham. "The woodwinds and horns executed the most difficult arabesques as Kreisler handles his violin. Really wonderful." Then he paused, playing with his cigar. "But for all this dexterity of technique, I found the players extraordinarily insensitive interpretively. No idea of an alluring phrase. . . ." He thought it over, readying the payoff. "Tell me," he finally said, "who has been conducting your orchestra lately?"

A Chip of the Old Block

A baritone known for such roles as Klingsor and Alberich asked Sir Thomas for advice about his son, who was about to leave Oxford without a shred of professional motivation.

"Aren't you going to make a singer of him?"

"Oh no, Sir Thomas. He hasn't got a voice. Not really."

"Ah, I see—a family failing."

Helpful Sir Thomas

When Beecham didn't like a singer he could be quite callous in his manner, even in purely artistic situations. Frieda Hempel, one soprano Beecham didn't care for, was singing Pamina in *Die Zauberflöte* under Sir Thomas and sent a deputy to inform him that she was not feeling her best. Would Sir Thomas transpose "Ach, ich fühl's" for her? Sir Thomas agreed. Obviously, she wanted it transposed down, so she wouldn't have to reach for the higher lines. But if the woman wants it transposed down, she should *say* she wants it transposed down.

Beecham told the orchestra to transpose it *up*.

Sir Thomas Accepts a Compliment

Beecham was celebrated for his Mozart. It had a grace, polish, and, above all, soul that other men's Mozart only hinted at. As long ago as 1937, Beecham conducted a recording of *Die Zauberflöte* that has been challenged but never surpassed, not even by Otto Klemperer and Herbert von Karajan.

After one such performance, Beecham's colleague Fritz Reiner came backstage to express his admiration.

"I want to thank you," says Reiner, "for a wonderful night with Mozart and Beecham."

"Why drag in Mozart?" Beecham replies.

Chrysothemis Appeals to Sir Thomas

Hilde Konetzni, a sizable woman, was singing Chrysothemis in Strauss's *Elektra* with Beecham in London in 1938. She was unsure of her entry at the line, "Kinder will ich haben bevor mein Leib verwelkt": I want to bear children before my body withers; and therefore moved closer to the conductor to discern his beat more easily. Seeing this hunk of soprano suddenly bearing down on him, Beecham called over his shoulder to Walter Legge and asked him what she was saying to him— she certainly seemed to be saying something.

"She wants you to be the father of her child," Legge translated.

"Send word to her," replied Beecham, still leading his men as he eyed Konetzni with bemusement, "that I'll reconsider her offer on some very cold winter's night."

Fun in Australia

Beecham has just concluded a tour down under, and a reporter asks, "When will you be returning to Australia?"

Replies Beecham, "Does anyone ever *return* to Australia?"

Music Is a Holy Art

This isn't precisely an opera anecdote, but it's too choice to lose. Rehearsing the *Messiah* with a soprano soloist who was shaky in her part, Sir Thomas warned her that she must apply herself to the music at once.

Later, she promised him, she'd be all right. "I've been studying the score for weeks," she said, "and I've been taking it to bed with me every evening."

"In that case," Sir Thomas told her, "I'm sure we shall have an immaculate conception."

Concerning the Mortality Rate Among Singers

In the finale of Massenet's *Don Quichotte*, Quixote dies as his devoted Sancho Panza keens and the voice of the unseen Dulcinea bathes the moment in pathetic nostalgia. Chalyapin, who created Massenet's knight, had a way of shifting the vocal line to suit his portrayal, and, at a rehearsal under Beecham, the bass's improvisations were throwing the Dulcinea off her beat. Beecham, however, was putting pressure on the mezzo to hold the scene together, and at last she said, "I cannot help it, Sir Thomas. Mr. Chalyapin always dies too soon."

"Madame," remarks Beecham, "you must be profoundly in error. No operatic star has yet died half soon enough for me!"

A Timely Pun

Beecham had been planning a withdrawal from England's musical life, but the outbreak of World War II brought him back to the lists. After a successful concert with the London Philharmonic, someone asked him why he had changed his plans.

"My dear fellow, we were given to understand that the country was in a state of emergency; and so I emerged."

The Virtue of Being Canadian

Jon Vickers met Beecham for the first time as they bumped into each other in a doorway just before starting rehearsals for a recording of *The Messiah.* It was a touchy moment, for the young and as yet unheralded Vickers was apprehensive about his ability to agree with Beecham on the matter of style.

The two traded compliments, and Beecham joked about this and that, but Vickers felt he must have it out with the maestro here and now. "First of all, Sir Thomas," Vickers began, "I'm not an English tenor." And Sir Thomas roared, "Thank *God!*"

Sir Thomas Coaches

Rehearsing the last scene of *La Bohème,* Beecham stopped the orchestra to tell the tenor that he could not be heard. Rodolpho had been lying on the bed, comforting the dying Mimì.

"How do you expect to sing my best in this position, Sir Thomas?"

"In that position, my dear fellow," Beecham advised him, "I have performed some of my greatest achievements."

RUDOLF BING

Bing brought back dash to the profession of impresario. Witty, despotic, and suave, he took over a house whose tradition was Great Voices and upheld it, while trying, fitfully, to develop new traditions of musical excellence and theatricality.

That neither took hold is not entirely Bing's fault. A great Met night in the early Bing years might be, say, an *Ernani* with Zinka Milanov, Mario del Monaco, Leonard Warren, and Cesare Siepi under Dimitri Mitropoulos. The conductor guaranteed musical excellence—no one found the song in early Verdi the way Mitropoulos did; it was like Toscanini with breathing spaces. But who on earth could teach theatricality to that cast?

What if Bing had come to the Met holding the assumption that less distinguished voices and more intent acting would serve Verdi better? Would he have given better opera? Better Verdi? Better anecdotes for collections like this one? Most Met-goers might suggest that better Verdi than Milanov's there isn't. At least what Bing did, and what Bing didn't, kept New York thinking about an impresario's choices; New York had taken Bing's predecessor Edward Johnson for granted. Bing, through the sense of confrontation he brought to all his dealings, ran the world's most international opera house on highly personal biases, and this in itself put the biases—artistic choices, really—into relief. The Bing Met was a seminar in The Mission of the Contemporary Impresario, and the stories bear out one's impression that much of Bing's tenure comprised his trying to get along with high-strung artists.

Some think he didn't try hard enough. The firing of Callas—when she was in Dallas blithely impeding the development of the coming season's schedule by not deciding which roles she would sing and when—remains Bing's most dubious achievement. The neglect of James McCracken, allotted only comprimario roles till he took himself to Europe and unveiled an important Heldentenor, typified the waste of young talent that Bing's regime actually took pride in. The disdain of Beverly Sills, after the City Opera's *Giulio Cesare* set her forth as America's favorite revealed voice, was fiercely questionable—though, as Sills herself points out, Bing's failure to enlist her at the Met helped define her identity as the Underdog Diva and contributed to rather than detracted from her reign.

When Bing did get along with a star, his or her fans would find the Met a pleasure dome. Renata Tebaldi, Franco Corelli, Birgit Nilsson, and a few others of the world's finest voices guaranteed wonderful nights. The repertory was limited, the stagings gruesome, and house tradition upheld every sloppy short-cut devised in the previous hundred years. But a Tebaldi-Corelli-Gobbi *Tosca,* or a Nilsson-Crespin-Ludwig-Vickers-Stewart *Walküre* gave Met audiences literally the greatest casts available in these operas—and the first performances of the von Karajan Ring had von Karajan in the pit. Bing reserved the right to view this momentous house debut of the world's most unavailable conductor with a sense of humor. When von Karajan mused proudly upon the nuances of gloom in one of his Vienna Wagner stagings, explaining that it took eight lighting rehearsals, Bing countered with, "I could have got it that dark in one."

Bing could get the best when he chose to, though he often waited too long. Seldom did Met audiences have the chance to welcome a wonderful new talent into fame; seldom was a debut a surprise. Newcomers to the stage tended to be either world-class veterans well-known through recordings or third-raters from exotic places such as Belgrade, Split, and Passaic. Yet Bing did move quickly in the matter of racial integration, pushing (against the express wishes of the Met Board of Directors) to invite Marian Anderson to join the company, if only for one role that she could slip in amidst her heavy recital schedule. Bing's first offer, in his first year, was for Azucena; not till 1955 did the contralto at last accept the opportunity to make a little Met history, as Ulrica in *Un Ballo in Maschera*—at that only because Bing and Anderson found themselves sitting next to each other at a concert and could pass an intermission talking terms. Other black singers followed Anderson, and by the late 1960s the Met had become special for its roster of black sopranos—Leontyne Price, Martina Arroyo, Grace Bumbry, Shirley Verrett. Like the young American Heldentenors who supported the Wagner wing in German houses, or like the designs of Nicola Benois at La Scala, the Met's black sopranos became an identifying element of company spirit, so much so that when one of the Met's periodic union troubles threatened a season, of all musicians' appeals to President John Kennedy to intervene, it was Leontyne Price's that seemed the most . . . well, appealing.

Bing was sly—as when he hired a claqueur to yell, "Brava, Callas!" when Leonie Rysanek made her entrance (and Met debut) as Lady Macbeth in the production Callas had been fired from, thus centering public sympathy on the debutante. Bing was clever—as each of these stories affirms. Bing was contentious; it comes with the territory. But Bing was a showman, too, and the Bing tales recall a time, not so long ago, when the Met seemed at times like the greatest opera house in the world.

Bing and the Conductors

An admitted weakness of Bing's regime was its conducting staff, strangely difficult to strengthen. Toscanini didn't answer Bing's letter. Erich Kleiber had committed himself to Covent Garden, Furtwängler was ailing. Guido Cantelli and Hans Knappertsbusch were booked up. Kleiber's wife suggested a German of some note, but Bing recalled him as "a mediocre conductor who was an outstanding Nazi." He was only willing to consider the reverse, an outstanding conductor who was a mediocre Nazi.

Bing's biggest disappointment was George Szell, who did come, but lasted for only four performances of *Tannhäuser.* Szell fought with everyone in the house, spoke disloyally to the press, and finally walked out.

"George Szell," someone told Bing, "is his own worst enemy."

Bing replied, "Not while I'm alive."

It's a popular comeback. More famously, George S. Kaufman said it of Broadway director Jed Harris.

Mr. Bing Has a Dream

Bing loves dogs, but he had a recurring nightmare haunted by dogs: divas' dogs. Callas's Toy, Tebaldi's New, and Milanov's Nickie—two poodles and a spitz—would advance on Bing and, in a burlesque of expressionistic music, sing, "Choose, choose, choose!"

He would wake up screaming.

Cecil Beaton's Faux Pas

The Met's first *Turandot,* which followed hard upon the Scala premiere, offered Maria Jeritza and Giacomo Lauri-Volpi under Tullio Serafin. Vigorous newspaper publicity and the performance itself made the work a sensation, but it fell out of the repertory till the rise of Birgit Nilsson drew Bing's attention to it. Some thirty years after the first production, a new one was unveiled, early in 1961, with Nilsson, Corelli, and Anna Moffo under Leopold Stokowski. Cecil Beaton designed the sets and costumes with special feeling for color—dark, nocturnal shades of blue and green in the first act; brilliant pastels for the Riddle Scene.

Imagine Beaton's horror on opening night when one of the chorus women accidentally came onstage in Act One not in her moonlit mandarin robes but in the burnt orange number assigned her for the Riddle Scene. Leaping out of his orchestra seat, Beaton dashed backstage in a fury; by then an alert stage manager had signaled the offending chorister into the wings. There Beaton ripped the costume off her while treating her to choice words on her sense of artistic discipline.

Bing enters here, determined to make peace among his Met family, especially among the offended chorister. "You like this opera, Cecil?" he asked.

Beaton did.

"You like this production?"

Certainly he liked it.

"You want to see the second act?"

Beaton paled.

"Well, you'd better get back there and apologize."

Beaton did. But the last word was Noël Coward's. The third Britisher in this tale of Englishmen in New York, Coward had been having a rough time for years from the London theatre critics, who called him a played-out dinosaur and were virtually trying to hunt him from the stage. Remarked Coward, "I wish just one critic had said, 'That dot of orange in the first act! What inspiration!' "

Bing Sings Opera

It was a mime part, actually, that of Sir Edgar in Hans Werner Henze's *Der Junge Lord* in 1973. Still it was Bing, in costume onstage; and on the stage of the City Opera, the Met's sometimes less than dear little brother. The event was considered so strategic to the fortunes of opera in the American *Hauptkulturstadt* that the *New York Times* ran the story, solemnly printing, in its entirety, the opening-night break-a-leg telegram that Birgit Nilsson sent Bing: EVEN IF YOUR ROLE IS SPEECHLESS, I'M SURE YOU WILL HAVE THE LAST WORD. LOVE BIRGIT. P.S. DON'T FORGET THAT MANY GREAT ARTISTS HAVE MADE THEIR WAY FROM THE CITY OPERA TO THE MET.

Precious Paper

If Bing did not extend himself professionally to Beverly Sills, they nonetheless got along personally. Once, when Sills was singing Violetta in San Antonio, an attendant announced a dressing-room visitor: Sir Rudolf, fresh from his City Opera stint as Sir Edgar. "I always knew," said Sills, "we'd both be working for the same opera company sometime."

The attendant had secured Bing's autograph; now he asked for Sills's, and got it. "Young man, that's an historic document," says Bing. "It's the only piece of paper in the world bearing the signatures of both Rudolf Bing and Beverly Sills."

Finale

Let us now page through the panorama of opera's onlie begetters in Fun with Composers Through the Ages, comprising, among other things, a deathbed comedy, assorted acts of arrogance, and one of Hector Berlioz's most scabrous proclamations:

The Passing of Lully

In 1686, Lully composed a Te Deum to celebrate the recovery of the king of France from a severe illness. While conducting, with his habitual great wooden staff, Lully struck his toe, suffered injury, and faced death. One noble family pledged a fortune to the doctor who could save him, but no treatment availed. Lully must die.

One thing remained for the greatest composer of France, to make his peace with God. Lully's confessor, long scandalized by the licentious character of opera, with its humorous couplets, ballet dancing, and other decadence, refused Lully absolution unless he agreed to burn the manuscript of his last opera, *Achille et Polyxène*. Lully agreed.

"How could you?" a friend sadly reproached him later. "To deny the world the last opera by Jean-Baptiste Lully! Why, it might have been your masterpiece!"

"Hush. I cheated the good father: I only burned a copy."

He died singing one of his own tunes, "Il faut mourir, pécheur, il faut mourir": Sinner, you too must die.

Rameau Is Honored

Louis XV decided to award Rameau's genius with letters of nobility, and to cap this honor with the Order of St. Michael. But sometime after receiving his letters-patent, Rameau failed to register them, as law requires, and the King wondered if the crusty old composer was simply unwilling to undergo the expense. Delicately, he offered to cover the registration cost himself.

"Let me have the money outright," said Rameau, "and I will apply it to some more useful purpose. Letters of nobility! Why, my *Castor* and *Dardanus* gave them to me long ago!"

Flirtation Scene

Drastic harmonic transitions were becoming fashionable in the opera of André Grétry's day. Purists fumed, but the public enjoyed hearing a violent turn of plot underscored in the orchestra. Grétry, however, seemed to be holding aloof from the trend.

"Someday I may give an audience something of the like," he told a
friend, "but not for the sake of being *au courant*. There must be a reason."

"Such as what?"

"Suppose an amorous young blade should attempt to make love to
a pretty miss. Love duet."

"Just so."

"Her father comes upon the two, unseen. Music of foreboding."

"Naturellement."

"He sneaks up from behind—crescendo—and fetches the young swain
a kick of the very best brand right where it belongs. Then, sir, I assure
you—I will modulate *very* abruptly!"

Flattery Gets You Nowhere

A painter, hoping to flatter Domenico Cimarosa, told him that he was
the greatest of composers, superior even to Mozart.

We all like praise, but this was too much. "What would you think,
sir," said Cimarosa, "of a musician who told you you were superior to
Raphael?"

Cherubini Defends Méhul

Someone showed Luigi Cherubini, the redoubtable pedant of the Paris
Conservatoire, a sample of score, alleging it to be the work of Etienne
Méhul.

"It's not good enough to be Méhul's," snapped Cherubini.

"It's mine, in fact."

"It can't be."

"Why not?"

"It's too good to be yours."

Cherubini Rates Rossini

"What do you say," asked some hack, waving the score of *Mosé* in the
air, "to this shocking chromatic passage by that libertine Rossini?"

Replies Cherubini, "I wish I had committed it."

Cherubini Flunks Halévy

Fromental Halévy took his former teacher Cherubini to Halévy's latest
opera. After the first act, he asked Cherubini what he thought.

No answer.

After the second, Halévy repeated the question.

No answer.

"Why don't you reply?" Halévy cried.

"To what? For two hours you've been saying absolutely nothing."

Now Berlioz Rates Cherubini

Berlioz was so disgusted by the lack of invention in Cherubini's *Ali Baba* that, during the first act, he cried out, "Twenty francs for an idea!"

In the second act, he called out, "Forty francs for an idea!"

Still later: "Eighty francs for an idea!"

Finally he rose and, saying "I give up—I'm not rich enough!," he stalked out.

A Keepsake

A countess visited Charles Gounod at his villa in St. Cloud while his family was taking the annual *vacances* by the sea. Arriving just after lunch, the countess happened to pass through the dining room, where the servants were clearing the table. A plate of cherry pits caught her eye; deftly she palmed a pit and hid it in her glove; returned to Paris, she had her jeweler fashion a brooch with the pit set off by diamonds.

Her brooch *en Gounod!*

When the great composer next visited her, she wore the brooch, with a sly smile. Every hostess in Paris was after this elusive celebrity, but she alone had captured his essence, in the most intimate of souvenirs.

Gounod was taken aback. "I never eat cherries, Madame," he explained. "It was my footman, Jean, whose pit you collected."

The countess was not amused.

Now It's Stravinsky Rating Handel

Listening to a recording of *Theodora*, Stravinsky says, "It's beautiful and boring. Too many pieces finish too long after the end."

Or Britten

"He's not a composer—he's a kleptomaniac."

Barber Congratulates Thomson

At the world premiere of Virgil Thomson's *The Mother of Us All*—on the life of feminist pioneer Susan B. Anthony and like much of Thomson an essay in boldly basic harmony—Samuel Barber approaches Thomson and says, dryly, "I hope you won't mind my stealing a few of your chords."

Now, some short takes from the world of the maestro:

Von Bülow on Tenors

Von Bülow praised a certain tenor and Henry Krehbiel demurred. The singer, he said, lacked virility.

"But, my dear fellow," Von Bülow answers, "a tenor *isn't* a man: it's a disease!"

Let's Talk Salary

Francis Robinson told this story, and insists that it happened: Cleofonte Campanini auditioned a useful if not superb tenor and asked him what his fee was.

"Two thousand dollars a performance."

"I'll give you two hundred."

"I'll take it!"

Klemperer versus Lehmann

Weimar Berlin delighted in three major opera houses: the official state theatre, Unter den Linden; the Städtische or Charlottenburg Opera; and the feisty, experimental Kroll Opera, under the musical direction of the exacting Otto Klemperer. When the Kroll closed down because of money troubles, Klemperer moved on to the big house, Unter den Linden, where his precision confronted the sometimes approximate attack of Lotte Lehmann, in from Vienna *als Gast* for *Der Rosenkavalier*. Tired of Klemperer's niggling corrections, Lehmann cried, "Don't keep on interrupting me! I'm only singing a few performances here, anyway, then I'm off to present my Marschallin at Covent Garden and the Chicago Opera!"

"Strauss," asked Klemperer, "or the Lehmann version?"

Careful Tenor

Bad enough were the sloppy singers; worse were the singers who liked to "mark" at rehearsals (singing in half-voice to save themselves for a paying audience). "Sing!" Klemperer told a tenor who was holding back. "*Sing,* I tell you!"

The tenor came to the edge of the stage and whispered (this tenor even marked when speaking), "I have but two high Cs left, Herr Doktor. Do you want to hear them now or tonight at the performance?"

Too Easy

Wilhelm Furtwängler's baton technique was the most ambiguous in the business. There was no denying the profundity of his performances— but did he have to wield such an unreadable beat?

"Anyone can conduct so square and straight," Furtwängler would say, when challenged thus. And he would demonstrate, leading his players in a perfectly unmannered delivery, clear beat, clear performance. Then he would drop his baton and shrug. "But that is so boring . . ."

That's a Good Question

Henry Holst, concertmaster of the Berlin Philharmonie, was asked, "How do you follow Furtwängler's beat?"

Smiling, Holst answered, "Do we?"

A Hometown Girl

Hans Knappertsbusch is having trouble getting a sense of character from Lisa della Casa. He wants *espressivo;* she gives *diretto.* He wants *accento;* she gives *senz'accento;* he wants *con slancio;* she gives *morbidezza.* He asks her where she was born.

"Bern, Herr Professor."

"I thought so."

East-West Diplomacy

Conducting the Bolshoi Opera on a visit to East Berlin, Mstislaf Rostropovich spent much of his free time blithely carting Western consumer goods through the Berlin Wall for members of the company in his Land-Rover. This was at a time when Soviet-West relations were on hold and the border guards tense and touchy.

In West Berlin for a competition of young conductors, John Culshaw questioned Rostropovich's audacity. "What if they won't let you through?" he asked.

"What," answered Rostropovich, "if I tell them I'm not going to conduct tonight?"

Let us conclude our tour with a fanfaronade of bons mots in no special order—just opera's people telling opera's tales. Some are witty, some angry, some classic, and some brand-new . . .

Our Most Savage Rating Yet: Berlioz on David

Félicien David was the forerunner of French opera's Oriental wing, which eventually produced, among our favorites, Bizet's *Les Pêcheurs de Perles,* Delibes's *Lakmé,* Massenet's *Le Roi de Lahore,* Rabaud's *Mârouf,* and Roussel's *Padmâvatî.* As the first of the line, David enjoyed a vogue, but Berlioz despised David's work as bourgeois vulgarity painted up in pseudo-Eastern modes with a lot of bells and cymbals going off. David's *Le Désert,* on the adventures of a caravan, gave Berlioz the opportunity for a choice *mot* when a friend asked him what he thought of this latest David opus.

"Il est descendu," said Berlioz, "de son chameau": It came out of his camel.

On Call

"Where to?" asks the cab driver as the World Famous Conductor gets in.

"Just drive," comes the reply. "I'm in demand everywhere."

House Seats

Someone wanted to buy a ticket to a performance at Bayreuth and someone had a ticket to sell—but the asking price seemed excessive for a seat way at the back on the side.

"It's the best seat in the house," the would-be seller insisted.

"How so?"

"Nearest the door."

Formal Dress

In the 1940s and 1950s, Mrs. John R. Orndorff decorated the opening night of each Chicago season by dressing as the heroine of the given opera. *Carmen* called up a black lace mantilla supported by a gold comb. *Aida* brought forth plumes and sequins answering to a gold motif. *Otello* inspired an Italian Renaissance gown in green velvet. There was one miscalculation, when Lily Pons's indisposition cancelled a *Lakmé* at the last minute and Mrs. Orndorff ended up attending a Milanov *Aida* in blue-and-gold Hindu pajamas with bare midriff.

A good sport, Mrs. Orndorff nonetheless drew the line at *La Fanciulla del West*, the 1956 premiere with Steber, Del Monaco, and Gobbi under Dimitri Mitropoulos. "I didn't want to attend the opening," she told the press, "as a barmaid."

Dean Swift Makes Comment

Most opera rivalries involve singers—Lotte Lehmann and Maria Jeritza, for instance, the two splitting the city of Vienna into warring camps; or Callas and Tebaldi, Callas gunning for the title of soprano assoluta and Tebaldi unsuccessfully trying to stay noncombatant. Handel himself officiated at one of opera's most gala feuds, between his two star sopranos Faustina Bordoni and Francesca Cuzzoni, the competition engaging the two singers so appetitively that one night they attacked each other on stage during the music, a scandal that delighted London and provided John Gay with a source for spoof in *The Beggar's Opera*, the battle duet of Polly and Lucy, "I'm bubbled, I'm bubbled."

When composers are rivals, the public seldom takes much interest, for the byline musicians lack the glamor of the thespians; anyway, composers can't give audience as singers can, and what's a rivalry without heated words and haughty looks? Composer rivalries are private affairs, like that of Bellini and Donizetti, or that among the Ricordi stable when Italy was looking for a thoroughbred to succeed Verdi. Every so often a rivalry does break into the public arena—as we saw with Gluck and Piccinni. Comparable to that ideological, virtually political dispute is the one that occupied Whig-and-Tory London in the 1720s, rooting for, respectively, Handel and Giovanni Battista Bononcini.

It was a silly feud, for if the tremendous Handel had a living rival, it would not be the sentimentalistic Bononcini. But at least the feud did inspire immortal lines from Jonathan Swift, who lacked the ear to tell the two apart:

Some say that Signor Bononcini
Compared to Handel is a ninny,
Whilst others say that to him Handel
Is hardly fit to hold a candle;
Strange that such difference should be
'Twixt tweedledum and tweedledee.

The Critic Criticized

George Bernard Shaw's music criticism is quotable and often ingenious, but filled with absurd judgments. One musician not impressed by Shaw was Ferruccio Busoni, a fascinatingly intellectual composer who also practiced romantic-hero virtuosity on the piano. Shaw's self-centered sarcasm offended Busoni the idealist; Shaw's lack of musicianship offended Busoni the pro. Worst of all was Shaw's facile jesting, even at the expense of his idols. Busoni didn't care for Wagner, but he was nonetheless disgusted when Shaw told him, posing for the quip, "I confess that I wish Tristan might die a little sooner."

"Why then," asks Busoni in frozen rage, "have you never *written* that?"

Arrested in his worthless irreverence, the garrulous Shaw had no retort.

The Last Prima Donna

Recently, a young American soprano was rehearsing for the world premiere of an opera by a distinguished American composer. In the old-fashioned manner, he worked with the singers himself to instill a sense of his style; but he was newfangled in his manners, in fact quite informal, and would express pleasure by enfolding the soprano in an embrace, complete with a deep, long kiss.

The soprano was glad for his pleasure, but not his kisses. She was further annoyed that he seemed unable to remember her name; he addressed her by the name of her character.

What was she to do? A young American singer is in no position to tell a distinguished American composer not to kiss her. Still, this was behavior unfit for the green room. Finally, a friend suggested that she outmaneuver the kiss by startling him. The next time he approached, she must wave him away imperiously and cry, "I am *Miss Diva!*"

In default of anything better, the soprano agreed to try it. Did it work?

"I did just as you outlined it," she told her friend later. "You should have heard me: 'I am *Miss Diva!*' "

"And?"

"He laughed, and then he grabbed me and kissed me just as before."

She sighed.

Her friend shrugged.

"Well," she said. "At least now he knows what to call me."

INDEX